I SEE JESUS

Three words that changed my life

D1453315

Quantity order requests can be emailed to: thebreathoflight@gmail.com

I See Jesus by Diane Nienas

Publishing services provided by FEW International Publications, a division of FEW International Organization, LLC. thefewwomen.com

Publishing Coordinator: Kimberly Krueger

Editor: Amy Oaks

Associate Editor: Matthew Nienas

Copyeditor: Matthew Nienas

Cover Designer: Trace Chiodo; Chiodo Design, chiododesign.com

Interior Layout: Trace Chiodo; Chiodo Design, chiododesign.com

Bible verses are taken from biblegateway.com ©1995-2017, The Zondervan Corporation. All Rights Reserved.

ISBN: 979-8-9869325-0-7

Categories:
Religion & Spirituality/Christian Books & Bibles/Literature & Fiction/Collections & Anthologies
Religion & Spirituality/Christian Books & Bibles/Biographies
Biographies & Memoirs/Reference & Collections

Breathing light into dark places by spreading the seed of hope

A division of Breath of Light, LLC,
Leo's Light Publications is a #1 Bestselling Publisher focusing on inclusion and sharing impactful stories to help guide others out of the darkness.

thebreathoflight.com

LEO'S LIGHT PUBLICATIONS ANNOUNCES:

The *Living Life with Leo* Children's Book Series!

This unique children's book series is based on Leo's life and is dedicated to Leo's honor and memory. Each *Living Life with Leo* story was written to provide hope and to encourage special needs families to be filled with "Leo's Light". In the midst of your struggles, Leo would want you to know you are not alone.

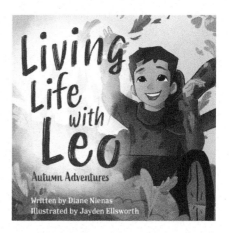

A #1 Bestseller on Amazon, *Living Life with Leo: Autumn Adventures*, is now available on Amazon.com or thebreathoflight.com. Watch for these forthcoming titles:

Living Life with Leo: Spring Adventures - Spring of 2023
Living Life with Leo: Winter Adventures - Fall Of 2023
Living Life with Leo: Summer Adventures - Spring of 2024

I SEE JESUS

Three words that changed my life

DIANE NIENAS

DEDICATION

To my son, Leo. Thank you for allowing me to see the love of Jesus through your eyes. To my son, Trent. Thank you for building my strength. To my husband, Tony, and my sons, Matthew and Oliver, thank you for uniting as a unit of love to build a brighter future with the pieces of our past.

TABLE OF CONTENTS

INTRODUCTION

"I am leaving you with a gift, peace of mind and heart. And the peace I give is a gift the world cannot give. So don't be troubled or afraid." (John 14:27)

The peace that fills my heart and makes it possible to carry on after the tremendous loss I suffered through the deaths of my sons, Leo and Trent, stems from this kind of love. It's sourced from the gift of peace Jesus gave us. This simple, yet impactful piece of Scripture sums up beautifully the way I moved forward in life. By surrendering and putting my trust in God, I was able to see past my failures and hardships, which allowed the things of the world to fade away.

Throughout the Bible, meaningful messages are revealed amongst the stories. As the pages are turned, hidden lessons and treasures of God's love lie within the words. Somehow, the stories from so long ago remain relevant to our own lives today. There are stories of betrayal and loyalty, stories of hope and dreams lost. Each page takes you either back to that moment in the past, or it opens your eyes to the life you are living now—or even what the future may hold.

This is a story of my awakening. As the pages unfold, it will take you along on a journey of transformation and self-discovery as you walk through my life, the life of my son, Leo, and my family. You will see how Leo's undefined illness of Leukodystrophy would not destroy his faith, but rather build mine, my husband's, my three remaining sons', along with many others. Leo held the love of Jesus in his heart despite the fact that the body that held his soul failed him. The slow deterioration process that manifested his disabilities gave him the ability to be still and trust in God. In a sense, Leo never had an opportunity to fully separate himself from God. His decline in health occurred while the innocence of a child was still intact. He was not allowed time to be tainted by the world; he remained in the world of God.

This story will provide inspiration and hope, letting you see how your circumstances don't have to define your happiness. My sons were seeded in a garden of hardship, yet they plowed through and cultivated a garden of glory. You will witness how the belief Leo held in his heart for Jesus ultimately saved the life of his brother, Trent. They both looked past the mountain in front of them and found peace in the promise of eternal life.

For years, I witnessed Leo's own experience with "the passion" as he went through life, beaten down by endless obstacles along his way. Little by little, functions were stripped away from him until he spent his teenage years mostly bedbound. He carried his cross to the end, doing it with grace and a love for God with a purpose greater than his own.

He stepped into the journey of hardship as a toddler and steadily maintained a balance between student and teacher, learning from Jesus as lessons were taught to him, and then guiding those around him toward the meaning of life. His passion was displayed along with strong compassion, never wanting anyone to be left out or behind, even when it was he who was often forgotten.

Leo's enthusiasm for Jesus overcame the pain he endured; he never lost sight of the mission to serve God. My tiny glimpse of Leo's pain and suffering opened my eyes to the pain and suffering of Jesus, as He laid down His life for all of us. It allowed me to take the visual experiences I witnessed daily and insert them into the words of the Bible, connecting for me something my heart could feel; a mother watching her son suffer, yet trusting it comes with a purpose and that it's following God's plan.

There were many moments when I could pinpoint God changing my course as we maneuvered through our lives, moments of darkness where He provided light. Leo became my light. He settled my thoughts, calmed my mind, and gave me the gift of seeing the world through the love of Jesus. As I grew in my faith, I knew we were given a story to share, one that could open the eyes of others and bring them to the light of hope.

This story is not intended to bring harm to any individual or portray anyone in a negative way. Rather, it is to cast a light on the shadow of darkness, to show God remains faithful and present in our lives with His love. We are surrounded by images and people who try to plant negative thoughts and sow doubt into our minds. I have learned to gently steer my thoughts back to God and regain control before they pull me down into destruction. My journey through brokenness is what built my faith. Only God had the power to allow me to witness, on such a personal level, His work flowing through the conduit He used in the form of my son. I had to be broken, mended, restored, and repaired in order to see that God had provided me with the armor of His love, before I could wear it and keep the enemy at bay.

Chapter One

LEO'S LIGHT

I awoke. A rising glow pushed through the blinds of the bedroom window and radiated up the bed. Stirring from an unsettling rest, I stared up at the ceiling and watched the sunlight flow across. I wiped the sleep from my eyes as I stretched and rolled from my back to my left side. My head slid with ease across the red silk pillowcase. Its embrace was tough to leave behind as I sat up and realized this wasn't a dream. The brown eyes that normally projected hope amidst the dark hours of morning were not looking back at me. An awareness of the space, once filled by my boy, consumed me with emptiness momentarily. Like a passing cloud over the rising sun, the darkness drifted by and exposed me to the upcoming events of the day.

My thoughts filled with what had occurred the previous days like marbles stacked together in Kerplunk to be released at once when triggered. Thinking back less than one week, I could see the reflection of my little boy, Leo, from the red orbs decorating our Christmas tree. It had been a day of strength and unity. There was warmth in the love shared by family and merriment in the conversations with Santa. The blessings of God sprinkled down on our home like snowflakes drifting together, forming a snowbank; a bank where love is its currency, and the people connect and remain present.

Even now, days later, as I rose with the day, I felt Leo's body shake with laughter and joy by running my hand through the left side of the bed. Leo's joy was felt in the spaces of the house through his voice and actions. His delicate words and fragile movements were embraced by the stillness of time, knowing each day was a gift to be near him. There had been months where words escaped like coals slipping from a melted snowman, but there were also special occasions where the true gift was being present near pure love. That is what made Leo so incredible to be around. His actions were intentional, and his determination to live each day to the fullest scattered amongst the hearts who stood by.

I sat there, one week from physically receiving his love, wondering where my strength would come from now that the ice thinned and steps became slippery. I slowly rolled out of bed, exhausted from days without sleep and little food nourishing my body, and made my way to the bathroom door. Stepping through, I looked at myself in the mirror and saw the eyes of Leo looking back at me in my reflection. He was smiling and beaming with light.

"You can do this, Mom."

Slowly, strength began to fill my soul. I took a deep breath and put careful thought into every movement I made. I began to run the water in the shower and stepped in, hoping to rinse the emptiness away. A hallowing feeling tickled my heart, like the spot on one's back that can't be reached, and washed over me. My eyes peered through the droplets toward the bath chair in the corner. Empty, no longer needed. The water continued flowing over me, making it difficult to breathe unless I dropped my head and avoided the current. I kept my chin up and held onto Leo's courage. Moments went by, and as I toweled off and brushed through my hair, I once again looked in the mirror.

Leo smiled back at me. "You've got this, Mom."

Numb to my surroundings, I stumbled through the motions of the morning routine, not focusing on much of anything. I stepped into my red dress; not typical attire for a funeral, but it allowed me to feel like I was carrying Leo with me. Red was his favorite color, after all. I began to do my makeup and hair, again questioning, *Why even bother?* since tears continued to fill my eyes. Yet, Leo gazed upon me in my reflection once again, and peace overcame me. I stood there for a moment, all put together on the outside, but crumbled within.

It was time to leave the reflections of my mirror, so I took a deep breath and exited the bathroom. The hallway led to an open living room featuring a 16-foot high stone fireplace built by the family, numerous big game trophies mounted on the walls, and comfortable furniture encasing an empty hospital bed that used to be the center point for gatherings. A few more steps past the kitchen and through the garage, I found myself alone in the car with Leo's belongings. I gathered my courage and briefly checked for brown eyes in the mirror once more. I backed out of the driveway while the rest of the family finished their preparations for a later departure. The open blue skies allowed the sun to continue to shine strong, and warmth filled the car from the unseasonably cozy day of winter. I felt Leo's love embrace me.

I pulled into the parking lot after a long ten-minute drive and found a spot close to the entrance door. Moments went by as I sat in silence. I turned my head to the left, and out of the corner of my eye, I saw the hearse pull in. Knowing it held the body of my child, a weight fell from the skies like a day's snowfall released at once. It was a quiet setting outside the church, but within, chaos ran rampant with loss and reality. I lifted my eyes to God and found peace.

Entering the lobby, I held in my arms the belongings of my sixteen-year-old son to display on the memorial tables for others to view. Some of our close family, touched by Leo's light, assembled the pieces of his life and displayed them for all. It was reassuring to capture his spirit, and the doubts of the morning faded away. The moment arrived to enter the church, so I began my approach, walking down the main aisle, arm in arm with my husband, Tony, and my remaining sons - Matthew, Trent, and Oliver. Leo's coffin was open and centered before the altar.

Above him was Jesus, and this sight reminded me of the numerous other times Jesus stood above Leo. I took a deep breath, stepped closer to the coffin, and fixed my eyes upon my son whom I hadn't seen in days. Leo lay peacefully in a position I had gazed upon for years, appearing only to be asleep. I felt his inner strength fill me, empowering me for not only what lay ahead in the hours to follow, but in the days still to come.

After an intimate gathering around Leo with my family, the church burst with life as those impacted by Leo flowed through the doors. A mixture of warm greetings and touching comments filled the air with a steady hum. To my right stood my sons, to my left, my husband, and in the middle of it all remained Leo. The crowd never waned as close to a thousand people made their way through the lobby in less than two hours. Loved ones who had known Leo for years, and others who were touched by only moments of time with him all came to pay their final respects to a boy who made a positive impact on their lives. As a family we stood, we embraced, we comforted others, and listened to stories of how our beautiful son provided hope and faith to them. I continued to be strengthened, the sun continued to shine upon me through the stained-glass window, and I had Leo by my side.

When the visitation ended, and silence overcame the air, the time came for those who stayed to find a seat, and for me to stand before them. Every center pew was filled. Every heart was filled with Leo's love.

My husband had told me, only days prior, that I needed to be the one to deliver Leo's eulogy stating, "Only you can capture the true essence of Leo's spirit. You need to find the strength to be able to do it."

My stomach fluttered and a lump surfaced in my throat as I replied, "I know."

I heard Leo's voice echoing in my mind, "I see Jesus," so I knew he was right. Yet, doubt crept into my mind for a brief moment, from a comment Tony had made months earlier that created tension in our relationship.

"When did the Leo updates become about you?"

I had been so hurt and taken aback by this statement from Tony. Over the course of the past 15 years, my weekly updates were a way to share Leo's story with hundreds of our closest friends and family and their acquaintances. I was always aware of excluding myself when I poured my thoughts out on paper to keep loved ones informed, drawing others into Leo's life. But the reality was, Leo's story was my story. We become one. Reluctant to move forward, I stepped into the role, knowing our story was one worth sharing.

I began the walk to the altar one step at a time, gaining strength from each stride. There I stood, legs steadily holding me firm; heart strong, not shaken. Only through the power of God could this have been possible. As I peered out into the crowd, I recalled how we all got here. The brokenness of my journey had been healed by a pure heart. I grabbed the microphone, adjusted my stance, and watched as a red hue shone in through the window and I found my voice. Before I found my words, I paused as the reel of my lifetime played out in my mind.

It was hard to believe that there could be a life without Leo. The experience of watching my son grow into an instrument of love and faith had changed me. His love had changed the lives of hundreds of people present in that church. Like the morning dew settling over a freshly mowed lawn, Leo's light settled on the hearts and minds of all present. A comfort poured from the vastness of time, soothing aching hearts yearning for a smile. His smile. Leo brought out the best in people, and without his physical presence to continue guiding us, it was up to us to build upon the foundation, create the best versions of ourselves, and carry on.

Chapter Two

IN THE BEGINNING

There was a time before Leo, too, where life felt different. Although the pieces of me were warped from the tears that fell upon them in death, there remained a core that held firm. That core was built through trials, faith, and maturity in my own experiences. But before that, the pieces were scattered in innocence. Whereas the sun beamed through stained glass in unison, pushing through the pieces and colors of the church window, the pieces of me were shattered and dim. No makeup or clothes could disguise the reality of what was transpiring inside of me. There were many things around me to be proud of, but there were also things within that stirred reality and purpose with experience.

I was broken. Without God in my life, I was failing. I walked alone and approached decisions without guidance, thinking I could hide or handle the choices I made alone. Things on the outside all appeared to be perfect, but internally I was vanquished by shame, suffering from guilt, deflated of self—worth, and harboring pain from various situations I went through. Some of these were by choice and some of them were out of my control. The dimly lit path I walked gave the illusion it was a path others wanted to take when in reality, it was one to steer clear of.

Then, this light of hope entered my life. This light was my son, Leo, and through his life struggle, I found my strength. When God created Leo, I now know He had a plan in mind; a purpose to fulfill. But back in the moment Leo arrived, this was not my belief. My spiritual awakening was still dormant and God was not the center in my life. Through the gift of my son, my eyes opened for the first time and they began to see all God had to offer. This offering came with a price. My son literally lay down his life for me, and ultimately, his journey transformed and saved me.

Before Leo, I was raised as part of a large family on a farm in southeastern Wisconsin. Things were always blooming and changing amongst our large family like the seasons when spring provided lush shades of green as the trees budded. Summer was typically comfortable, as the sun kissed your skin refreshed by a cool breeze. As fall rolled in, shades of brilliant color cast along the ridge, swooshed away with the harsh winter winds. Trees stripped of their leaves stood desolate as everything was left bare. Then everything was transformed by a blanket of white, freshly fallen snow, and repeated over again the following year.

My mother was an only child, suffering the loss of both her sisters shortly after birth. Along with my father, who was raised with his two siblings, they decided together they wanted love to abundantly surround them with children. When they began their family together, I am not positive they had a number in mind (I was later told a dozen), but that number turned into 15 children: 10 girls and five boys over the course of 22 years, with me being number 14. I guess I should be grateful that they created more than a baker's dozen, or I wouldn't be here. With this many kids came a certain status that was almost intimidating in a sort of power—in—numbers kind of thing. There was an image to uphold, *the family way*, where everything appeared perfect and everything was unspoken. Private thoughts remained just that—private.

My mother was a selfless woman who not only attended to her family but was also a devoted and loyal servant to God. She was a peaceful lady who put her needs on hold continuously throughout her life to care for others. She took a backseat and lovingly allowed everyone else around her to shine. No one was ever turned away from her altruistic offerings. My mom's nurturing nature welcomed everyone and anyone into her home. With her faith, she instilled in all of us the importance of being true to yourself while being good to others.

That, combined with my father's dedicated work ethic, humbling himself to take on jobs that would provide for his family which gave my mom the gift of staying home to raise their children, led to the foundation of strong family values that eventually applied in my life. That said, my dad wasn't a perfect man, but he was a man of integrity, loyalty, and love who also sacrificed so often in his lifetime to see none of his children go without the necessities. We may not have had the newest and latest things, but my dad was a man I looked up to and we were shown and taught how to love the land and appreciate the simple things in life through his actions.

The house was often filled with commotion and, just like the family, it grew. What started as a two-bedroom house blossomed into an eight-bedroom home, making it hard to find stillness. At one point, my older siblings were assisting with projects like caring for the chickens, plowing the corn fields, milking the cows, and occasionally cleaning the pig pen. The commitment of the working farm ceased before I was of age to take part in any of the chores. Fortunately for me and my younger siblings, it became more of a casual undertaking. As you can imagine, with that many kids, someone was always coming and going, leading my dad to often state that the door appeared to be on a hinge, yet ironically, it got slammed often. My dad would yell out, "Quit slamming the door!" Then he himself would slam it shut, and bam, the door snugly fit to the frame. With the flow of people in and out of the door, it amazed me how I could still often feel unseen and unheard.

The grocery store became a second home in order to keep the pantry full. My mom even had a regular spot in line at the checkout lane and was known by name. These frequent visits turned into meal preparations which were more of a grab and go, or eat as quickly as you can lest you will be left with nothing. Rarely, mostly on holidays, we had an opportunity to gather around one table and eat as a family. Even these events made it difficult to do such a thing; is there even a table big enough for that many children to gather? Plates and cups were strewn about from the different eating times of us children. There were always dishes left on the counters and even though we each had chores to attend to, it appeared my mom left imprints of her feet at the base of the kitchen sink. The busyness of the home typically left most things out of place, and keeping it clean was as difficult as keeping up with the laundry. With so many people living under one roof, cleanliness was like reaching the finish of a marathon on flat land: seeing it ahead, but finding it to be unobtainable.

The strength in numbers also made finding alone time next to impossible. Someone was always crowding your personal space, and even though the home consisted of many rooms on two floors, we often shared one. It wasn't until I began high school that I obtained a room I could call my own. Even then, it is funny how you can long to have something, and then once you receive it, realize how much you miss the sister that was your roommate for so many years. As this newfound freedom entered my life at home, it also took a hold of me as my high school years began. By that point, many of my older siblings had moved out and started families of their own, which made the house feel easier to get lost in.

I was an untamed spirit, always feeling older than my age. There were multiple things that led to this development; experiences in my childhood that impacted me like dark secrets that held residency in my soul and shaped me probably more than I realized. So often in life, we don't see the impact of our daily choices and experiences until later. Sometimes, they are buried deep in our souls, and when new circumstances arise, the layers are peeled, and memories resurface. I am not sure how significant of a role my birth order played in opening my eyes, but I have seen, in my own parenting as a mother of four boys, that it had an impact.

Similarities between my siblings and my sons show that the oldest one tends to start off being shyer and more hesitant whereas the younger siblings tend to dive right in and find their adventurous side earlier. Well, considering how many older siblings I had, I am sure you can imagine my eyes were exposed to experiences earlier than most. My sisters and brothers demonstrated beautiful values and weren't necessarily doing anything wrong, but when you factor in the age span of our family, it is like a kindergartener riding the bus with a college student, and that sounds like trouble.

There are scars in my past that shaped the person I was, and the person that I try to continue to heal. In a house filled with so much love and life, it was easy to trust and remain loyal. Bonds of sisterhood were established quickly as we learned from our parents, and the land, how to find joy in the little things. The building blocks of youth were stacked delicately with the passing years, trusting the stability of family roots to prevent them from falling over, only to be tipped in an unlikely direction. As a young girl, I lost a piece of my innocence. Led to a room with a whisper of *shhh* followed by the door shutting out the hallway lights, I followed, blindly trusting an individual who should have respected me. Yet, I was violated. My youth was taken before I found my voice. I was left silenced without value.

Having been interrupted from the day-to-day, I then participated in actions that led to situations I shouldn't have been involved in. I was naive in not knowing it was wrong, but sometimes when something is introduced, it becomes the natural order of things. Why did I continue to allow it to happen? After being silenced and having to do things that didn't feel right to me, why would I once again go down the hall that led to a room where I felt myself being shut in, and yet still follow? A cycle was formed. A cycle that needed to be broken.

This early introduction could account for some of the decisions I made along the way. The who, the what, and the where are not important. What is, is that it changed me, often making me feel closed in, held down, and without a voice. But ultimately, God gifted me a mind with thoughts to determine right from wrong. At that time, I wasn't allowing God to be part of my life.

I found myself thrust into the world of boys in middle school, loving the attention I received. Although I took school seriously, cared about my grades, and had perfect attendance; I found myself daydreaming, caring about my social time, and getting into trouble like skipping class to kiss my boyfriend. I even had a teacher intervene at one point, expressing her concern about the choices I made. I started to drift in a direction that could potentially lead me the wrong way, but what I was not expecting was that the rock bottom I thought I had fallen onto could be lowered even further.

When I was in eighth grade, my twenty-one-year-old sister, Patty, was injured in a car accident. As a family, we were all gathering to celebrate the birthday of my brother—in—law. The event carried on into the late hours of the night at my sister's home. Occasions like these were always exciting, due to the large number of family members present. The next morning, however, when I woke up and stepped off the last stair from the upper level and placed my foot onto the linoleum floor leading into the kitchen, I could sense a heaviness in the air.

My mom greeted me with tears in her eyes. "There has been an accident. Your sister, Patty, is in the hospital." So many emotions overcame me, and honestly, there was this feeling of being frozen, as if what was said really wasn't.

"How bad is it?" I asked the question, but wasn't prepared for the answer. My mom's frame looked too weak to hold the weight of the news she delivered next.

"She is non-responsive. It is not looking promising."

Patty suffered severe head trauma caused by striking the pavement, but instead of taking her to the hospital, her boyfriend, uncertain of what to do, took her back to my sister's home where the party was held. Time wasted. Precious minutes that could have potentially altered her outcome.

There was a weight crushing me into the earth like gravity multiplied. This feeling was all too familiar and added onto my baggage. I can't even recall if I embraced my mother into my arms at that moment, but it is what I should have done. As I look back, I can see the immaturity I exhibited during that time. So many thoughts were only about me.

These were gloomy times. Her death wasn't instant, and she was kept alive for days with the assistance of life support. Waiting for the arrival of each of us kids to make it back home, in addition to realizing that my parents were not ready to let go of her just yet, they faced an incredibly difficult decision. As we all stood surrounding her bedside, they contemplated whether or not we should pull the plug on the machine that sustained her life.

I remember the pain that filled my mother's heart when the doctors approached her.

"Are you willing to donate your daughter's organs?" The anguish my mom felt as she watched and knew her child was slipping away from her was difficult to observe. How absurd it was in her mind to think of saving a life, while the one she gave life to was slipping from her grasp.

My mom released the words, "No knife in my baby's body." She looked upon my sister, seeing all the wounds. "No more." Yet, this was a decision my parents did not take lightly or make alone. Looking at all of us in the room as we stood in silence, she asked, "What should we do?"

Unable to hold the incredible weight of this decision on their shoulders alone, they sought the advice of each of us one by one.

"Should we pull the plug?"

So much of life during those ages of middle school and high school, we often find it hard to look past ourselves. We see only the way a situation will impact our day, but not the whole picture. I remember a thought that came to mind about how this was going to ruin my perfect attendance at school. Her death occurred at the end of April, and I was only weeks away from earning a perfect attendance award for not missing school from kindergarten through eighth grade. A piece of paper with an inscription of perfect attendance and my name; how could that possibly hold more significance in my mind than the life of my sister? I guess this reaction disappointed me even more and brought to light how even though I was attending religious classes, preparing me for my sacrament of confirmation, I didn't have God in my life. I believed in God, but I didn't know God.

Even standing at my sister's bedside, watching her breathing fade, seeing it was only the machine that was aiding her body, I had no thoughts of God or the degree of loss that was in front of me. Nothing in the world mattered anymore. I became numb. Experiencing this death was my first exposure to loss, and it wasn't sinking in that this was permanent. Patty was not going to return and physically be a part of my life. Memories of these times are ones that I have suppressed and ones that I have not fully come to know. Details of that night resurfaced only in pieces. It wasn't until years later that scenes from that dark night came to light for me as I sought out the truth.

Questions bubbled up like a spring bursting through the earth, but whenever answers were found, it was as if only more questions flowed out of me. Multiple explanations were given as to what happened on that late—April day that changed the dynamics of my family forever. Keep in mind, it was 1985, which was a time before cell phones. This was in a place where nothing other than fields of corn and other crops lined the roadway. It was rumored that Patty's boyfriend might have pushed her out of the car following an argument they had while leaving the party. I also heard that Patty jumped from the moving vehicle. Her tenacity and free spirit could have led you to believe this was true, yet logically, neither made sense. My mother didn't want the incident investigated and begged my dad not to pursue charges. Despite the years that haunted my dad from the lack of closure, he abided by her wishes to move on.

Patty had incredible beauty. Long flowing auburn hair with hazel eyes that captivated you. These stunning features were unable to be viewed the way that we siblings were used to seeing her as she lay in her final resting place. Due to her trauma, her head was partially shaved and a hole was drilled through the skull to relieve the pressure of her swollen brain. As a result, her hair was swooped to the side while lying in the coffin, trying to disguise her bruising and scars. I recall one of my sisters saying, "Patty would be so upset with her hair." Patty was a beautician by trade and always put together well, so her final reveal was not living up to what we came to know of her.

We were united as a family, greeting visitors as they came to pay their final respects. My parents stood together, alone by Patty's coffin, as an endless line of love came to their side. The pain was so deep that few words were spoken. My parents grieved the loss of their child so differently from one another. One held it all in, demonstrating her incredible weakness through strength, while the other, crumbled from the haunting of the unknown, turned to isolation and alcohol, often retreating to the basement and sitting in darkness, alone with his own thoughts.

I didn't only lose a sister that spring, I also lost a piece of my mom and dad. My parents changed, and I no longer felt like a careless young girl wandering through the hallways and fields of our home. After this loss, and while experiencing the loss of my voice, I became even more isolated. As I watched life carry on for others, I felt life being sucked out of me. There was an emptiness that filled me. I didn't know another individual who understood what I was going through (someone outside of my family I could unload on), and I believe this left me looking for something to fill the void.

Love is what I found to begin to mend my heart. I was a young girl, only fourteen, when I believed I fell in love. I remember, vividly, standing at my locker when he came up behind me. I caught a glimpse of him approaching from the mirror attached to my locker door. He tapped my shoulder, my heart began to flutter, and my eyes met his. There before me stood an irresistible Italian young man named Tony. He was a junior, and instantly, I was his. There was an immediate connection. I was drawn into his smile and dark hair and eyes like a magnetic force. I fell quickly and I fell hard and nothing else in my life mattered. The days at school seemed to grow longer, and even though we had brief moments in the hall between classes together, I only wanted the school day to end so we could spend time with one another.

Tony's upbringing was quite different from mine. He was the youngest of three in his family with enough of an age gap between him and his older two siblings that they really didn't have any common ground. His parents divorced when he was in seventh grade, leaving him to decide which one of them he wanted to live with. It honestly didn't seem like a winning decision either way, but he ultimately picked his dad, based on the sole factor of not wanting to leave his home or his friends. This decision left his mom absent more than present in his life.

Eventually, he was living alone with his dad since both of his siblings were old enough to be on their own. This lifestyle wasn't ideal, and it not only lacked the loving compassion of a mother, but his dad worked long hours which left Tony alone to fend for himself. This led to some positive traits: Tony learned how to cook, do laundry, and attend to his basic needs. However, it also led to time unsupervised. With his home located right across the street from the high school, it became a party house, which for Tony, filled a void in his life of loneliness. It wasn't uncommon for us to gather with our friends on weekends, after school, or even prior to school at Tony's home. I remember on more than one occasion having a few drinks and heading off to school. This did not make for an ideal mind for learning.

This freedom seemed to also escalate our relationship. We were a young couple sort of playing house, exposed to the positive aspects of having a place to hang out without the responsibilities of paying for it. This carefree accessibility took the innocence of our love and developed it into an intimate situation. Once we introduced that level of intimacy into our relationship, it opened a whole realm of issues, and we couldn't go back. The innocence of love was gone. Although sex took our relationship to a deeper level, it was not always processed correctly from the mind of a teenager. It tested my trust and brought questions into the space that was once free-spirited.

It is interesting what triggered internally to make me feel like I was ready to give a piece of myself away. Even though we were incredibly young, our love felt established and mature. When it came to Tony, his family, or lack of, played a big role in our relationship. His family was broken, he was lonely, and I filled the void for him. Together, we found ways to create the pieces of ourselves that could be built to form an image of our determination. The resulting image may not have come with instructions, but we pieced together the broken parts of ourselves to form a complete masterpiece. Seventeen years of my life were raised on that farm, and now the years ahead were destined to be spent with Tony.

Chapter Three

LOST SOULS
IN THE DARK

The bell rang, and the halls became flooded with commotion. Conversations bounced off the walls as teenagers scrambled to gather their materials from their lockers to make it to their classes on time. Lost in the chaos of it all, I tried to settle into my second year of high school, feeling more secure with freshman year under my belt. I started to find my way. I thought I was gaining confidence as I tried to make a name for myself (both in sports and academics), despite following so many footsteps of older siblings who walked the hallways prior. I portrayed myself as comfortable in my own skin, yet I was still insecure and immature.

I was surrounded by hundreds of other teenagers who were just trying to find their way too. So many fish swimming in the same school following the direction of the leader, yet remaining individual amidst group pressures. For me, high school was a time that easily trapped me into worrying about what others thought, and I was occasionally caught up in waves of gossip. It was difficult not to react or be impacted by what was said, especially when relying on yourself to sort through things.

There was an age difference between Tony and me. Even though it was only two years, in the world of high school, that seemed significant. We each had our own core of friends, but also tried to fit into the other's spaces. With so many moving parts to the student body, Tony and I fit best together when we spent time alone. Like two gears in rotation, coming together, and creating energy for something bigger to work, we moved together flawlessly. Alone, our world seemed to be so perfectly formed. The amount of time we shared resulted in us facing a decision that was not meant for teenagers. We discovered I was pregnant.

I was only a sophomore in high school, a child myself, living in a whimsical way, until I was struck with an adult situation. I put myself there, unprotected and unaware this could happen to me. I honestly never had *the talk* with either of my parents about sex or anything else, for that matter. Even when it came to my period, I learned what I needed to learn from sisters and friends. I initially walked around as a young teenage girl, utilizing a maxi pad that was way too "much" for me. I didn't realize that they came in different sizes and thicknesses. My only accessibility was to rummage through the bathroom cupboards in hopes of finding the supplies I needed. It took years before I had any understanding of tampons. Yet, there I was, this young girl somehow managing to "figure out" how to have sex, finding herself carrying unexpected news.

Tony, at this pivotal moment, was a senior with plans to go away to college. The baby was not part of the plan, or an option to discuss, or potentially move forward with. Still being young ourselves, he felt that there was much to be experienced in life before bringing another one into it. My mind concluded that I had only one choice. His choice. I told myself that if I wanted to maintain this relationship with one whose arms gave me comfort in a trying world, the life that was beginning inside of me needed to end. This decision affected me physically and tied my stomach in knots. Once again, I felt unable to breathe, trapped in a situation where I had to remain silent. I felt myself slipping back to the violated little girl being led down a long hallway, shutting the door, being held down, told to be quiet, and then instructed what to do. Even with my thirteen remaining siblings and dear friends surrounding me, I felt alone, and I was overtaken by fear and shame.

The years of learning to hold secrets in, most too painful to admit aloud, left me unable to speak to anyone; even to those who loved me and cared about me. This left me to decide between choices my youthful mind was not equipped to make. My heart has carried this secret for all of these years, unable to be revealed to a single soul. My lack of self-worth and my inability to recognize God in my life led me to think I had no other option, resulting in a child I would never know and losing a part of me.

As I turned the pages of the telephone book, the crisp sound of the pages flipping drew me closer to what I was in search of. With Tony alongside me, I placed my pointer finger on the page and began to dial the number that corresponded with the clinic. The sound of the retraction alarmed me each time as the rotation made its way back to the start position. My heart beat fast as I placed the receiver to my ear and it began to ring. The friendly voice on the other end startled me as I was lost in the tone of the ring.

"Hello, how can I help you?"

"I need to schedule an appointment."

"And what would this appointment be for?"

My body trembled. I was unable to form the words. Tony gently grabbed the phone from me and stated, "We need to schedule an abortion."

"Okay. I will need to gather some information from you."

"Okay, please let me know what you need."

I watched Tony calmly engage in a conversation as I shrunk myself in disgrace on the couch next to him, in hopes of being unseen. Once all the relevant information was collected, Tony handed the phone back to me and stated, "They need to confirm the details with you." When I eventually hung up the phone, the conversation hung in silence along with it.

When the day arrived, I recall holding Tony's hand in the waiting room. Our eyes met one another and I felt a sense of fear and relief at the same time. We were taken into a room and asked to watch a video. A video that left nothing to the imagination, fully depicting an abortion being performed. Shame weighed me down again, as the enemy dwelling in my heart whispered, *There is no turning back now.*

Tony and I were then separated. He was asked to wait outside, and I was led down a hall into a room. The door was shut. Those words once again, *Shhh, stay still,* filled my mind and I was silenced. I was instructed to disrobe from the waist down and lay upon the table. The room was cold, I felt numb and ashamed and frozen, without a voice. The life inside of me had no clue that even with a struggle or a fight, it had no chance. It was about to end. The machine was turned on, and the dreadful sound that can't escape my mind even all these years later, took only moments to terminate what God intended to be a lifetime.

As the procedure came to an end, tears rolled down my face. The coldness of the room matched the coldness in my heart. Like the slow drip of melting snow from the rooftop, my heart hardened in my wrongdoing, and I was left frozen, alone, like a single icicle hanging in the midst of a vast space of loneliness. I lay there, lost in my own thoughts, desperately seeking someone or something to bring softness and love back to it. I couldn't see it then, but Leo was the salt, the flavor of God's love, that would be sent to sprinkle my soul and break down the density of my heart.

Abruptly, I was startled from my thoughts with a knock on the door and asked to get dressed. I began my walk down the hall, my body hunched over, my head held down in disgrace. As I walked closer to the waiting room, my head lifted, and my eyes met Tony's gaze. Initially, I found it hard to meet his look, but those eyes drew me in again like the first time I saw them. Yet, it was different this time. His eyes were uncertain, as opposed to the confidence I regularly became lost in.

He tried to comfort me, asking, "Are you okay?"

I answered only in my thoughts, *How could I be okay after what I just did?* Again, he tried to comfort me as we began our drive home, but I pulled away from his comfort, shifting my indignity from myself, blaming him, and we drove in silence. My mind raced faster than the car itself. I finally opened up when I couldn't hold it in any longer.

I expressed angrily, "Nothing happened to you! It wasn't your body that just experienced loss! You are not the one bleeding, seeing the reminder of your actions." I quivered as I shifted all my guilt, all my pain, upon him.

"I am sorry," he replied.

"Sorry, can't erase the scar on my heart."

This guilt has stayed with me my whole life. It weighed heavily on my soul for so many reasons, but mostly because of the God I have come to know and because of what I have faced and overcome since. I know now I could have altered my choice, but at that time, Tony and I were just two young kids who were scared and unable to fully process a decision of this magnitude. Our young love knew only one another. Even though we thought we were mature enough to enter into an intimate relationship, our lack of maturity made us both feel alone and unable to talk to someone with more experience who could have helped guide us to a different outcome. We kept it unspoken. Much of my pain I held within me was not given a voice.

A woman's heart is like a vault of secrets, and honestly, my soul has grown tired of carrying the weight of it around. The vault is not meant to deceive; it is rather the space where I hid my shame and guilt resulting from choices I knew were wrong. Although I was able to hide events from those who surrounded me, I was unable to keep God from knowing the truth. My lack of self—worth and confidence held me captive and, as a result, held my wrongdoings imprisoned too. But God saw me, and He wanted to free me from the weight. I wanted to lay it down at the foot of the cross and hand it over to Him, but I didn't know Him.

I didn't know it then, but I know now, that it took my son, Leo, and his life experiences, to open my eyes and finally release my failures to God. Unfortunately, at this point in my life my failures, not my faith, layered together to build the platform on which I stood.

Unlike the Virgin Mother Mary, who, with grace and a humble heart willingly accepted what God asked of her, I rejected His gift. Although I was similar in age to the young girl who allowed God to bestow upon her the miracle of our Savior, I ran from His offering out of fear of not knowing Him, taking what I assumed to be the easier solution. Little did I know at that moment that my decision would follow me, and I would never escape from it. It is not an event I revisit daily, but it is one that guides my decision—making. God allowed me to be lost. He allowed me to make my own way. God knew what was coming in my life. He was aware of the light He was sending to me, so even though I couldn't see it yet, I would be saved.

As I disclose this information for the first time, I can feel the judgment placed upon me. Yet, what I have come to recognize is that God is the One ultimately holding the gavel. I don't want the responsibility of judging someone. Rather, I want to understand them and show compassion and love with my choice of words, so I can focus on helping those who are in a dark place find their way back to the light. God is the only One I have to answer to. God is the only One who can restore me, build me up, and then use both my successes and my failures to shape me into the spirit that I was meant to be. I have come to see now that my mistakes and failures in life can be, and have been, very beneficial in helping others through difficult situations.

Carrying around a vault is not an easy task. Why would I want darkness to gain control over me, keeping me from living in happiness? Releasing my wrongdoings is not easy to do. Saying something aloud makes it real, making it a truth in some way. But, there is healing that comes from release. Ironically, this whole trial didn't fix my relationship with Tony. I became even more broken, and things just didn't feel the same between us. Our gears developed too many rough edges, and what was once running smoothly, began to jam up. Similar to how my dad responded to the uncertainty of my sister's passing, we weren't allowing each other to grieve or express our pain. Frankly, we just didn't know what the grieving process should be. We tried to make things work, but there just seemed to be a strain on our relationship that stemmed from a lack of communication, not understanding that this choice impacted us differently. As the months went by, I felt him slipping away. I wasn't ready to be in a world where I lost so much, and thought I was losing him as well.

I was no longer whole. I felt myself being pulled down into a life of despair. Piece by piece, fragments of myself were chipped away like a sculptor holding a chisel, yet I was not becoming a masterpiece, I became mass destruction. I held it in, and silently I began to fade. Something overtook me; guilt, shame, a dark force. I unknowingly drifted into the bathroom and pulled the door shut behind me. I stood at the vanity, numb to my surroundings. I watched myself in the mirror, moving, as I remained still. The cabinet door opened, and I observed myself grabbing bottles of pills from the shelf inside. My eyes met my own in the mirror and I did not like what was looking back at me.

It was darkness, a flat reflection with no spark; an image looked back, but no life or light dwelled within it. I reached out to touch my reflection and saw myself reaching back, but was unable to feel anything, unable to wake myself up from the trance of darkness that took hold of me. There was a person looking back at me that I couldn't fully recognize, and it was hard to meet her gaze with mine. A gaze stared into a pit at rock bottom, instead of giving a glimpse of the stars.

I tipped the bottle over into my hand. I started swallowing a couple of pills, then a couple more. A slight pause. Then handfuls fit into my mouth. The reflection was still unrecognizable, and the pain and sadness weren't going away. I obviously wasn't myself, and without giving it much thought, I left the bathroom and headed to the car, as if there would be no repercussions for what I had just done.

I began my ten-minute drive and found myself at softball practice, numb and not understanding the severity of my actions. My mind shifted and something came over me, and at that moment, I was positive death wasn't what I was seeking. I was crying for help, and I turned to my friend and disclosed to her what I had done.

"I need your help. I took multiple handfuls of pills before coming to practice."

"Oh, Diane, what have you done? Don't move."

My friend quickly ran to tell our coach. I chose to listen to the voice in my mind, the Spirit that was fighting for me despite my lack of fighting for Him; the voice that saved me. I find it so frightening to see the battle of thoughts that can enter one's mind, appearing almost out of nowhere and presenting itself as the only option. I tried to do life on my own; God didn't hold a prominent position in my world, so I was floundering without direction and didn't have a focal point on which to hold myself accountable. I was ultimately failing because God wasn't the center of my being; He wasn't even present, because I wasn't letting Him be.

It saddens me to imagine the pain I put my parents through as my stomach was being pumped in the emergency room of the hospital, not to mention the unneeded financial burden placed on them while trying to raise all of us kids on a single income. What I experienced when I was in recovery, however, was the purest form of love from my mom. This scene wasn't unfamiliar to her. She had been at the bedside of a daughter fighting for her life once before. We embraced.

"Oh, sweetheart." I tried to sink into the bed and fade away.

"I am sorry, Mom." The grip of her embrace lifted me from my shame.

"Just rest." All the unknown answers from that circumstance still lingered in her mind as she gazed at me with a new set of questions that would remain unknown. Yet, in that moment, she was able to hold me.

My dad looked at me with more uncertainty. He remained silent. I imagine that endless thoughts of the possibility of another lost child rushed through his mind as endless thoughts flooded my own. I was unable to detect if he was angry, relieved, frustrated, or filled with such a variety of emotions that just one could not reveal itself. My dad still wasn't himself, alcohol controlled the man he became, trying to block out the pain of reality still lingering from the loss of my sister. Overall, what I felt was distance. This moment left me sad, not knowing if I could repair the trust and the relationship with my dad that I so foolishly compromised. He sat beside me in silence.

My parents were unaware of the level of desperation and never asked, nor did I ever offer details as to what got me to that point, because I didn't allow them into my thoughts. They didn't know the events in my life that brought me to feel hopelessness, unaware of the innocence taken from me as a little girl, the emotions that consumed me after the mysteries of my sister's sudden death, and the lost grandchild they never were able to hold in their arms and grow to love. What they saw was only reckless behavior from an inexperienced and careless young love, because I held everything else in, remaining silent.

Chapter Four

SECOND CHANCES

Slowly, the darkness that held me captive and obscured my vision began to slip from my eyes, like a night mask that could no longer shield my view from the morning sun. I began to regain stability as I buried my heartache in the vault of my troubles. As I tried to move forward, a powerful force drew Tony and me back together. This magnetic pull seemed to be bigger than both of us, and eventually healed our wounded hearts, uniting us once again.

As a present for his high school graduation, Tony's sister invited him to stay with her at her home in Las Vegas. After being there for a few days, Tony became anxious and called me. The distance must have made him realize how close he wanted to be to me.

"Hi, been thinking about you … it's fun to be in Vegas, but something is missing." A moment passed with a sigh of courage, "Can you come join me?"

Heart fluttering with desire, a smile crept up from my stomach and portrayed itself on my face. Even so, I replied, "That's a great idea! I don't think my parents will let me though."

"This experience will be more enjoyable with you. You won't know for sure unless you ask, and then you can be with me!"

I hung up the phone and quickly began to seek out information about a flight. An exhilarating feeling spread throughout my being with a warmth that shook away the cold and replaced it with hope. I put together a few options before I approached my mom.

I sheepishly stepped forward, knowing she was the only chance if I wanted the answer to be yes, "Can I go to Vegas to meet up with Tony?"

"Is this really the best thing to do?" She looked at me inquisitively.

"I love him, Mom." My eyes emitted the love I had in my heart, and I hoped it showed in my expression. That, paired with a daughter's smile, must have been enough of a nudge to tumble her wall of concerns.

"Your father is not going to be happy about this."

I feel like I put my mom in a very difficult spot. After all, it had only been several months since my attempt on my life. If she refused, it could have led her to believe I would attempt again, yet the fear to let me go was equally daunting.

"Okay, Diane. Let's look at booking you a flight."

She said yes! My ticket was booked, and I called Tony to share the good news. Soon after, I arrived at his sister's apartment and into a new world. This was literally the first time I had ventured out of the state of Wisconsin, and out of my county if I am being honest. Tony was eager to meet me at the airport and he quickly showed me around. It was much different from the life I had come to know. Instead of the smell of open pastures, it was one of city life — a confusing medley of urban aromas took the place of the pure smell of green open pastures I was used to back home, and the white stars of the country sky were replaced by the bright colorful lights of buildings taller than I had ever seen.

Unable to book a flight home, we spent a month together which revived our relationship and built a new foundation of love. We had a beautiful balance of adventure and quiet time together. It gave us the space we needed to grow deeper in our trust. We learned how to respect and understand what led each of us to feel what we experienced, both individually and as a couple. Our relationship was in a good place, and the scattered pieces were formed together once more.

After arriving home, it became a long distance relationship as Tony went back to college while I remained behind to complete my junior and senior years of high school. At first, Tony was lonely, attending college in the middle of Southwestern Wisconsin with little surrounding the campus grounds as a means of entertainment. When he called, I would grasp the handle of the phone and stretch the coiled cord as far as it would extend. Closing the door behind me, I sat on the bottom step of the staircase and held the receiver close to my ear.

"I miss you." Hearing those words made it possible to make it through another day.

"How is your week going?" I would press the earpiece even more snugly against my skin as if it was him I was holding. These conversations were fulfilling, but they didn't fill the void I had in my heart, longing to be held by him.

"It's been alright so far, but it'll be better this weekend when I get to see you."

He came home often, and I loved the comfort of his arms. Then, a change of plans occurred, and he decided to transfer to a university closer to our hometown. This change reunited Tony with a group of high school friends who also attended. The loneliness that Tony felt while away at his first college was no longer filled solely by me, but rather in the familiarity of his old friends. Strain was put on our relationship, as often occurs in long distance situations, and once again, we spent time apart. That said, this time gave me a chance to reconnect with my own friends. The yo—yo relationship between us had its ups and downs, but it was held together by a strong string that always seemed to pull us back to one another.

Our love was tested, once again, when I discovered I was pregnant for a second time. I was the total cliche; so naive, immature, and uneducated about the fact that this could happen to me once again. I was in complete denial that just because I was pregnant once, what were the odds that it would happen again? Apparently, when it came to me, the chances were 100%. I guess some lessons in life just don't seem to be learned the first time through.

I was frozen, petrified about the position I was in, yet certain I could not go down the same path I had already traveled. Flashbacks flooded my mind, and once again, I felt myself in a cold room with the door shut. It took months for me to gather the courage to reveal my situation (maybe subconsciously, I considered if I was too far along when I told

Tony, we for sure wouldn't be able to do anything other than proceed) but eventually, my body changed too much to hide this secret.

As I looked at myself in the mirror, I saw life. My ever-changing body was more than extra pounds added to my frame, I visualized a child fighting for its life much in the same way that I was fighting for my own. As I gently rubbed the palms of my hands over my belly, I felt a connection. I was scared beyond anything I could comprehend. What will my parents think? How will my friends react? Will I find comfort and protection within my family? Will Tony remain by my side, or will I be left alone? So many questions, but one constant that planted my feet firmly on the ground was the reflection of me and the baby was one I could see and be proud of. No longer was I numb to my reflection; rather, proud to stand up for life.

"Tony, I am pregnant."

Literally the hardest words I had expressed up to this point in my life. The heaviness of silence filled the air as I sat trying to make myself feel small and unnoticed. Looking at me, he could see the decision had been made and no response was needed. Thankfully, I found support in some family members and friends to help me through months of attending school as a teenage mother. I even managed to continue my volleyball season! Setting and bumping the ball as my own bump began to grow, I remember literally hearing my mom gasp from the stands each time I dove to save a spike. This bump also caused commotion in the classroom. I recall one occasion when I became stuck in my desk.

As the bell rang and my classmates began to exit the room, there I was, pinned within the wooden frame of a student desk. I slid my bottom forward while guiding my belly safely out of the wedged position that it took under the desktop. Of course, there was no discrete and graceful way to do this, so it didn't go unnoticed by those who lingered around me. I tried to balance my world, staying engaged in the life of a high school teenager, while embracing the reality of my adult life situation.

Going through this time was extremely difficult. The whispers, the glances, the attention I couldn't hide from. Tony was living a carefree life away at college with friends, almost able to escape the reality of it. Meanwhile, I was home amongst loved ones, feeling isolated and alone. My hormones and immaturity often got the best of me as I was filled with resentment and anger. Even when Tony visited, our time was overshadowed with irrelevant accusations from me. So, instead of enjoying our time together, I wasted it on pushing him away. Even so, the decision to have my child became one of the stepping stones that built the foundation of my strength, beginning my path as a single parent and preparing me for what still lay ahead in my future.

Having a baby at a young age is not a plan for which I am advocating, but in my story, it worked out. I was blessed with my firstborn son, Matthew, and eventually, his birth strengthened my bond with Tony. It took time, and many emotions needed to heal. Although Tony missed Matthew's birth due to being away at college, he was by my side and held him in his arms shortly after.

My mom's loving support and willingness to help me graduate high school is something for which I am forever grateful. She allowed me time to figure out how to balance school, a baby, and some sort of social life. The relationship with my dad took more time to heal. It was hard to move forward when you're not speaking, but his immediate love for Matthew was apparent the first time he held him in his arms, and most likely the key that mended what was broken between us. I thought this segment of my life was going to be my greatest challenge, yet I was unaware of the events still to come. With each new obstacle placed before me, I was built, and as the events unfolded, each one became a cornerstone of my foundation.

Tony and I managed to remain united, and after I finished high school, we found an apartment. Shortly after, we realized getting married was the direction we both knew was right for us. Our struggles became our strength and, in a weird way, the glue that held us together. Although we were extremely young, we had this inner connection of love that seemed to be wise beyond our years. His proposal to me was nothing extravagant, yet it was meaningful as he extended his promise to love me forever. We were living in an apartment, cuddled up in bed together, when he offered me that promise in the form of a ring. A circle, showing that our love had no end.

"Will you marry me?"

I responded quickly, before he had a chance to change his mind. "Yes!"

He slid the gold band with a tiny diamond over my finger where it fit securely past my knuckle. He pulled me close into his arms, and in that space, I felt safe.

As we began to plan our wedding, we discovered, once again, I was pregnant. I literally must have been the most fertile myrtle.

Tony said, upon hearing the news, "Just looking at you makes you pregnant."

Thankfully, even though these pregnancies were not planned, I was at least growing and learning to make better decisions with each one. I don't condone this particular order of things, but I also know now that this was part of God's plan. What this discovery did for us was just move our plan along a little more quickly. Instead of getting married in September, we made it official in July and welcomed our second born son, Trent, the following January.

The struggles were real—we were just kids ourselves, now living on our own and raising two boys three years apart. The world of sacrifice really set in as we struggled to provide food, mostly living on ring bologna and macaroni and cheese, and barely making enough money to pay rent. During those early years of marriage, we didn't have any savings or safety net. We were just getting by, but we had love and a commitment to make it work. Despite the fact we struggled financially, our boys never longed for anything. They were able to experience a variety of activities and were raised in a loving environment with a flair of simplicity. Slowly, things became steadier, and we were able to feel a sense of security.

The following year, Tony found a summer job in the mortgage industry at which he excelled. He decided to pursue it further and didn't return to college that fall. I, too, found a job, and we started to find balance in our life with the help of my parents watching the boys while we worked. We were so young, and our responsibilities threw us into adult life without ever having an opportunity to discover who we really were. Like most marriages, we had our ups and downs, remaining pulled together by the string of our compatibility. There were many times that it seemed like ending our relationship would be the easier thing to do, but what you can't always see in those moments, is the beauty of the rainbow that is hidden out of sight, until you fight for it.

Through these early lessons, not only was I able to witness the beginning of my own transformation, but I also stood next to my husband; the boy that I watched turned into a man. I witnessed Tony begin his own spiritual journey. We knew the good, the bad, the struggles, and the triumph that each of us faced because we faced them together, never ceasing to learn from our experiences. Even to this day, we continue to learn along the way, trying hard never to feel hopeless, because even in the moments of despair, an unexpected gift may be waiting to be unwrapped.

Chapter Five

GOD CREATED LEO

Life became busy, exposing Matthew and Trent to as many opportunities as we could. There was no time to relax on a honeymoon, but we grabbed life by the horns and went with it. We began to find a rhythm in our relationship and, as the years passed by, everything seemed to fall into place. Tony's job developed into a career (one that he has remained committed to, to this day) and we were able to establish our roots in an area we believed was thriving and a great environment to raise a family. A gift presented itself as a piece of land at the end of the rainbow where we drew up plans to build our dream home and dug in. Like giddy leprechauns, Tony and I passionately grasped at the chance to create value out of nothing, which was incredible, considering the shaky start to our relationship and the fact that we were only in our mid-twenties. The universe seemed to be lining everything up in a path ahead. The challenges we faced faded into the past and we put them behind us.

With our cozy, blue, Cape Cod style home nestled at the top of a hill, we felt refreshed and renewed with a sense of freedom. We were dealt a difficult hand at a young age, but Tony and I rallied and created a space that was safe for our boys to dwell within. In the late hours of night, when all should be still, we would hear Matthew and Trent laughing together in their beds. This brought peace to my worrying heart. An unbreakable brotherly bond formed that made time more meaningful with each passing day.

The years went by, and we watched our boys grow with our marriage.

Matthew was an observant little boy who liked to lead Trent around in their imaginative world. They spent most of their time in the yard of our dream home, exploring lands beyond. Both boys excelled at school, took an interest in sports, and established strong ties with friends. Tony and I instilled strong family values and open communication to keep them aware that they were loved and supported through life's trials. The four of us had a good system going at the house, ensuring chores were completed and chances were taken for adventures. Even though money was tight, we were able to experience several excursions, including a week stay out west in the foothills of Wyoming. There, we watched our first rodeo together before viewing Mount Rushmore in South Dakota. All of our faces beamed as we captured a family picture in front of the presidents' portraits.

In the blink of an eye, Matthew was eleven and Trent eight. Constantly full of energy, the two of them would return from school and throw their backpacks on the table while looking for something to eat. Their menu expanded from the macaroni days much like their stomachs expanded as well. It seemed as though there were constantly cups and plates strewn about, reminding me of my mom and the way she was always posted at the kitchen sink. Not to mention an additional burst of energy we added to our space in the form of a yellow Labrador puppy named Mylo. I recall one winter where my primary responsibility was preparing hot cocoa after hours of playtime in the snow. Sometimes, when Wisconsin winter winds were bearable, I would poke my head out the door to listen to their adventure.

"Trent, come over here with the shovel! We need to dig deeper to make a tunnel."

Trent came hustling over and handed Matthew the spade. Mylo, meanwhile, sniffed and scratched the spot they marked. "Here you go, brother."

"Thanks. Okay, you go on the other side while I dig this side and we'll meet in the middle."

Trent ran around the mound of snow at the top of the driveway and slid on his knees. Following the guidance of Matthew, while wrestling Mylo away in excitement, Trent dug an entrance on his half of the mound. Eventually, their hands joined at the center, and they carved out the remaining snow that allowed all three of them to crawl into their tunnel.

"Well, this is a good spot," Trent stated.

"For sure, this is the biggest tunnel I've ever seen."

When the cold settled into their bones and the snow melted into cloth, they would stomp into the house and shed their layers. Mylo came trotting in moments later, leaving a trail of snow crumbs through the kitchen that quickly became puddles of water. Even though all my boys were messy, my life wasn't.

Then, one unexpected day, Tony approached me and said, "What do you think about having another baby?"

I was stunned.

The thought of starting over again wasn't something I was jumping up and down about. We experienced multiple broken moments in our relationship, moments we initially thought we couldn't work through, and even considered ending our marriage several times. It took Tony about a year to convince me, and then it took another year for us to conceive (which shocked me, given my previous track record). This brought me back to those naive thoughts that I could control the outcome, when really, things were on God's time.

I was thirty during this third pregnancy, and my perspective on it was so different from what I encountered with my previous experiences. There was an obvious growth and maturity that developed in me, not only from being older, but also from being a mother. I fully understood this time that there was a life growing inside of me. After having time with my older boys, I could see the joy they brought, and the adventure they gave my life. All of us were excited about having another member join our family. The decision wasn't taken lightly, and knowing it was ultimately going to change the lives of all four of us, we involved Matthew and Trent in the decision process. Little did we know at that moment just how much.

I felt so healthy and strong during all the stages of this particular pregnancy. I had a better understanding of the importance of nutrition and exercise, not only for keeping me healthy, but also to develop a healthy child. I still indulged in treats, but let's just say I didn't get stuck in any desks this time. I remember the moment I revealed to my parents that I was pregnant. I was a bit nervous, like the same child who had to approach them from the pregnancies before. My parents were able to witness the growth and maturity in my marriage and in my parenting skills, and they were beyond thrilled to hear the news embracing me with love and excitement.

Our third born son, Leo, entered our lives on New Year's Day of 2002. We made for a speedy exit to leave a New Year's Eve party we attended to head home and get cleaned up while grabbing our packed bag. My delivery with him was quick (about a two-hour span), so we literally made it to the hospital with little time to spare. The speed of Leo's entry was as if he knew he had a message to deliver and only a short period of time to do it. It was a good thing his delivery was not delayed because he arrived with the cord wrapped around his neck (which the doctor tried to discreetly remove) and, had he endured a long-term delivery, he could have potentially sustained some side effects. Thankfully, that wasn't the case and instant joy filled our hearts as we heard the sound of his strong voice released in his first cry.

He was a beautiful baby, and the first thing I said to my husband as Leo was placed in my arms was, "He is perfect." What is funny about that moment is, although those words spilled from my lips with such ease, I didn't realize how perfect he was really going to be. As we looked at each other for the first time, together we could not have begun to anticipate the journey that lay before us. Things in life are not always as they seem. A package which appears perfectly wrapped on the outside could hold something completely unexpected within, much like the outer shell of myself that I was trying to display, while the inner-self remained broken. Leo was such a package, a special gift! He somehow managed to emerge from the darkness of the womb as a light just waiting to be lit and seen.

Tony could barely contain his excitement as he stood at my bedside. "Let's call your parents and share the great news!"

"Maybe we can wait a little bit. After all, it is only four in the morning." Moments later, Tony was dialing the phone.

"He is here! You have another grandson." Bliss filled Tony's chest, and with a release of air, he declared, "He is perfect. She is amazing!

Delivered him like a pro." Standing proudly, holding him in his arms, he then said, "Leo."

My pregnancy with Leo brought me so much joy. Although I have nothing but love for my first two children, this delight stemmed from a difference in my own individual growth and maturity. I felt strong and confident, I believed I was finding myself and my way. Tony and I were in a position where we could financially take care of ourselves, and this brought a new level of contentment. In addition to how I felt, I was so excited to see how involved both our older sons would be. I was not in this alone. I was not the little girl unable to have my voice heard. I was now part of something bigger; a family—a family I created.

Trent was thrilled about having a baby brother, stating, "I knew it."

As a newborn, Leo desired to always be held and cried when he wasn't. He required constant attention and, because I wasn't producing enough milk leaving him unsatisfied, he would finally give up and fall asleep from exhaustion. These challenges didn't help things as I also experienced postpartum depression after his delivery. I was very uncertain about the range of emotions I experienced. I didn't realize at that moment exactly what I was dealing with. I was sleep deprived and I felt moody, which led me to believe I was simply experiencing symptoms of being a new mom.

As I healed from the physical and mental effects of the pregnancy, Tony worked from his office out of our home. I found myself with my newborn all the time while feeling far away from him. To add to my insecure thoughts, Tony was training another employee. Every time I stepped close to his office, I heard laughter coming from the two of them. It made me angry and suspicious, and my mind created scenarios like those I experienced during his college years.

It put me in a dark place. The commotion of Matthew and Trent ceased during the day while they attended school, leaving me alone in our home with Leo in my arms. I noticed a pattern; my emotional growth was not lining up with my physical growth. I was stuck in a little girl's mindset. The unresolved trauma from my childhood lived in my bones and continued to resurface, not allowing me to move forward in life. Although I told myself that I was fine, it was obviously affecting my relationships and my self-esteem.

This was my first experience with postpartum depression, and it became a pattern of mine to deflect my unresolved issues onto Tony. After all, he was the one who wanted to expand our family, and in my mind, I was only seeing my new limitations and viewing things from a very narrow-minded perspective. I wasn't extending gratitude to Tony for his hard work which allowed me to be a stay-at-home mother. I wallowed in my own self-pity, trying to change Tony's behavior, blinded by the fact it was me, who needed to change. I needed redemption. I needed a Savior.

I was brought up in a family that went to church, and I was taught to believe in Jesus. It was a routine; something I had to do and get through, but I didn't have a fellowship with God. I went about my day, believing I was a decent person. Looking at me from the outside, it appeared I had it together, but I didn't have a stable moral compass. I often justified to myself that the wrong decisions I made from time to time were not a big deal. I thought, *Everyone does things like this.*

We had real struggles, and our lack of communication made it hard to work through multiple issues to regain and strengthen our marriage. They were just pushed down, the way I learned to cope, with the thought that if they were not spoken about, then they don't exist. I battled in my mind that he didn't see me as an equal, often mentioning he was the provider, the one who brought in the income. I felt controlled, occurrences of my youth resurfaced, and once again, I felt held down without a voice.

Thankfully, with the help of family, we were able to work through this uncertainty which developed from a lack of communication. By openly discussing our issues, we learned that it was okay to ask for help and allow others to see our weakness instead of sweeping them under the rug. Somehow, through these times when it seemed like we were just tolerating each other, we managed to have intimate moments that led to us discovering baby number four was on the way. When we initially discussed having another child, we hoped that they would have a sibling close in age to grow up with, but we just didn't anticipate it was going to happen so quickly.

Oliver was born in May of 2003. Upon arriving at the hospital, he was born about fifty-five minutes later. Oliver made a splash into our lives. As he exited the canal, his departure was followed by a heavy flow of water. It wasn't long after he entered our lives that I was whisked away to have an emergency dilation and curettage (D&C) where the doctor opens the cervix and uses a surgical instrument to remove tissue from inside the uterus. Shortly after Oliver was born, my uterus released a significant blood clot and this procedure was performed to eliminate further concerns.

Oliver's arrival made him and Leo only seventeen months apart. He was such a happy baby; often content and full of smiles. Having the boys this close in age was so special and they formed an amazing bond. Leo and Oliver did everything together as the three of us enjoyed outings and adventures.

As their lives began, Matthew was going through his own transition. He was involved in a lot of school activities and held a part-time job. He was independent as his high school days flourished. Or so I thought. Just months after Oliver arrived into our family, Matthew was preparing for college. My life was so full. There were so many demands competing for my attention that this moment of void, from a child eventually leaving home, didn't have time to fully set in. I couldn't see how Matthew was treading water, trying to stay afloat. He noticed the weight of life on my shoulders and held his struggles in, much like my own pattern. He desperately wanted to share choices he made, yet simultaneously, didn't want to disappoint us. For example, he thought that he would let us down by not showing an interest in school sports.

Trent was heavily involved in ice hockey during this time. He didn't seem to slow down and really take in the dynamics of how our family was changing. He stayed focused on himself, which possibly protected him from the reality of what was happening around him. Sports was an area that separated our family. While Tony attended to Trent, getting him where he needed to be, I continued developing my bond with both Leo and Oliver.

There were plenty of challenges that came with the dynamics of our family. With that big of an age span, it sometimes was difficult to find outings we could all do together and enjoy. What this did for our family was enable Matthew and Trent time to extend their youth, giving them an "excuse" to still engage in childhood games they enjoyed. It was so beautiful to watch the playful nature arise in them, keeping them in touch with their inner child.

Everything in life seemed to be the way it was meant to be; happiness enveloped the walls of our home and there was a level of calmness that surrounded us. Our boys were all healthy. Matthew and Trent were discovering their journeys that lay ahead. Leo and Oliver were thriving and exposure to their older brothers seemed to push them along their voyage. All the struggles in life that led to this moment allowed me to exhale. Like true wind pushes the sails of a boat, we felt at peace; at last, we reached the summit of life's mountain we had been climbing. But with calmness, a storm is often brewing.

Chapter Six

EXHILE WITH NO TIME TO EXHALE

The moment of exhalation was short-lived. At age two, Leo's life took a drastic turn and, as a result, so did our family. Leo's body began to fail him. We noticed the change in January of 2004, while attending a family gathering. Leo began tripping over his left foot, and as the day progressed, it happened more frequently. This subtle change in his physical abilities didn't seem to affect his attitude. He happily engaged with all his cousins and enjoyed the party.

When we arrived back home, it was late. After tucking Leo into bed, my hope was that the morning would bring resolution. Unfortunately, our journey took us in a different direction and Leo's foot was worse as he was then unable to bear weight on it. I reached out to his doctor immediately. My heart raced with endless possibilities as I worried about what could be wrong. Again, I found myself dialing the numbers on the phone, fearing what may answer on the other side. We were able to schedule an appointment for later that day and I was relieved to have it looked at before further damage occurred. That visit became the moment that forever changed our lives.

I entered the room with Leo in my arms, assuming he possibly sprained his ankle, but nothing could have prepared me for the news that was actually presented to me. I was told Leo had a dropped left foot and nystagmus, a term used for eyes shifting quickly side to side. Based on those symptoms, I was instructed to go to the hospital for a CT scan of his brain. None of this made any sense to me. What did his brain have to do with what I was still thinking was a sprained ankle? My mind couldn't grasp the words spoken to me. It was a moment frozen in time as I tried to make out what was so unexpected and so unnerving. Leo sat in my lap, smiling, unable to make out what was wrong in the first place.

I left the office feeling so confused, wishing I would have had another set of ears listening in on what was said. I called Tony to make arrangements for him to meet me at the hospital. The hallways seemed to swallow our steps as we left. I proceeded to load Leo back into the car and exhaled. On the thirty—minute drive, my thoughts kept looping with the words that were told to me. My heart was pounding, and my eyes filled with tears, making it difficult to see clearly, both for the road and for what my life had in store for me. The weeks that led up to this moment didn't show any reason for concern or indicate any significant change was occurring.

As I parked the car in the structure, I turned off the ignition and felt something within myself also disconnect. I peered into the rearview mirror and saw the same emptiness staring back at me that my reflection had displayed in years past. My eyes shifted, Leo came into focus, and my mind was fueled with determination to help my son. His serene nature calmed me. I opened the car door and tried to keep my mind from making assumptions until answers were found. I embraced Leo into my arms, hoping that my footing remained strong enough to walk the pavement that separated me from the entrance of the hospital doors.

Shortly after Leo and I arrived, Tony made his way to the check-in area. He left Matthew and Trent at home to watch Oliver so we could get answers together. As our eyes met, we felt each other's pain and uncertainty. It was nice to have him close to me. He felt like home, and at least we were in this together.

"Hi, sweetheart." Tony leaned in and connected with Leo's eyes.

Tony grabbed Leo from my arms as I addressed the endless questions to get Leo admitted. I could hear myself going through the routine, but my mind was elsewhere. I looked back at Leo and saw his hands playing with Tony's shirt and was motivated to do what I could to get him help.

We were led to an exam room. The lighting omitted an unpleasant glow as I searched for the panel to dim them. The chill in the room, along with the sterile smell, emphasized the lack of coziness that our home provided. With the hospital being a learning facility, endless doctors paraded in and out of the room. Each one asked the same questions to the point of both exhaustion and frustration. Things moved so slowly, and yet quickly all at the same time as we tried to trust and process the procedures being laid out before us.

The three of us were moved into another room. The same feeling encapsulated the space. This room, however, held a bed instead of an exam table. The bed felt more like a cage, with bars surrounding it on all four sides. Leo's tiny body was placed inside of it. He looked so diminutive, like the bed was absorbing him to the point of being lost within. A free-spirited little boy shouldn't be put in a cage. It didn't seem natural and that feeling had me on edge.

I felt so helpless as I sat at his bedside, lost and uncertain of what lay ahead. I felt strapped down to my chair, unable to hold him in my arms while cords engulfed him. So many things were being monitored that it was hard to find Leo, entangled in all the equipment. Torn between staying at his side and the tug of my heart as my two teenage boys remained home with my baby, I found it to be a difficult time to be a mom to all. I recognized the need to feel loved, and I wanted to be able to give that to all of my sons in a moment where one desperately needed me more.

As tests were prescribed, things seemed to escalate quickly. The frantic display of movement swirled around me as doctors tried to figure out what was happening to Leo. He was pulled in multiple directions for bloodwork, a CT scan, and an MRI. Charts were being documented, medical findings were being explained, but nothing was resonating. The explanations felt like a jumble of words bouncing around in my mind.

The doctor entered the room once again. Leo's body lay limp and exhausted in his bed.

I recall seeing the life slip from Leo's eyes, replaced with cold dark puddles that didn't reflect light back, the same dull look I remember seeing in my own reflection prior to my attempt to end my own life. There was a source at this moment, though, that kept us calm. It felt distant, but we knew it was there. The following day we needed to run another test and, dreadfully, it was a spinal tap.

The doctor's words still replay in my ear. "We will be inserting a needle into the lower back to obtain a sample of the cerebrospinal fluid. This is the clear fluid that surrounds the spine and brain."

The panel of blood work previously taken indicated high levels of lactic acid. Basically, Leo's body appeared as if he was running a nonstop marathon. They hoped this test would eliminate other conditions that were in consideration and narrow down what they believed was occurring. My heart ached that only one of us could accompany Leo. I went to Leo's side, kissed him tenderly on the lips, and whispered, "Momma loves you." I turned to Tony, and without a word spoken, held him in my embrace. I knew I needed to check in on my other sons and knew that Tony would be there for Leo while I was away. I watched Tony hold Leo in his arms where a toddler should have been able to walk beside his father. I exited the room, and left a piece of my heart with them.

They made their way to the operating room as I left the hospital. Later, when I was reunited with Tony, he filled me in on how tears streamed down his face as the cries of Leo's fears echoed off the walls of the room. Gently, Tony had laid Leo on the bed. Positioning his tense body on his right side, Tony remained at his side throughout the procedure. He held Leo's hand, gazing into the eyes of his child who did not understand what was happening to him. The doctor approached from the other side of the bed. The blood shattering screams that exerted from Leo's tiny existence made it feel as if the doctors forgot to give Leo the local anesthetic to numb the puncture site. As the thin, hollow needle was inserted between the two lower vertebrae, through the spinal membrane, and into the spinal canal, Tony felt the piercing in his heart. As the fluid was withdrawn and the needle removed, the puncture site was covered with a bandage. Yet, no bandage could ever cover what Tony witnessed.

Tony can still hear the screams of our son. Tony can still feel the piercing of his heart. This so-called routine procedure left scars in Tony's mind. He felt helpless and unable to protect Leo from the pain he endured. The suddenness of the whole ordeal was tough to process. We went from a day with little worry, to one filled with anguish and fear. A fear that brought in dark clouds, flooding our clear paths with rain and hail. Anguish that took that rain and churned it into mud to make a mess of the foundation on which we stood. Although I may not have been there physically during this procedure, my tears poured forth, knowing it wasn't a sunny carefree day.

After a week's stay at the hospital, they gathered all of the information and revealed our worst fears. That evening became the first day of our journey on the path as a "special needs" family. The prognosis: the decline of Leo's body was inevitable. They released us from the hospital with a child who was broken. Leo was in worse condition than the moment we had arrived days prior. A child was brought to the hospital, but the remains of experiments were left with us. Just processing it all ourselves, it was difficult to assure Leo it would be okay, and we were concerned about how our other sons would react.

We were sent home with a heavy dose of steroids, concluding Leo most likely had ADEM, acute disseminating encephalomyelitis. The doctor hoped the steroids would reverse the declines to his motor functions and that he would regain stability. It was anticipated these improvements would occur within a few weeks. Their explanation was delivered in a manner that left us unsettled and our minds clouded. The forecast was delivered, but the accuracy remained as uncertain as the sun on a partly cloudy day. It was a long car ride, but at least there was the fact that we were bringing Leo home, where he belonged.

I remember the day we brought Leo home from the hospital days after his birth, holding him in my arms, uncertain of where our lives were leading. This same feeling came over me once again, as I walked into our home, holding him in my arms, this time as a toddler. Stepping through the door with more than just uncertainty this time, we had little reason for hope. We were given no instruction, no guidance. Wait and see. *Wait, and see?* This was my son, not a science experiment at school. We were left abandoned, isolated, with no one to show us the way. I know now we were never alone, but medically, we had nothing to lean on. Spiritually, God had everything under control. Tony and I had no point of reference, no baseline, and no other case to compare our experience with. We stumbled, we experimented, we succeeded and failed, all for the love of our son.

Then, the moment arrived to have a conversation with Matthew, Trent, and Oliver. Tony and I gathered the boys in the living room and tried to shake off our nerves. They suspected something was wrong due to our weeklong visit at the hospital, but putting the words with our actions made it more real. Mom and Dad were away off and on for a week, but now this news was going to alter the reality of years to come.

I glanced over at Tony as the boys seated themselves on the couch, and turned back to look at Oliver. His eyes were bright with youth. I opened my mouth to speak and tried to explain what was not explained very well to us to begin with. Fear filled their faces, matching the same fear within Leo's own eyes, and electrified the room with anxiety. His reality became our reality. It not only altered his life, but transformed the lives of each of his siblings along the way. While the world all around us was moving, inside our home, things were brought to a halt like gears wedged by a stick.

Jaws dropped, and tears puddled together, streaking the furniture with their love. As a family, we embraced Leo in the center of the room and remained together for a few minutes in silence. Our dog, Mylo, even entered the room and placed his head on my lap to sympathize with us. After the initial shock, Matthew and Trent took it upon themselves to bring movement into the stillness of despair that hung over our home.

Matthew coped with the situation with compassion and understanding. The day we brought Leo home from the hospital was also Matthew's sweet sixteenth birthday. A day that should have been celebrated in honor of him was overshadowed by dark times. He was a sophomore in high school and suddenly his home life was in disarray. Trent was in seventh grade, in the midst of pivotal years of growth and self—discovery. Nevertheless, recognizing the pain in my face, they sprang into action to give me a moment of peace.

"Come on, Leo! Let's go downstairs."

"Okay," Leo replied.

Matthew smiled and walked over to his brother. Leo's arms extended to the high ceiling as he awaited his brother's hands. Lefty hung a little lower, but held onto just as much longing to be lifted.

"Trent and Oliver, come down too!" Matthew positioned Leo onto his waist and opened the basement door. "Let's make sure you get the red engine, Leo."

"Yeah, yeah, yeah!" Leo laughed while Matthew's footsteps trotted to the lower level. Soon after, the other brothers followed. I took this opportunity to catch up with Tony before heading downstairs myself to see if the boys were okay. As my presence joined theirs, it became apparent quickly that, although the situation was heavy, Leo's light heart still united them with peace.

"So, what kind of track do you want today, brother?" I overheard Trent ask.

"A big loop with five trains."

"A big loop," Matthew interjected, "but where will we all fit?"

Laughter filled Leo's lungs before he replied, "Right there!"

"Oh, my bad, I did not see that space there."

The brothers entered the toy space and stared in awe at the totes stacked on the shelves. Within, there were all sorts of games waiting to be played and all kinds of memories yearning to be shared. There was the tote that held blocks and Legos, the box that contained army guys and action figures, and a basket holding miscellaneous balls. What they were looking for, however, was scattered across the floor already from the previous day's journey. Matthew placed Leo on the floor and helped him stabilize.

"The red one!" Leo blurted out while Matthew and Trent assembled the pieces. Oliver lost himself in the piles of toys next to the brothers as he patiently waited.

There were straight pieces, curved ones, and even those that branched out to allow multiple connections. These tracks built numerous possibilities, but it was up to the conductors themselves to make such a build that the tracks would be legendary. After all, only the best would be sufficient for Leo, and the brotherhood did not want to let him down. This set came with motorized train engines, each having its own base to start, and each with some cargo to haul.

Trent connected a few pieces to form the straight edge of the course and held it up to Leo. Finding it hard to judge the tracks from his position, Leo scooted his butt closer to the brothers to take a good look. His brown eyes examined it closely before he agreed it would do.

"Okay, Leo, do you want the engines over here?"

"Yeah."

Trent brought out more pieces and assembled them carefully, following Leo's instructions. Corner pieces clicked together with straight edges and engine stations were locked in on the side. After several more minutes of contemplating the design, they all gazed at the completed loop in awe and sat back with pride. The red engine was at Leo's side near the black, brown, green and blue ones. All they needed was a conductor to give them the go ahead.

"Turn them on!" Leo shouted.

Each of the boys held onto the controllers that gave the engines fuel. All at once, they pulled the triggers and watched their trains spring into motion. Leo sat with his red controller in hand, gently supported by Trent's, and followed the trains loop after loop until they were all exhausted from play. The engines returned to their stations and the boys moved to the couch.

Matthew and Trent tapped into their creativity and built marble tracks, towers and structures from Legos, and endless tracks of railway for Leo over the following weeks. They built forts from couch cushions, danced to loud music, and made a pet shop using Leo's stuffed animals he collected from being in the hospital. Sometimes, Mylo would even be involved as a sea monster or lion in the jungle. These games allowed Leo to travel in his imagination where his body was limited in motion.

These activities encouraged Leo to engage over the following weeks. He began to find his footing and attempted to take steps. His brothers were so proud of him when he attempted to be more involved than just a bystander laughing at their jokes. The steps he did manage to take were so precious and filled with such intention. Even though he was improving, unfortunately by the time our follow—up visit came, the doctors were not seeing the developments they hoped would be occurring. This news didn't surprise me. Leo made some strides in the few weeks that passed since we were released from the hospital, but not to the level they expected the steroids would have provided.

This once again seemed to have them puzzled and we obtained a second opinion from another local neurologist. Leo's files were also then sent to doctors from around the world, including Amsterdam, the Netherlands, and Johns Hopkins. Even once they examined his MRI and file, they still didn't have a decisive diagnosis. They moved away from the initial ADEM diagnosis after further review. They concluded that the diffused white matter disease that was symmetrical on the scan was actually marked symmetry which would not be common in ADEM.

They then began to consider Leukodystrophy, a brain disorder where the myelin or white matter of the brain deteriorates. Within this illness there are several categories: Alexander disease, megalencephalic, Krabbe disease, and vanishing white differential. Leo showed symptoms of each, but didn't seem to fit into any one in particular. They also considered a Mitochondrial disease, yet that too, wasn't conclusive. Bottom line was Leo's findings didn't "fit" into any one category and it appeared as if they were grasping for answers. Leo's findings were just so rare. We were told at the time, the way his scans read, it made Leo one of only five cases in the entire world known!

Things changed quickly for Leo. In only a month's time from the initial hospital admission, the once energized little pack of power became a lifeless body locked with fear. Everything that physically made Leo "Leo" was stripped away. He lost the ability to walk, stand, crawl, swallow, speak, and use his left hand. His right hand was weakening, and he was only able to sit on his own for short periods of time. Leo was locked in a still body with only the capability of eye movement, which held fear and screamed, "Help me!"

The decline took hold and he lost so much of himself. We all lost so much of ourselves, seeing him deteriorate right in front of our eyes. It was a helpless feeling to see his loss reach such an extent in such a short window of time. His health was escaping and all we could do was continue to try to find ways to make each day matter. I believe in that moment, although it wasn't yet revealed to me, my little two-year-old boy found Jesus, and guided my thoughts to Him as well. Silently, within the depths of Leo's soul, Jesus settled in and kept him calm through the rigorous journey of his life.

It was heartwrenching to look at a bottle of steroids and have to administer it to such a small child, yet we made an effort to trust the process. Nevertheless, Leo still tried to engage in activities he loved. With the loving support of his brothers, we all assisted to bring life back into his world. One of his favorite activities was knee hockey. This game consisted of a miniature hockey net, played with tiny sticks and a ball while playing on your knees. Matthew and Trent were ball retrievers, careful to avoid the swings of Leo's stick to score a goal. Once the ball hit the net, the entire family would erupt with cheer and the smile would return to his face.

I took Leo into the other room to rest. He was so delicate as I lay him on his pillow. His weight felt different. When I reentered the living room, my sons were sprawled out on the floor with the dog, consoling one another and trying to make sense of it all.

We entered the wilderness season, as Leo's health declined. A tidal wave of change pressed us against the rocks, and then pulled us back under. Fear surged in the crashing waves, exploding with energy, then retreating back to its depths. Like the sand trying to remain on solid ground, the boys masked their fears to avoid afflicting more pain.

As others in high school worried about passing their driver's education course, attending athletic events, and school dances, Matthew and Trent were concerned with much more. They felt wise beyond their years, unable to relate to the carefree nature of their peers, much like I had experienced in high school as well. The path ahead may have been difficult to see, but together, as a family, we were asked to trust God. It was in this trust that my faith grew. I believed He had me in His arms, and wasn't going to let go.

Chapter Seven

HARD TO SWALLOW

In the stillness of the morning, I awoke to a heaviness in my heart. Like fog casting shadows over a meadow, I was unable to think or see clearly, as the density clouded my thoughts. Leo's health changed so quickly—just as I processed one loss of ability, another occurred. It wasn't only externally; internally, drastic changes impacted his ability to swallow safely. There were multiple occasions when a sip of water resulted in aspiration, and as this reaction continued, we had genuine concern with his lack of nutrition intake. Life was slipping away from him, and measures needed to be taken to help him survive.

After discussion with his team of doctors, it was determined that we needed to include a gastroenterologist on his case. The need for more opinions weighed heavily on my shoulders and the speed of change made Leo's body appear to wither away before my eyes. He was confused, knowing that he could perform habitual tasks up to this point, only to now struggle with life's basic needs. After some contemplation, Tony and I scheduled the appointment with the GI doctor.

"We need to place a temporary feeding tube through Leo's nose and down his throat. This will bypass the normal means of eating, which will deposit formula directly into his stomach."

Stunned for a moment, I eventually replied, "Is he put under for this?"

"No. I will gently guide the tubing through the nasal passage. It is a simple procedure."

I felt the heat of anxiety overtake my body. The last time we were told something was simple, blood curdling screams filled our souls. In such a short period of time, we knew nothing was simple and that most procedures came with a price. A price that was slowly depleting the life from my son while trying to save it.

"Okay, what happens then?"

"Once we are able to stabilize Leo's decline, he will need to undergo surgery to have a permanent G-tube placed to assist in his nutrition."

I looked at Leo, "Momma is here. Let me hold your hand."

The tube was fed through Leo's nose, allowing him to ingest formula and put his stomach at ease. For the rest of us, back home, the knots worsened as our anxiety took over. Feeding Leo became a process that took hours to complete. In an effort to keep him calm, while allowing gravity to pull the formula down the tube, we each took turns walking around the house. Leo was held firmly in one arm while the other held the formula sac in the air. This was a chance for us to sing to Leo and speak kind words to a boy who was fighting for each drop. Around and around we went, hoping each feeding was a success, while fighting the urge to rest. This bonding experience made *Leo's fight our fight* knowing we were important to the success of his recovery.

When his body stabilized just months after his release, we returned to the hospital and Leo underwent surgery. As we entered the familiar halls, I felt them closing in upon me, like a vice securely clamped down on a piece of wood. I struggled to breathe. It was hard for me to find trust with the doctors as they consistently scrambled for answers that appeared to never be found. Tony and I kissed Leo and watched as his stable, yet fragile body stretched out on a bed and was wheeled off to the operating room. Nervously, we waited side by side in the waiting room staring at the doors, hoping they would once again open with our baby in tow.

While under general anesthesia, the doctors placed the tube lapa-roscopically. Utilizing a small camera, an incision was made inside the belly button and an instrument was used to bring the stomach closer to the abdomen wall. This allowed the tube to be placed into the stomach from the outside. A small balloon was then inflated on the inside of the button to hold it in place. While he was under, they decided to also obtain a skin sample. The physicians wanted to consider, and eliminate, the possibilities of other medical reasons as to why Leo's body was spiraling downward without answers, and since skin was already being impacted, they saw an opportunity to use it. Finally, after we memorized the design of the clock on the wall, the doctor surfaced.

"Everything went smoothly. You will be able to see Leo shortly in the observation room."

"Thank you," Tony replied as I clung to his hand.

We were escorted to a room at the end of a long walkway. Leo lay upon the bed, a bit disoriented, but smiled at the sound of my voice as we approached.

"Hi, Leo. It's Momma."

His deep chocolate eyes appeared to be more of a cocoa color, clouded by the grogginess of the anesthesia. As I gazed upon him, his body was limp, fully extended across the stiff, white sheets.

"It won't be long before we can go home, sweetheart." A spark of light appeared in his eyes. The word "home" appeared to trigger relief.

Prior to being discharged, we received all the necessary supplies to care for the healing of the wound, in addition to instructions on how to use the tube. So much information was thrown at us. I felt overwhelmed. What was common practice to the hospital staff was completely foreign to us. Leo was less than thrilled about this change, but remarkably, began to understand this new device sticking out from his belly was actually making his tummy feel full.

Just off center from his belly button, a long tube extended from the incision. At the base was a clamp that sealed the opening of the tube. At the other end was a shut-off valve. This initial feeding tube was cumbersome. The weight and the length pulled at the tender opening, making it difficult for the skin to heal. We had to continue to change the gauze that surrounded the insertion point due to the fluid that oozed from the rawness of the procedure.

Meeting Leo's basic needs became very time consuming. Administering the fluid into his G-tube was a slow process, one we lovingly did for him, yet it was hard to also meet the needs of Oliver, who was only about ten months at the time. He also needed the love and attention of his mother. This was the moment we realized we desperately needed help.

Our church stepped in, and two ladies from their women's group came to our aid. These ladies willingly walked into our circumstances and, without really knowing who we were or the situation they were coming into, provided unconditional love and assistance to a family in need. This became one of many situations when Leo drew someone into our world, and they became friends. Leo had that effect on people; once they were pulled into our life, the blessings were revealed, and they wanted to stay.

With life slipping away so quickly from Leo, we began to expose him to all life's possibilities. We also saw an urgency to capture images of Leo and our family before physical abilities slipped too far away from him. So, my very first encounter with one of the ladies from church was a whirlwind of a meeting. She stepped into our home, and even before uttering a full sentence of, *Nice to meet you, I am Diane*, I whisked her into my vehicle. I had an appointment scheduled at a photography studio in the mall and was already running a bit late from the previous appointment with Leo.

As we made the thirty-minute drive to the appointment, I tried to familiarize myself with her and vice versa, to build some sort of platform of trust so each of us could find comfort in the other. When we arrived at the studio, we took multiple photos of Leo and Oliver together and then, as I attempted to obtain some of Leo individually, I asked if she could take Oliver for a stroller ride around the mall, and she agreed.

I gently placed Oliver in the stroller and quietly mentioned to her, "Do not let Oliver see that it is you pushing the stroller, or he might panic."

"Okay." A look of shock came over her face.

"Thank you." I was a woman of desperation, sending my ten-month old child out into the mall with basically a stranger. As the reality of life slipped away from Leo so quickly, I wanted and needed something to hold onto, a photo capturing him before he no longer would be.

This beautiful woman, who became a lifelong friend, later shared her insight on that crazy day, a day a mother handed her child over to her and said go. It is funny how we can laugh and cry at the same time about this moment in a time we shared. A frantic event where clothes were flying in the studio, as if I were dressing a ticking time bomb ready to explode at any moment. Desperation filled my body, not knowing if another photo opportunity would present itself. In reality, I was trying to capture something that was already lost. Things changed so quickly, even if I were to have taken a photo hourly, things would have been different.

I remember having lunch with her right after the photo shoot, the panic subsiding, but the uncertainty still weighed heavily on my heart. Being so caught up in the event of the day, I almost let the importance of my toddler's nutrition slip from my mind. As I fed Leo through his feeding tube, my new friend sat by my side, asking if it was okay to let Oliver have some of her soup. His big, beautiful blue eyes staring into hers reminded me that he, too, was hungry. Such an overwhelming day had made me so out of sorts that the simplest requirements of mother-hood almost went undone.

As I continued to capitalize on life, I researched ways to have Leo exposed to the animals that he loved so much. Leo cherished visits to the zoo, but it quickly became difficult for him to get close and see the animals from his stroller. We discovered the local pet shop, and took Leo for weekly visits where he was able to handle the puppies and kittens that were for sale.

This exposure brought him so much joy, and before his abilities were completely stripped from him, we found an amazing therapy source nearby, called hippotherapy. Within a few miles of our home, there was an indoor arena where physical and occupational therapists utilized horses for a variety of therapies. As I explained the urgency of Leo's situation to the therapists, there was hesitation. They seemed uncertain that they could make this possible for him. I believe they felt my anguish over the phone and were willing to allow a trial run. Leo's body was extremely weak, but boy, did he sit proudly upon that horse when the time came.

His first visit only lasted about ten minutes, but the smile that spread across his face warmed our hearts and filled our souls with contentment. As we walked in a big circle around the arena, I felt the weight of the situation lift from my shoulders and rest upon the back of the horse. It was a majestic animal, willing to pace itself to keep the people around him safe.

The therapist looked tenderly at Leo after completing the first loop and asked, "How are you doing?"

Leo answered with a flash of his smile. Without even knowing him, the gravity of his charm captured their hearts. They adjusted their schedules to accommodate Leo, knowing that his endurance was only going to take up minutes of their day. Leo's presence managed to once again pull at the heartstrings of complete strangers and transform them from someone we just met into lifelong friends.

Despite this success while in the saddle, Leo's body continued to decline. His ability to hold his head up, and the obvious weakening in his right hand, added a layer of frustration for Leo. We also began to see changes in his vision. Each week, we watched our little boy deteriorate more and more before our eyes, but somehow, there remained an inner calmness. What I believe was happening then was a divine revelation, where Jesus came to Leo. The spirit within him allowed Leo to have peace, and those who surrounded him directly were able to also take on some of that serenity. Months passed, and as the days came and went, so did the sound of hearing Leo speak.

Days passed in silence. Weeks weakened our hearts without the comfort of Leo's words. A boy whose laughter could lift a sorrowful heart was unable to express his love.

Then the day arrived, and our hearts were filled with delight, when the tension broke and from it sprung life. Mimicking the sounds of Oliver, "Da-Da" and "Momma" formed from his mouth and were released from his lips. Every time Oliver said something, Leo tried to repeat it. The power of words, the impact they have when used, became more evident in their interactions. The simplest things in life that we took for granted became the most rewarding events of our day. The sound of his voice, the smile on his face, the gentle kisses, and the need to be held and hugged brought peace.

We slowed our lives down. Everyday needs took time, and in order to allow Leo's body time to absorb and take in the nutrition from his feeding tube, we noticed we needed a distraction. We ended up pairing walks with eating to let Leo see the world around him while he endured a task he wasn't really fond of. We explored bike trails, subdivisions, parks, lakes, farms, museums, the Milwaukee Domes, and zoos, all to help keep Leo's focus on something other than the feeding tube.

I remember a particular walk with a friend on the trail near my home. We walked side by side as I pushed both Leo and Oliver in the double stroller. While the drip of the liquid flowed from the bag into Leo's feeding tube, he enjoyed the flavor of a dum-dum sucker settled upon his tongue. While we are able to take pleasure in the taste of the foods we eat in a natural way, Leo's intake bypassed the sensations, the sucker was a substitute of enjoyment as his tummy was filled. Caught in conversation and flowing in stride, I peered over the top of the stroller and noticed I no longer saw the stick from the sucker. Pausing for a moment, I noticed the sucker had begun to slide down Leo's throat. With a quick thrust to his back, the sucker popped out. I placed it back into his mouth and began to walk again.

My friend looked at me, "What the hell?"

"What?" I stopped to look at her, taken back by her words.

"How can you be so calm? Leo almost choked."

"But he didn't."

"Seriously, why are you not more shaken?"

"After everything we have been through, how can I possibly let a sucker be what shakes me?"

The feeding tube really became a focal part of our day. The initial tube was somewhat temporary until the MIC-KEY tube, which was more of a button style, could be put in place. This really was an extension of Leo. We did our best to tuck it under his shirt to protect it, and him, when not in use. Unfortunately, we did have some mishaps that added to our concern for his well being.

The first feeding tube malfunction occurred when we arrived at one of Leo's early sessions of horseback riding. Panic was a constant companion, feeling the presence of time slipping away. Anxiety took hold of me and sometimes had me frantic, and the added awareness of Leo's pain often caused me to move quickly to get him into a position of comfort. When we arrived at the parking lot of the arena that day, I went to get Leo out of his car seat. In doing so, I unbuckled him and scooped him up, but somehow the extended tubing got hooked in one of the crevices. I pulled Leo up, and ripped the tube right out of his tummy.

"Oh my, how did that happen? Leo, are you okay?!"

"Yes, Momma."

Complete horror set in. I imagined fluid would begin to pour out from within him. To my surprise, there was nothing, just a little bit of blood extracted, but what was pouring out were my tears. I couldn't believe what I had just done, and I was also petrified as to how this would get resolved, assuming Leo would have to undergo another surgery to repair the damage. So instead of enjoying time on the horse, I refastened Leo into the car seat, and we headed to the doctor. I was relieved to discover this was more common than not and I wasn't the first one to ever do this to their child.

"This is an easy fix. Let's get an x-ray and we will proceed from there."

I released a heavy sigh. "What a relief."

"Let's get Leo prepped."

This accident ended up being a benefit as it technically moved along the process of installing the more efficient (I mean less cumbersome and more discrete) feeding tube. For some reason, this minor change seemed to make a big difference in Leo's attitude about the accessory he was sporting on his midsection. The reality was, he no longer had this foreign object visible to him and it no longer added weight to his stoma or tugged on the skin in that area.

Unfortunately, I can't say this ordeal was the only mishap with the feeding tube. Thankfully, the next time we had an issue, I was more prepared and a lot more laid back about the scenario. While attending a family celebration, I decided to take Leo onto the trampoline in the backyard of my sister's home. With Leo in my arms, we began to jump up and down and laughter developed from both of us.

"Higher, higher," he exclaimed.

We continued to jump, as I tried to maintain control of my bladder, and I heard a noise that sounded like air being released from a balloon. I asked everyone else jumping along with us to stop for a moment and as I looked down at the mesh, there lay the button portion of Leo's feeding tube with a deflated balloon attached to the other side.

Somehow, Leo's tube malfunctioned, and thankfully, due to the previous experience, I knew things were going to be okay and no need to panic. However, I knew I had a small window of time to address the situation before the hole in his tummy started to seal. So once again, I scooped him up and said our goodbyes, getting both Oliver and Leo buckled into the backseat, and we began our drive to have a replacement tube put back in. Although I was calm, I apparently was speeding and as I came up over the hill on one of the back country roads, I saw the lights and heard the siren of the local police.

I couldn't believe I was being stopped at a time like this! I slowly pulled over to the shoulder of the road, and through my rearview mirror, I watched the officer approach my vehicle. I anxiously awaited while he seemed to move slower with each step. He stopped when he reached my door and I proceeded to roll down my window.

"Hello, ma'am," he said. "Do you know why I pulled you over?"

"No," I replied. "But I am just in a bit of a time crunch. My son's feeding tube just fell out and I desperately need to get a new one in place."

The anxiety shifted from me to the officer as he peered over my shoulder into the backseat and gazed upon Leo. "Feeding tube?"

I tried hard not to reveal my inner annoyance with him. "Yes. Can I show you?"

The officer stepped back as I exited the front door and opened the door where Leo was seated. I lifted his shirt to reveal the hole in my son's tummy, where the feeding tube once was, and explained that I needed a new tube before it sealed. Ironically, in the area where I was pulled over, there just happened to be a fire station, so the officer inquired if they had a feeding tube in stock. I was trying to be appreciative and, at the same time, knew it would be easier if he would just let me be on my way.

No luck with a replacement (after spending what seemed like an hour searching when in reality it was probably only five minutes), so he allowed me to get on my way. He instructed me to drive carefully and let me off with just a warning. By the way, this wasn't the only time Leo managed to get me out of a ticket, never intentionally, but he was definitely my lucky charm.

So many things in life revolve around the comfort of food, and that had been taken away from Leo. I remember a particular visit to my parents' home, during which my dad made himself a sherbet cone. They had a large freezer in the garage which stored a few gallons of frozen treats. It had been months without the joy of taste for Leo at this point, and he was looking longingly at the cone as it was being devoured quickly with the rainbow colors melting off the side. My dad noticed his desire, and acted on instinct to share the wealth with his grandson.

He gently pressed the sherbet up against Leo's lips. Leo's tongue flicked, and his lips reacted to the cool touch. The smile that overtook his face as the flavor hit his mouth was priceless. Enjoyment briefly awakened Leo's taste buds, and he found complete bliss. Requesting more, my dad agreed, and gave Leo another taste. The slight coating of sherbet covered Leo's tongue, and like the saliva that formed naturally within his mouth, he managed to swallow. The sweet sounds of delight filled the room, and we all enjoyed a moment of one of life's simple pleasures. Like a child finding a golden ticket within a candy bar's wrapping, Leo found elation from the simple taste of food, beyond the limitations of the tube.

Chapter Eight

THREE SIMPLE WORDS

As we continued to move forward, it felt like we had our own version of plagues settling upon us. With every success Leo endured, he would then take two steps back. To find a sense of stability, Leo began working with a variety of therapists to help maintain some of his abilities. What had been so natural for Leo to do on his second birthday now became a gamble of what could go next. We already saw how swallowing changed his days and behavior, which is why seeing him struggle with his extremities and words broke my heart.

For every gain he made, he would unfortunately come down with a cold or fever and then weaken and lose strength. It honestly felt like we, too, were in the wilderness and couldn't be led out. God was in our hearts, but we hadn't yet truly accepted Him to see us through this. Everything that was occurring was just so real and so raw that to think beyond how to get through that day escaped thoughts. The ups and downs were the focus of the family, and the older boys were torn between time with their friends and staying home to lend a hand, while Tony balanced work with family to support us as well. The sad days affected us all, but when those good days came with Leo's smile, we all found strength.

As a family, we ran through open meadows in search of joy and comfort from existence when, in reality, our hike was an inclined slope. Each day, we faced a new uncertainty with every turn on the path. Leo had a mystery of life unfolding inside him. Darkness hovered over us, only allowing us to see the physical defeats, while he lay unable to communicate the pain he experienced at times. What I wasn't aware of, due to racing thoughts of his health, was that God planted a seed in Leo's soul and, just like any other seed, it took time to grow. As it began to reach toward the surface, looking for light to guide its way, Leo became the light, for God created Leo and Leo became our beginning.

As we established a new way of life raising a child with special needs, our biggest struggle initially was finding the proper medication. Trial and error found balance in managing Leo's pain without inhibiting his daily life activities. One of these early moments occurred when we first visited the palliative care doctor at the hospital. Once again, we walked down a long hallway, eventually to be seated in a cold, sterile room that had no feeling of life. The door shut behind us. Moments passed before it opened again, bringing in a new white coat with questions about our situation.

The doctor shook my hand and greeted, "Good afternoon, what brings you in today?"

I began to explain, "Our son is in a great deal of pain, and we are looking for some relief."

He turned toward my boy. "You must be Leo." He proceeded to administer several muscle tests, checking Leo's reflexes. "Can you feel that, Leo?"

He intently looked into Leo's eyes as he tapped the bottom of his foot. He studied Leo's face and, upon finishing his evaluation, he held up a chart that indicated the facial expressions that one releases, based on the pain they are experiencing. There were ten faces illustrated.

He declared his findings, "Leo seems to be at pain level nine."

Leo's pain was a nine! The doctor indicated this was an extreme level of pain, but yet again, we left that visit without a care plan and without any medications to ease his pain. The doctors just didn't seem to know where to begin with Leo or what to do. Things were so foreign to us, and we didn't know how to advocate for our son to get what he needed. The examinations were so quick to find results, but the follow through lacked, and that's where a patient truly needs aid.

Appointment after appointment, Leo left multiple doctors uncertain of his disease and uncertain of a plan of action. It was such a lonely time.

I felt lost and uncertain about how to care for Leo, knowing we had no other cases to compare him to. Time and time again, we were told that he just didn't fit into any one category and that he showed signs of this diagnosis and had pieces of this other illness too. From a medical standpoint, they gave up on Leo, which also meant giving up on us. We felt dismissed and abandoned.

I released my frustrations to a family friend who just happened to be a doctor. She was appalled by the lack of attention Leo received for his pain management. She insisted that I make a follow up appointment so she could attend with me. It was her assertiveness, and level of expectations, that helped us achieve the care Leo deserved. This time, we left with what became our initial pain management plan.

At this point, Leo remained still, and blinking was his only way to communicate (even that was uncertain at times). Everything vibrant about him was withdrawn from his frame, yet there was something inside that appeared to be screaming, *Help me*! Not wanting any regrets, we took a leap of faith and left our comfort zone of traditional medicine, which led to an unknown pathway of holistic practice. Somewhat skeptical, I took Leo, with Oliver in tow while Tony worked and Matthew and Trent were at school, to see a woman nearby who practiced out of her home. As we entered her workspace, it appeared it had been an outbuilding of some sort. It was bright with a lot of light filtering through the windows. The space felt positive and it held hope.

She began to administer several tests, including retrieving a hair sample. She was very kind in the manner she retrieved samples from Leo and explained her work to us as she went. I felt a bit overwhelmed as I tried to listen to what she described while Oliver wandered around the space, observing the knick-knacks and books displayed. After some time went by, Oliver made his way back to me and climbed up onto my lap as she presented her findings.

"On this chart, you can see the different metals that are present. These lines indicate safe levels of each. You can see here that his readings for iron are fine, for example." She paused, moved her finger, and continued, "What I don't like to see are these readings of aluminum and mercury which are extremely elevated and bad for your blood."

The results astonished me, indicating that Leo tested so high in various metals in his body. Leo had undergone so many lab tests in the hospital, yet they had never once mentioned the high levels of metal before, so this news flabbergasted me. Leo had a variety of spikes in different metals as if they were feeding off one another. Measures of aluminum and mercury were off the charts and indicated that Leo possibly had a reaction to his eighteen—month MMR vaccination series where the thimerosal, or mercury, that is used to prolong the shelf life of the vaccine, reacted negatively with Leo's system. Instead of being able to excrete this out of his body, he accumulated it, ultimately suffering a form of metal poisoning.

This new information did shed some light as to potentially why the doctors had such difficulty diagnosing Leo. Ultimately, the severity of Leo's condition was out of the comfort zone of the holistic woman testing him, so she referred us to two other practitioners who specialized in nutrition and detoxification, along with biomechanics and holistic cranial sacral treatment. The process of integrating these two treatment options into Leo's day was slow, but steady. We saw positive signs that the plan was showing improvement in his health, enough to be faithful in continuing to see where it would lead us.

The nutritionist, a beautiful slender lady, caught Leo's eye from the moment I carried him into her downtown office. She spoke softly to Leo, providing him with a sense of calmness. As she referred to her notes from the previous healer, she proceeded to refine her findings by testing a few of her own techniques on Leo. She, too, confirmed the high levels of metal and began using a specialized treatment for Leo that not only pulled metal from his body, but also provided better nutrition for his system.

In the beginning of this treatment plan, Leo was still utilizing a feeding tube, so our options were pretty slim. What she discovered was that the liquid supplement, PediaSure, we were using for his feedings was not suitable for Leo's body. Tony and I acted quickly on this information. We were able to get Prime Greens into Leo's system, which was a supplement of mixed green vegetables that we made into a liquid form, and pushed through his feeding tube.

After making these nutritional adjustments, we saw a change in Leo's overall appearance and mood almost immediately. His skin color blushed, and his eyes had life in them that we hadn't seen for months. When we first saw the nutritionist, Leo's eyes were one of the first indicators of poor health. The whites of his eyes were clouded, lacking clarity and shine. To see that clarity return was one of the most celebrated successes we shared as a family. The metal detox treatments were pretty hard on Leo's system, causing severe diarrhea and leaving us with a lot of laundry.

As for the second practitioner, a ray of hope shined upon us, literally. While working with the nutritionist to detoxify his body, Leo began working faithfully with a natural healer to help his nervous system and mind. After years of working as a practicing physician, Dr. Ray realized he had more to offer than traditional medicine. He felt an inner gift of connecting to one's body and healing through touch and techniques that didn't require medication. This process with Ray elevated my trust and hope as we continued to say yes to new strategies.

I had to really dig deep in my soul to have confidence in Ray's techniques. It was so out of our comfort zone to resort to holistic measures, yet traditional medicine was failing us. On the first visit, for example, Tony and I arrived at the address, looked at each other, and agreed it couldn't be the right one. It was an abandoned medical office building. I confirmed the address as Tony unbuckled Leo from the car seat. He carried him securely in his arms, almost squeezing him, as we walked into the unknown.

"Trust the process," I said before we reached the door.

"Trust the process," Tony repeated to Leo.

We took the stairs to the second level and began our walk down the long hallway. My heart pounded, reflecting on the results of my past journeys. Ray's office happened to be the last door on the left. We entered, and we were greeted by a tall, gentle man. He extended his hand out, offering help, as we placed Leo upon his table. He began to work on Leo with a gift of manipulation by touch. There was confidence in his mannerisms that filled the space with safety and assurance.

Little by little, we saw improvement in Leo, tiny indications his body was responding to Ray's techniques. After watching Leo remain motionless, depleted from tests of all sorts, it was hard to think progress could be made. We were told otherwise by Ray saying Leo should be able to wiggle his fingers by the next session. It was beyond imagination that we could find such joy in seeing a finger move. But session after session, we witnessed what Ray said would possibly happen—actually happen. He helped Leo transition from a motionless body back to a boy with life. Ray was the actual "ray of hope" that we were looking for. God crossed our paths and, what began as a leap of faith, turned into years of treatment, love, friendship, and hope. Ray became more than just Leo's healer, and Leo went from a patient to a teacher. God brought them together, and together, they built an unbreakable bond.

Our mindset shifted as time went on and we discovered that things were what they were. Acceptance was a big key in us being able to move forward. At a certain point, we started looking at life moment by moment instead of focusing on the vast future. Our goal was to put a smile on Leo's face and make the most out of the trials we were given. It was our moment of surrender that led us to discover what the distant source was. It was God.

As the challenges continued to outweigh the moments of peace, there was a purity that began to seep through the pores of Leo's being. Although uncertainty weighed heavily in our thoughts, it was revealed that Leo came into this world perfectly created the way God intended him to be. Leo's body began to change internally and unnoticed; the white matter of the brain (the myelin) deteriorating slowly, silently taking away abilities without allowing a visible change to be seen. Hidden below the surface of flesh and bone, his body transformed into what eventually became noticeable, a mind full of life, a body lacking motion, and a soul filled with the love of God.

At that precious age of two, as so many toddlers begin to explore the environment that surrounds them, Leo's life reverted to complete dependence. I see so much value in the lessons Leo expressed over the years because they were not tainted from outside social aspects, and I was by no means educated in the Word of God to implant thoughts into Leo's mind. I was more of a "surface" Catholic, retaining information that was delivered to me over the years and trying to be a good person, but failing most of the time. It wasn't until this "still" teacher, the one who remained by my side, motionless, began to utter phrases and simple messages that

I really began to feel and see God surround me. I came from a place where I believed there was a God, and began to transform to a place where I *felt* God.

After about nine months of treatment from more natural methods, we were able to remove the feeding tube, which, I have to admit, was very scary. It was the source that kept Leo alive during this transition of detox, and at the same time, it was exciting to see how far he had come regaining the ability to swallow safely. In the back of my mind, I had reservations. What if he lost his ability to eat food again, and then we would have to put him through all of this once more? The voice in my mind kept saying, *Move forward and trust that things will be okay.* Having the tube removed brought more life back to Leo's composure and lifted our spirits as well. Being able to hear Leo speak and feed him with a spoon were welcomed victories that made our home a little cozier.

As Leo started regaining some abilities, although short-lived, we tried to capitalize on it. After months of working with the natural healers, Leo found his footing and began to utilize a walker to assist in relearning his steps. We knew it was important to retain as much movement and muscle mass as possible, considering it would deteriorate quickly if not used. One of the ways we did this was by taking Leo to the grocery store so he could walk the smooth surface of the aisles in his walker. This was an outing that Tony delighted in.

He would yell out to Leo, "Leo, it's time to get some exercise!"

"Okay, Papa," Leo replied as Oliver scurried off to the car.

Tony always enjoyed telling me about these excursions when they got home. I think both of the boys enjoyed these outings as much as Tony. Once they arrived, Tony unbuckled Leo and carried him in, while Oliver assisted by walking the walker into the store. Once inside, Tony positioned Leo in front of the walker and helped him grasp the handles while grabbing a shopping cart for himself.

"Let's go, boys."

As Tony began to select items from the shelves, Oliver encouraged Leo to follow him. "Come on, brother."

"I am trying."

Leo held tight to the handles. His stomping motion was a result of the cumbersome shoes he needed to wear. He had to trade in his stylish footwear and replace them with orthopedic shoes. The white color contrasted with many of the outfits that Leo enjoyed wearing, which drew attention to his feet. A bit bigger than he was accustomed to, which allowed for his AFOs (orthopedic braces) to be on prior to the shoe sliding over, which was secured with two Velcro straps. The extra weight and length often had him dragging the toe of his left foot, especially as he tried to keep up with Oliver.

Tony looked over his shoulder. "Where are you boys?"

A distant giggle followed before Oliver replied, "Over here, Papa."

"Okay, stay close."

Tony continued to grab the items on his list as the boys continued their adventure. As they rounded into the next aisle, Oliver ran ahead. Leo became tired and took a quick break as he sat on the flip—down seat that was attached to the walker.

His eyes glanced at the items in view and, as Tony came into sight, Leo requested, "Can we get these, Papa?" His eyes were laser focused on a box of Teddy Grahams.

"How can I resist?" Tony pointed to the shelf to make sure that he grabbed the right item.

Feeling recharged, Leo lifted his bottom to regain his footing. Once he was stable, he looked down at his foot and said, "Come on, lefty." Encouraged by his words, his left foot went into motion.

"Boo!" Oliver jumped from behind a mid—aisle display, almost causing Leo to fall.

"You scared me."

"Sorry." The word came out sincere, yet the mischievous smile indicated otherwise.

Workers and other customers came to know about this activity and most people were patient, encouraging, and kind. Although, we did come across a few who were less than accepting.

One time, Leo and I were walking side by side, shopping. The gentleman behind us sounded off numerous heavy sighs. I glanced back from time to time, then carried on with encouraging Leo. This man was impatient and irritated and made his presence known to us. He was displeased with the fact that we were blocking his way, when in reality, he had room to go around us. Finally, the protective mom in me stepped in. I turned around and explained the situation, yet he showed little to no empathy.

"Why don't you stop being a jackass?" I guided Leo to the side and waved the guy on. He seemed to be taken back by my rudeness, yet unaware of his own.

When we got home, Tony asked Leo, "How was shopping?"

Leo simply replied, "There was a jackass there."

I looked at Tony. "I will explain later."

Although we did run across those who were less amiable, I am grateful we had more experiences of acceptance and love. People began to notice the ripple effect of how Leo impacted the way everyone around him viewed things. Leo's gentle nature and light within him opened the hearts of everyone he encountered and, one soul at a time, Leo brought Jesus to their days.

Leo transformed me. He took me from being the person who would have possibly looked away and walked on the other side of the street, and brought me face to face with God. Leo was my driving force. He was the piece of me that inspired single words to become stories; stories that inspired others to see the world in a brighter light. He showed me that being alone doesn't mean loneliness, but rather, it gives you time to know who you are, and possibly reveal a "silent" friend.

One day, I found myself seated next to Leo in the living room with the television playing one of his favorite shows. The house was quiet, besides what came from the screen, as the two of us sat alone. While he gazed at the TV, I remained focused on him and felt happy when he was happy. Every little reaction was precious, and I adored having him close by my side. I leaned in and kissed his forehead before fast-forwarding through commercials.

I pushed play and the show continued. Leo took a deep breath and watched with delight. There was a soft sun sprinkling its way in through the blinds and birds whistled by the windows in search of grub. Warmth was shared between locked hands.

Leo looked toward the hallway, beyond me, and said, "I see Jesus."

I instinctively replied, "Well, don't go by Him."

Leo looked in that direction a bit longer before turning back. I was so afraid of losing Leo that I assumed Jesus was there to take him. I thought this was his calling home. Needless to say, Tony wasn't exactly happy with my response.

"Why didn't you ask questions?"

"Leo's words startled me."

"Well, if it happens again, take a deep breath and ask questions."

"What do you mean, if it happens again?" My grip on Leo's hand tightened.

It did happen again, just a short time later. I was a bit calmer, and allowed for a different state of mind to set in. We were upstairs in Leo's room this time. The lights were dim, and I kissed Oliver after I got him all nestled in his own bed. I turned back to tuck Leo in, and gave him a kiss too, but noticed he was looking at the wall by the closet door. I paused to watch, unable to see what he was looking at myself.

"I see Jesus."

My stomach leapt into my throat. It was happening again. These three simple words, uttered from the youthful lips of my son, expressed with confidence and conviction as his eyes shifted from the wall and met mine. This day had played out like so many before it, with me positioned at the side of Leo's bed. The gift of language was one I did not take for granted, especially from the one whose words were at one point muted.

This is the moment that saved me. At the time, I didn't even realize I needed saving.

I softly asked Leo, "What does he look like?"

Leo then turned his head back to the wall and stated one word slowly at a time, "He – has – long – dark – hair, blue – eyes, a nose, and – he — is smiling, but – I – don't – see – his – teeth."

Leo's response, considering that he was only around three years old and had endured a great deal of brain and body trauma, amazed me. As Leo described Jesus' features, he never once took his eyes off the area he was focused on to look at me. He clearly stated what he saw at that moment. A calmness settled over me as the room became more still.

"Can you share more?"

"He has legs – and – He is wearing white – and – is bright."

The vision was so clear. The words that Leo expressed were from an image that definitely stood before him. He lay there, looking above at a figure who shared the same space we resided. "Blessed are the pure in heart, for they will see God." (Matthew, 5:8)

Leo was pure.

Chapter Nine

SURRENDER

Leo let Jesus settle into his heart and his mind, and as a result, his whole being was aglow with love. His ability to find calmness in his own storm was such a beautiful demonstration of his faith in God. Witnessing his relationship with Jesus left me feeling so inspired to persevere through our daily challenges, yet because I am human, I still failed.

So many changes continued to occur, but losing his capability to use the bathroom was physiologically challenging for Leo and emotionally draining for us. He was potty trained before age two; he was such a quick learner. Then after the onset of his symptoms, he lost that ability, too. Once he regained some strength and was utilizing a walker, he again learned how to make it to the restroom. Leo was so proud of doing this task on his own.

"I gotta go potty," he announced.

"Let's get in there quickly, Leo." I walked behind as my mind quietly prayed that he would make it there in time.

"Okay." Holding tight to the bars on the walker, Leo stomped down the hall, cautiously transitioning from the carpet to the wood floor.

"Let me help you get your underwear and pants down." Leo continued to hold tight to the handles as I wiggled his clothing down to his ankles.

He stood before the toilet, then minutes later, he pivoted his head and looked up to me, "False alarm," he exclaimed in a matter-of-fact kind of way.

"Good try." I helped him pull up his undergarments, released an inner sigh, knowing it would only be moments later that this would all replay itself out again as we made our way back to play. It was tiresome, not knowing if it was going to happen or not and not wanting to risk ignoring it and having him feel the shame of an accident. Leo did have success with this for a small period, until once again, it was stripped away from him. It was hard for me to surrender this ability. Leo was so proud when he had success. Yet, once we began to utilize pull ups, some relief from failure brought peace to him.

No matter how hard we tried to be patient and do the right thing, moments of weakness set in. Any time I gave my focus to something else, Leo always wanted to make his presence known. In the midst of a conversation with a friend, Leo began to seek my attention by repeating something over and over, resulting in me having to halt my conversation and bring my awareness back to him.

"Leo, just hold on," my voice raised.

His big, beautiful eyes stared at me, unable to express what he most likely wanted to say back. When complete exhaustion consumed me, I hit my lowest moment with Leo. Although I never raised my hand to him, I found myself over him. Firmly taking both of my hands and gripping his arms, holding them to the bed.

"I can't do this anymore!"

Yelling these words of anger. Anger at the situation, not at him. I pinned him down, placed him in a position that I had been held in. I took away his voice. His innocent face just looked back at me, locked in a body that was unable to free himself from me to leave the room. When so many issues compounded, I felt I was being pulled down with no sight of relief in front of me. My lack of sleep and my lack of true belief wasn't allowing God to see me through anything. Those tiny moments, when I took my eyes off God and felt alone, were the exact moments my eyes should have been fixed upon Him to see me through. But, I continued to watch and learn from Leo's example.

Any moment of weakness on my behalf, when it came to Leo, was immediately followed by remorse, expressing my apologies. I was incapable of looking into his eyes and not seeing the love of Jesus staring back at me. It was like I lost my patience with Him and that feeling shook me. The purity of Leo's being, the complete reliance he had in me was such a powerful display of God's presence in my life. Having Leo in my days helped keep me centered. Leo brought my focus to my faith as I watched Jesus shine through him daily. I then began to recognize that the difference between Leo and myself was the ability to surrender.

"I have been crucified with Christ. It is no longer I who live, but Christ who lives in me. And the life I now live in the flesh I live in faith in the Son of God, who loved me and gave himself for me." (Galatians 2:20)

For years, I slept with Leo at my side, extending my left hand and resting it upon his right thigh, reassuring him I was close as we lay in the dark with the faint glow of his projector casting colorful stars across the ceiling.

"Hi, Momma," he softly whispered.

"It's time for sleeping. Momma is tired."

He released a "Hmmmm." In that moment, I knew his mind was thinking and wanting to express more, but I tried to remain quiet and still in hopes of receiving the sleep that my body needed.

I couldn't pull myself away from Leo and his needs during his initial decline. I spent nights sleeping in his crib, confined close to him, or alongside the edge with my hand fed through the rail. My inability to separate from him separated me from my husband. This behavior increased over the years, leaving me torn about where my love should fall. As a mother, I had endless love, I tried to spread it amongst all who needed it. The struggle came when an individual child required more than the others. In that moment, I gave it all to him, hoping the other loved ones realized he just needed me more at that time.

This tug between wanting to meet everyone's needs took a toll on my heart, not wanting to let anyone down. The *I can do it all myself* attitude had to adapt. At a certain point, doing it all might be possible, but doing any of it well becomes questionable. It appeared my two older boys adjusted to the circumstances, yet no one can ever be inside the mind of another.

Trent, at the time, had just turned 13. He took to the situation differently than his older brother, with more of what you would expect from a young teenager who thinks life revolves solely around himself. Matthew felt a responsibility most kids in high school can't relate to by caring for his brother in between studies. Trent, however, wasn't thrilled about the fact that our comfortably united family was being somewhat pulled apart. Leo's circumstances made it more challenging for us to do all of our typical family outings, and on many occasions, I would stay back and do something with Leo and Oliver so Tony could attend to the older boys' needs. Trent appeared to hold some resentment. He wasn't mean to Leo, but he wasn't happy about the situation either. He had a hard time moving forward from this traumatic situation and needed more reassurance and love to make it seem like life was going to be okay. Even moving into adulthood, Trent still seemed to hold more of the *take care of me* view on life and, to some extent, never really became self-sufficient.

Nothing was lacking in Matthew's and Trent's lives as they were still able to explore their options and be involved in all the hobbies they enjoyed. Matthew participated in several after school activities and Trent pursued an athletic trajectory. Trent was receiving endless hours of attention from Tony because they both shared a common love of hockey. His time with me was more limited, but nothing skipped a beat in time, as far as the things that brought him enjoyment. Yet, something didn't allow Trent to move past this new life change.

Our youngest, Oliver, never knew any different and, in a sense, seemed to rise with Leo's fall. I mean this in the most loving of ways, for everything Leo lacked, Oliver picked up the slack. This extension of himself helped to satisfy Leo's needs and, at the same time, develop characteristics that a person just can't come to know without the proper environment. He watched, observed, and was able to witness a variety of situations most toddlers don't see their older siblings struggle with. He adapted as Leo adapted and was able to learn traits of compassion as Leo would "face plant" while attempting to crawl, and Oliver would come to his aid.

I witnessed a beautiful bond of brotherly love between Leo and Oliver. With Oliver being the younger brother (Leo made sure Oliver was well aware of this fact), he never knew Leo any other way. He looked upon Leo with a child's eyes and there was an instant acceptance of how things were. Oliver spent countless hours side by side with Leo and there was rarely distance between them while they attempted and tackled each adventure together. They spent so much time using their imaginations and learning from each other, much like Matthew and Trent when they grew together. Their laughter always filled my heart with satisfaction.

There was a point in their childhood where Oliver's skills surpassed Leo's, making Leo try harder to keep up with his brother (not wanting to be outdone in anything). Although Oliver had extensive compassion and patience with Leo, he also had a normal brotherly rivalry with him. As they grew, Oliver didn't let Leo's limitations keep him from doing his best. He wanted to be the first one to make it to the other end of the slip and slide, but at the mere thought of Leo being hurt, Oliver was the first one to his side to guide him back to balance (sometimes, it was a gentle nudge and, other times, it was an aggressive pull). Their brotherly bond went beyond competition, and it was apparent that they loved each other like two puppies playing with a bone. Play time was all the time, and their minds raced together to form new games and new ways to laugh.

The extreme level of love Oliver had for Leo was one of the most beautiful gifts that I watched blossom over the years. There were few selfish moments in Oliver's childhood. He never wanted Leo left behind and was willing to have Leo be a part of his own achievements. For example, there was a year Oliver's ice hockey team went to state and, even though Oliver was the one who obtained the right to be there with his team, he shared this special moment with Leo. His coach and teammates allowed Leo to be honorary captain and share in the experience. Like an assist to a goal scored by a teammate, victories can be shared and still mean something to both.

Every aspect of Oliver's time and development from the years spent with Leo transformed him into a well—rounded young man. He adored his brother and was there to assist him often. This loving sacrifice, that became a strong characteristic, got him into trouble at school. I noticed a pattern year after year when it came time to meet for teacher conferences. Oliver was praised in many areas, and then there seemed to be this common denominator that was put in the "needs improvement" category. You see, Oliver often does things for others and doesn't allow them to attempt them on their own. At first glance, it sounds like a good thing, but from the teachers' perspectives, he was not allowing classmates to flourish and bloom into new growth themselves.

With this feedback appearing to be negative traits of his, I realized some explanation was needed. Oliver only knew one way of life by helping, doing, and assisting Leo. He was Leo's voice when Leo didn't have one. He was Leo's body when Leo's failed to comply. He took what was Leo's mind—Leo's thoughts—and he made them possible. This was a positive quality of his character, not a flaw. At the same time, we needed to explain to Oliver that, while this is an extraordinary act of love that you show your brother, you need to allow and be patient with your classmates, giving them the opportunity to do things on their own. This was such an important lesson in life because, more often than not, we may be unaware of why people act the way they do. We may not know the backstory to what shaped them into the people they have become.

Oliver knows the fragility of time; he has come to understand if something isn't making you happy, leave it behind and search for a new joy. He doesn't stay stuck in the past; he experiences, learns, and moves on. He is a sponge absorbing all life has to offer, learning to carve his own path and taking the imprint of lessons learned from Leo to apply to his own journey.

With Oliver being so bound to Leo, he didn't lack time with me. The two of them were sort of a bundle package. In addition to me, he was also supported by a variety of other adults coming to my aid. I quickly realized that not only was this assistance helping me, but it was also helping them, and my family, by letting people into our world. Seeking aid and finding comfort from friends and strangers, who became friends, built a connection with people that filled a void I didn't even know was there. In helping us, it also helped them, allowing them an outlet for giving and helping others. These moments were my first exposure to God appearing to me through the love He instilled in others with a mission of helping.

During moments of stability in Leo's health, I felt confident that if I were absent for a few hours, he would be okay. Tony and I were able to break away and have time for just us. Like many married couples with kids, this so-called time away usually led to talking about the kids. In our case, even more so, because we truly couldn't let go. There is only one person who can have the ability to give "mother's love," and that is the mother. Even though I had amazing individuals who willingly stepped in and gave of their time, I couldn't help but wonder if they were doing it right. These moments of uncertainty didn't just lie with those who came to help. My mind couldn't completely relax, even when it was Tony.

Leo not only was my son, he was my terminally ill son, who was fighting for his life and literally an extension of me. As his primary care-taker, I had a system, a certain order and way of things, and Tony's way was different from mine. There were times when I found myself correct-ing him and inquiring why he was doing it like that, rather than trying it my way. Then, eventually, I learned his way was exactly what Leo needed to add variety in his life. Just like when my older sons would help out, they played with Leo in creative ways I hadn't tried or thought of, and in the end, Leo benefited from it.

So as these opportunities came and went to try to have time alone with my husband, I found we both struggled to be present with each oth-er. In addition to the demands of work, and running a household with four kids, we drifted apart, as many marriages do when raising children. On top of the normal circumstances many couples face, we also were coping with the uncertainty of Leo's life, and the fact that Leo had be-come my bedtime sleeping partner. We not only lost time together and lacked communication on a regular basis, but we then lost intimacy. We were functioning, we were committed to each other and our love, but also drifted in separate directions and became comfortable with it.

We were doing what we needed to do to survive, but in surviving, our ability to know each other was dying. We would go through the motions of the day, each doing our parts, but doing them separately in hopes to regroup prior to bed. Exhaustion would inevitably take hold. We slowly drifted into a functional marriage, losing so much of ourselves. Tony tried to meet the financial needs of the family and I desperately tried to maintain a family unit in something that was so disrupted.

We applied so many band-aids on situations that needed to be ad-dressed and deserved attention. Eventually, the stickiness gave way and the wounds reopened, never really getting their chance to heal. Other things took precedence, and our relationship was set on the back burner, simmering, until a moment of boiling over surfaced. Our ability to process things logically lessened as stress levels heightened. We suppressed emotions over and over and eventually they scorched us.

Tony and I had the experiences of more than one obstacle in our lives to learn from. We allowed the space that each of us needed and we seemed to realize that our ways of processing and grieving weren't always going to line up with each other. By giving the grace each of us deserved, we found a way to climb yet another mountain, maybe not at the same pace, but we willingly waited for the other one to catch up. It was through this level of patience that we were able to see things from such opposite perspectives at times, and yet still find each other by the other's side.

There is always going to be work to do to make a marriage succeed, rarely does it run smoothly. The best thing I discovered about my spouse was actually what I discovered about myself. I needed to look with an honest heart at the type of person I was before I could fully accept and appreciate the one who chose to stand beside me. The struggles we faced in these moments prepared us for what God planned for us. So, I began to look at the hardships in our marriage as a blessing, and discovered the areas of myself that needed work to fulfill God's plan.

I have come to learn that life is meant to be shared, having each stride align with others while being willing to pick others up from the ground if they stumble and fall. Life isn't a race to win, rather it is an experience, gaining insight on how to live for God. By sharing experiences, struggles, and triumphs, perspective is gained, enhancing the ability to see ahead more clearly. Vulnerability provides strength. By being transparent in my own life, I realized my moments helped build and strengthen others, which in return strengthened me. This behavior took away the control of fear from the evil one. I've recognized that fear froze me by clouding my judgment and limiting my ability to believe I could do anything with the love and guidance of God.

By being vulnerable, I became more approachable. People let down their guards and saw me in a more relatable perspective. By showing my flaws and insecurities, I actually helped others from trying to cover up or hide theirs. I tried to display these weaknesses while we were out in the community, allowing others in. We often found ourselves being looked at. Eyes observing us, I invited them in, in hopes I could knock down any barrier that could potentially be formed.

People were drawn to Leo, yet some would hesitate to approach, perhaps uncertain of their own selves, afraid they may say something wrong. When I felt those opportunities upon us, the glances that wanted to become more, I welcomed them by approaching them.

"Hi, would you like to meet my son, Leo?"

I would introduce myself and Leo, express what his situation was, and pause for a moment, waiting for their response. Most conversations were followed up with, *What is wrong with him?* or, *Why is he in a wheelchair or using a walker?* These situations didn't only occur with children, but with adults as well, sometimes not understanding why they were being drawn to Leo. Sometimes I wondered if Leo had insight into what my future held. It was as if he was gathering a crew of women who would continue to hold me up in the time of his absence. By breaking down the fear of the unknown, people were able to see Leo for who he really was, a happy little boy enjoying life's blessings, just in a different way.

This presence Leo exuded was impactful, and most people who crossed paths with him were left with his imprint upon them. I saw it with my own family and friends, along with strangers and among Leo's teachers and classmates. Initially, fear was at the forefront, but once they had a chance to spend time with Leo, they were transformed. While I assisted at school as his aide, I witnessed his peers embrace him with kindness and acceptance. Children may hesitate when something is different, but I strongly believe their natural instinct is kindness. Unfortunately, fear is taught to them. If we could all live through the eyes of an innocent child, imagine the amount of peace that would surround us!

Leo's vulnerability was transparent, a visible limitation that could be seen by all. If we could look at our lives; our insecurities, the things we try to hide from others, the secrets we don't want people to know, and view them from a physical perspective as something we couldn't hide, maybe it would alter the decisions we make. We all have things we don't want people to know about: challenges in our marriage, addictions we try to cover up, events that we pretend didn't happen. As these things build and take hold of your heart, they claim valuable space that doesn't allow for God to settle in. Guilt and shame take hold, not allowing us to be open and honest about the events in our lives. How much better it feels to release that guilt and let go of that shame. It may not be in the form of a public statement, but at the very least, say it out loud to God. He already knows, but there is something magical that occurs in your heart and mind when you actually verbalize the things that are troubling your heart.

It takes courage to be honest not only with yourself, but with others. It makes you vulnerable when you let others into your thoughts and actions, but if you can trust those moments, one may just be the moment someone else needed to release their own claim. It is very important to be mindful of words spoken, choosing to say things that are thought out and truthful. Words have amazing power and sometimes less is more.

Leo was a perfect example of that. He was a boy of very few words, but his words left an impact. Because his speech was limited and difficult to release, his word choices were mindfully spoken. He had messages to share and lessons to teach. I hung on every word uttered from his lips. It was a whole—body experience to deliver each sound, everything from the top of his head to the tip of his toes would engage to form words.

I learned not to take for granted the relationships I had and the experiences I partook in, no matter how grand or how small; each moment is precious and no moments can be lived again. Time is one thing we all share and when someone gives the gift of their time to you, remember they gave a moment of their life and chose to spend it with you.

I believe that when we keep running from who we are instead of expressing and sharing who we are authentically, we are doing the world a disservice. In order to improve and change this way of life, we need to come together and learn from one another. If we can just be real, raw, and honest with one another, allowing people to see who we really are by opening up and revealing the layers of what makes us who we are, we would limit the ability for the evil one to get into our minds and take away the intimate relationship we have with one another and God.

Leo made every person feel special. When you were in his presence, you were his focus. His attentive gaze upon you made you know that you had his complete attention. He listened with not only his ears, but with his whole self. You mattered to him and were worth his time. When it came to listening to a story, Leo listened with his whole body. Some of the most tender moments I witnessed were shared between Tony and

Leo; a father returning from a hunting excursion, giving every detail to Leo to make it seem as if he, too, had been there. His ears absorbed the information as Tony began to talk. His body translated his excitement.

Tony began his story on one occasion, "It was early, before the sun had a chance to rise..." My eyes shifted to Leo as I saw the impact each word had on his frame. Tension filled Leo's limbs to the point of complete stiffness. "I walked quietly out to my stand..." Leo's body became covered in goosebumps, tingling across his face as the suspense of what was going to be expressed next could hardly be contained. "I heard a snap of a limb."

"It's him!" Leo blissfully exclaimed. Tony allowed the excitement to build and continued with his story. Everything from which way the direction the wind was blowing to the sounds of all the other critters in the area. Then Tony reached the climax of the story.

"The bear came into view. His soft padded paws were unheard, but he made the mistake of turning broadside and, BAM, he went down."

The whole bed shook as Leo's body quivered, hanging on to every word as he released a triumphant, "Hurray!" Laughter filled our entire home from the success of the hunt.

The stories shared with Leo that were more humorous often caused me to remind him to breathe, because the inhale held him in a frozen position before he remembered to exhale the noise that coincided with laughter. Getting Leo to this state was a great indicator that you had a story worth sharing with others.

As a family, we witnessed Leo's acceptance of his life change and began to loosen our grip on the reins of control. We surrendered to fate and saddled our horses, preparing ourselves for the unknown journey ahead. Living one moment at a time, and doing our best to put a smile on Leo's face each day, we trotted faithfully next to Leo.

Chapter Ten

LITTLE SPIRIT WASHED AWAY

Leo's awareness heightened as movement slipped away. The creak of my chair, as I leaned forward to lift myself away from his bedside, had him shift his head in my direction. I lay my hand upon his head to comfort him.

"I will be right back," I whispered.

I hoped to sneak away for a moment undetected, but his ears didn't let a single vibration go unnoticed. I observed how certain senses became profound when others seemed lacking. His hearing was keen and even a whisper from the other room made him clue into the fact that something was up. We often teased him, saying he had *grandma ears*, in reference to my mother. My mom was gifted with being able to listen, engage, and respond to multiple conversations while being on the phone. She still knew what was being said two rooms away, and Leo too, was able to hear the whisper of conversations that occurred in a different room.

I imagine God with *grandma ears*, as He listens to the prayers of all people. How hard it must be for Him to know all the wrongs we will do in our lives. Hearing that inner whisper in our minds, but proceeding to do it our own way. Giving us the most precious gift of free will and hope, we ought to make wise decisions with it. As a parent, I prayed the lessons I taught my children would guide them to make good choices. I tried to shelter and protect them from pain and harm, yet, at the same time, allow them to fail in order to learn. Oh how I rejoiced when they succeeded! I knew in my heart that I gave God moments to feel pride in my choices, but I knew I broke His heart as well.

My own heart was half-full as it weighed heavily on the realization of what had been removed from my life, but balanced by what remained. Loss is a deep emotion that mends over time like a lesion; the scar is left visible, so it never fully heals. There is never a comparison of one's loss to another. The connection of love and moments shared cannot be laid side by side. What has helped me is to have understanding and compassion, and the ability to see through the eyes of others, as they mourn pieces of their hearts stripped away from their lives. It doesn't matter how I view an individual, what matters is how Jesus viewed them and knowing He looks upon every soul with love. Then I should strive to obtain that as well.

I have come to believe that the period of time you spend with someone impacts the reality of the loss, because there will be more memories embedded in your heart and mind. Yet, loss in general appears to be something that never fully leaves you. I have no memories from the child I never met, choosing not to allow them to occur. I have endless memories with Leo, allowing them to be built. And then, I also have uncertainty hovering in my mind regarding a miscarriage that took place a year after Leo's diagnosis.

When Leo was only three, and Oliver a rambunctious two-year old, I discovered I was pregnant. I stared at the in-home pregnancy test and thought, *Is this really happening?* The weight of life's demands sat upon my shoulders. The thought of balancing a visible presence in both Matthew's and Trent's lives, while supporting the energy of Oliver and keeping up with Leo's physical changes, was a lot to take in.

I saw the pressure of this new reality hitting Tony, uncertain if he could maintain not only a financially stable life, but also an emotional one. All I could see was darkness. As I looked at myself in the mirror, I could see that same little fourteen-year old girl looking back again. I saw her fear and it entered me. I was looking ahead into a future that I couldn't see, and I assumed it was more than I could bear. Then I exhaled, and for a brief moment, the fear left me as I remembered God was with me.

The following week, I entered the doctor's office to confirm what the home pregnancy test indicated. As I sat in the exam room, my anxiety began to build. We were still uncertain at this moment in time if Leo's health decline was one of chance or one of genetics. The thought of taking on another challenge brought me to my knees.

The doctor entered. "How are you doing today?" He could see in my eyes the concerns I had. "It looks like you are correct. You are about ten weeks pregnant."

"Are you sure?" I sighed heavily.

"I take it, this news isn't what you were hoping to hear."

"With so much uncertainty with Leo right now, I guess I have some fear."

"Lay back. Let's begin the exam." Endless thoughts raced through my mind. I played out every possible scenario that I could imagine.

As I lay upon the table, I remember experiencing a few extremely painful moments during the exam, but left the office with pain only in my heart. The thought of bringing a new life into the world at the same time another was fighting to stay in it troubled me. Soon after the visit, I experienced sharp pains, those that resembled labor pains. I found myself in the bathroom, passing the fetus of my child. I lay on the floor, curled up in pain, both physically and emotionally, while Leo and Oliver watched cartoons in the other room.

What I had come to accept in my mind, a child due to be born late October, now lay upon the floor, wrapped in tissue, pieces of a story that would never be told. My physical pain consumed me, and emotionally, I was frozen. Tony then opened the door abruptly.

"What is happening?"

I lost the baby. I tried to form the words, but could only sob. Instead of offering the comfort and support I needed, Tony abruptly swooped up the remains wrapped in tissue and flushed them away. My heart was shattered, the coldness in his heart crushed me. I know now the level of stress that we faced was more than he could take. He thought he was helping me by allowing me to move on, but in fact, what he took from me was the opportunity to grieve our loss.

He helped me get cleaned up and into bed, but my mind couldn't stop replaying my thoughts from the recent office visit. Why did this pregnancy end so suddenly? The heartbeat was strong and, physically, my health was stable. Did something occur during my exam? What was the extreme pain I felt? Unanswered questions circled in my thoughts.

I needed to pull myself together. So many little ones were dependent on me. I had to allow my body to heal, but emotionally, I had to be present and proceed with the challenges that waited for me. I once again bottled up emotions and placed them safely in the vault of my heart in hopes I could process them later. My bottle of emotions was getting full, but there were others who needed me, so my own needs would have to wait.

As time went on, my attention traveled back to the lives of two children I never had a relationship with. I fought so hard to help Leo survive against all the odds stacked against him, but I hadn't given that same fight to the lives that began within me, but never had the chance to breathe the breath of life. God's forgiving grace settled upon my heart as He allowed me to heal and grow during my time with Leo. Although I had made a poor decision in my childhood, I learned from my mistake. I also knew at the core of my being I had not personally caused my miscarriage, and needed to release that unknown to God for Him to sort out for me.

My womb was the home to the beginning of six lives. They all fought to exist, yet only four captured their first breaths. When I reflect on the lives of my sons and the tremendous amount of worth they gifted to my life, I mourn for the tiny existence that was not able to see the light of day. I mourn my inability at such a young age to understand a child was forming within me, not just a situation; one I was not mentally able to accept and physically equipped to handle. I think of the tiny body that was trying to form to encase the beautiful soul God so lovingly entrusted to me, and I declined.

I also envision a life that tries to be whole, yet never receives the opportunity to see the world. Did the doctor hear the drowning desperation in my voice, and try to assist in my survival, claiming to believe I couldn't find the surface alone? Did he completely misconstrue the situation or did the life within me come to an end because it was the way it was destined to be? All these battles engaged in a war within my mind.

Regret and uncertainty all tried to occupy space in my heart, body, and soul. They weighed heavily on me, yet I eventually laid them at the foot of the cross. Jesus took my sins and allowed me to look at myself with love, repairing a few of my broken pieces in order to rebuild my shattered self.

Leo then helped me to find my footing once again. In my moment of feeling lost, he directed me back to Jesus. He encapsulated the gift of being so insightful. He knew about things from before he was even in existence, or he wasn't present when they occurred. One time, Tony and I were driving in the car, and Leo was in the backseat with Oliver. He was young at the time, maybe around kindergarten age. I mentioned something casually to Tony about my sister Patty.

As I said her name, Leo stated, "I know Patty."

"Oh, honey, you have a lot of aunts, but you don't know Aunt Patty. She died before you were born."

Leo seemed a bit irritated with me. "I do know her. She has long, auburn hair."

"Oh, Leo." I was held with amazement by his knowledge and use of words.

"She has hazel eyes," he stated as my eyes met him through the rearview mirror.

"How do you know this, Leo?"

"I told you. I know her."

Tony and I looked at each other in complete astonishment. We had barely spoken of Patty prior, and I am pretty certain I never mentioned her in front of Leo. Furthermore, he had never seen photos of her as there were few to begin with (from a time before cell phones).

As I looked at him, once again, in the rearview mirror, I was stunned that Leo knew about my sister. Somehow, Leo was able to describe her features, just like he had described what Jesus looked like. Our belief in Leo, and the abilities that he continued to reveal, made it hard to discount what he said. There was just no way he could know the things he told us without his relationship with Jesus. As I shared this encounter with my mom and dad, I saw such peace wash over them. The uncertainty of Patty's death and the investigation that didn't take place never allowed my parents to heal and move forward. Something ate away at them, especially my dad, until Leo showed them Patty was safe — that she was home with Jesus.

A few years later, Leo once again brought up my sister Patty, this time in a completely different reference. He was being a bit sassy with me. I drew my face close to his and looked him directly in the eyes.

I said, "Be nice to me. I am the only mommy you have."

Leo was unshaken by my statement and looked right back at me. With intensity in his voice, he stated, "Not in Heaven."

I became extremely concerned about this comment. It was obvious Leo was going to Heaven, but was I? I composed myself and asked, while my heart was beating fast, "Who is your mommy going to be in Heaven?"

"Jesus said, 'Aunt Patty.'"

Tears rolled down my face. I couldn't think of anyone better than my own sister to step in until I could rejoin him, considering she was unable to experience motherhood.

Leo continued his intense look as he finished by saying, "Guess who will be my papa? Jesus."

These moments of hope often came without warning. Leo would lean into God's love and reveal precious details that stopped me in my tracks.

Leo gave insight on another young girl to me one night. While lying in bed next to me, he told me, "I have a sister in Heaven."

"You do?"

"Yes." This conversation brought me to tears. I was unable to compose myself to the point of asking further questions at that moment, but Leo continued by saying, "Her name is Leah. Do you like that name?"

"Yes, sweetheart, I do."

My heart sank to the pit of my gut. Leah was a name Tony and I had discussed when we were pregnant with Oliver. Once again, a detail Leo would not have known.

"Leah's wings are yellow with red edges."

"That sounds beautiful."

"They are."

As we continued to lay next to each other, I asked, "Do you know what color my sister Patty's wings are?"

Without hesitation, he replied, "Purple."

I sat in silence with my eyes closed and envisioned these beautiful images. The rapid flutter of angel wings soaring high above me. Peace filled my heart as I envisioned purple wings flapping a slight breeze over me. And peace was also provided by the angel beside me.

No loss is easy. Not one that happens suddenly, nor one that is slowly pulled from your grip over a course of time. It is impossible to compare the void from one you were given years to build memories with, versus one you were never able to hold. Love has endless value. So, anytime someone holds value and a place in your heart, a piece of your heart will leave with them.

Chapter Eleven

REDEMPTION

Standing on the porch, I felt the whisper of the wind brush against my skin, blowing my long hair off the side of my cheek. I stared off into the distance, and although I couldn't see the wind, I knew it existed as a floating feather drifted by. As I turned to look at Leo, I saw that he too held a whisper of the wind as we were unable to see at the time God strategically working His ways within him. Yet, it eventually became visible to us. Through each and every struggle Leo faced, he did it with grace and a smile on his face.

God saved us from the slavery of the illness by showing us the light of His love. Leo's illness had the ability to control us. We could have fallen into the pit of self-destruction and become angry with everything and everyone in life. Somehow, God lit a light within Leo that was unmistakable. Normally, you would have to turn away from something so brilliant, but like a moth to a flame, Leo's light was a transcendent splendor. He drew us in, and the child became the teacher.

All of us have the capability of being "chosen", we only need to be open to it. God wants to provide a fulfilling life of happiness, and that happiness comes in different forms. Not all of us are going to be celebrities, professional athletes, or high-ranking executives of notable companies. Some of us are going to live simple lives, do simple things. I have learned that when we do them as if Jesus was standing right before us and we do them with love, the simple things become extraordinary.

Through these simple acts, a transformation occurred not only in Leo, but in myself, and in many who experienced him in their lives.

I believe we each have a calling, but because we have a right to choose, only a few of us will actually be chosen. Leo was called and Leo was chosen. He responded when God called him, and he chose to listen and follow God's plan. Leo was determined to be one who lived his life for Jesus so others could witness, and then hopefully want to seek God for themselves.

Leo accepted the invitation to his calling and responded without hesitation. Through his belief and his actions, his calling became a living dedication of being chosen. He took what God laid out before him and made it his testimony of life so others could also find their way. Leo built an intimate relationship with Jesus, and the peace that overcame him through his outer shell outweighed the pain and agony of what his body experienced internally. Leo sacrificed what we would consider to be a normal childhood, so we could get a visual glimpse into the love God has for us.

God never left Leo's side throughout his whole journey and somehow managed to strengthen me from the inside out. No matter how much was piled upon us, no matter the uncertainty and endless obstacles we faced, God provided the strength we needed each day to keep us from being crushed, despite how broken we felt emotionally and physically. God somehow managed to keep our emotions in check. Every time the devil wanted to invite us into his pity party of despair, God let down His golden rope of hope and pulled us to steady ground, keeping firm hold of our hands.

I used to believe God doesn't test us or give us more than we can handle. To me, that sounded like a god of deception, especially when people asked me how much more my family could handle. Thankfully, my perception shifted as I grew to know God more intimately, and I realized I was worth testing. He saw a strength in me that He planned to use. He saw a strength that could show others what faith could do in their lives. Showing that loss doesn't have to feel like you are losing, it is quite the opposite; if you believe in God, you will be able to see loss as a gain. "But I say, walk by the Spirit, and you will not carry out the desire of the flesh." (Galatians 5:16) With every hardship, struggle, and loss, I gained strength, I gained confidence, and most importantly, I gained a more intimate relationship with God.

I trust in His plan, and I confidently believe Leo is in a place of indescribable beauty, surrounded by peace and love, where pain and suffering no longer exist. This confident belief stems from the visions and conversations Leo exchanged with Jesus and shared with us. Leo taught me a life worth living is one lived to please God. The things of the past are the things of old, they need to be cleared away to make room for the things of now. I made my share of poor choices in the past, and my present self is disappointed in the decisions I made. Yet, I have shed that layer of me and tried to move forward in life by not looking back by using my inner light to light the way for me and others to God. I want to shine brightly. I want to imbue that same inner glow Leo had and embraced. People were drawn to him because the purity of God's love exuded from his pores. From the moment Leo was placed in my arms, to the moment he left me for Jesus', he embodied a glow of life.

Through an illness, something that could have broken us, God led us on a journey of redemption. Prior to Leo's illness, I saw my family going down a path that could have led to self-righteousness. Things were going smoothly in our lives, and instead of God being the center of our days, other things took precedence. Leo's change of health became a wakeup call, to some extent, that we needed to refocus. Little by little, God revealed Himself, gently nudging us in the direction of finding Him. He took what could have been the fall of my family and turned it into the core of our life. We started to uncover the beauty in the simple things. We slowed down and discovered a new awareness of life.

Throughout Scripture, many of God's servants were tested. They faced all sorts of extensive challenges they had to overcome. He used the strong, He used the loyal, He used the trustworthy, and He also used the ordinary; the ones who were less obvious in choice. There was no mold that an individual fit which said, "This is God's type." We are all His children, and He is willing to use each of us. The key is remembering it is for His plan. I try to keep in mind, when I am lost and wandering around without direction, it is because I am either disobedient or I am not listening. My life was an example of that, but Leo spent a lifetime listening.

We coped with Leo's illness because he lit the way. Leo patiently guided us through our unknown, and we discovered life was a lot more doable when we surrendered and allowed God to take control. Day by day, moment by moment, we entered the world of special needs and learned how to adapt to meet Leo's needs. With time, we found out all things were possible. We could give Leo the life that most people experience, we just needed a different way of looking at opportunities and becoming creative to make them work for him.

Leo longed to be surrounded by others as much as possible. His heart filled with joy to experience life in a "normal" way. Tony and I both wanted Leo to partake in school to give him that feeling of inclusion. There was a great deal of trust in order to release him into the care of another adult, not only because he was my child, but my child with multiple limitations both physically and verbally.

The elementary years of Leo's life included plenty of opportunities to attend school. Although he had to hurdle multiple developmental challenges, he was equipped with drive and charm. After I enrolled him in preschool, I met with the two teachers who were assigned to his small class, only about ten children. Initially, the nerves got the best of them, uncertain if they could manage Leo's needs. I reassured them I would stay on as his aide, but wanted him to be included in the class experiences. As the weeks passed and their comfort levels grew, I was able to step back a bit and let Leo thrive. He utilized a walker at this time and loved the independence of stomping around the room among peers.

This experience helped with Leo's transition to kindergarten. The elementary school was set back away from the busy city street. Nestled into the hill, this three-story building had a welcoming appearance. The blue rooftop captured your attention as you drove up the winding entranceway to the front of the building. Although pavement surrounded the structure, the rolling hills and emerald green grass highlighting the landscape made you feel as if you were attending a retreat. Then there were the playgrounds and the soccer fields and space for children to play and run around to be kids—to be themselves. And that was so reassuring.

Once again, I sensed an overwhelming concern as to how to meet his needs, but Leo's ability to captivate others quickly stole the heart of his teacher. It started in the classroom where beautiful relationships developed, not just with the staff, but with his classmates. This was a space where motivational posters, alphabet stickers, artwork and post-its were scattered on the walls to brighten the room. Energy was seen and felt everywhere.

At first, it was difficult for Leo to see the teacher, surrounded by all the kids sitting in a circle on the floor, because Leo couldn't sit as they did. His core lost strength and his legs didn't bend with ease. However, he was able to sit on a little wooden chair with arms to support him and be amongst the other children. This gave him the chance to be a part of things, but he was always in the back. So even though this was a success, it showed that there was always room for improvement. Our minds learned from this simple victory that if there was a way, we could find it. It may not have been perfect, but at the very least, Leo was experiencing life.

The activities in the classroom continued to flow, and as his peers transitioned from story time to playtime, Leo transitioned from his wooden chair into his walker. Leo commanded the stage once again. He flipped down the seat of his walker and acted as if he was the foreman of playtime, especially in the block corner.

"Put that one over there," he instructed one of the kids to move a block.

"Right here, Leo?" The willingness to obey his instructions brought laughter to his teacher.

"Yes. Now, put that one over there."

This roleplay allowed what Leo saw in his mind to be played out in the actions of their movements. Remarkably, the other children wanted to participate in his requests and were eager to please him. This early interaction with his peers developed into acceptance and friendships. Inclusion early on eliminated certain unknowns and fears that could have settled in. Leo's classmates saw Leo as Leo. When questions arose, I did my best, along with the teachers, to answer honestly so that a level of comfort was obtained. The desire to spend time with Leo led to teachers having to develop a schedule for being Leo's helper. Kids loved assisting him and wanted to push his wheelchair when that time came. This wasn't only limited to the natural nurturing of little girls, but the young boys in Leo's class also enjoyed the opportunities to help.

First grade expanded Leo's love for adventure. The class attended a variety of field trips. With the concept of inclusion, Leo was able to participate in experiences when some may have expressed that it would be better for Leo to stay behind. What a shame it would have been for not only Leo, but his peers and teachers as well, to miss out on opportunities to see him laugh. He enjoyed time at the farm, nature hikes, visits to Old World Wisconsin, and even crawfish catching in the river.

We were with a group positioned at the banks of the Fox River. After receiving instructions from the nature reserve volunteer, Tony and I began our preparations to get Leo ready. There was a crisp chill in the air. Tony got himself ready as I grabbed a pair of waders.

"Do you think these will fit you, Leo?" I held up a pair that were meant for a very tall person.

"No." He giggled. "Those are too big."

"Okay, I will keep looking. How about these?"

"Momma, I am bigger than that."

"You are?" I held them up next to his body. "I guess you are. This pair looks perfect."

Meanwhile, Tony was completely dressed and ready to assist me. Tony held Leo under his armpits and lifted him while I slid the waders up his legs. I kept making my way up and over Leo's bottom and looped the straps over his shoulders. Tony placed him back onto a chair and made final adjustments. I quickly put on my waders and made my way to the stream. We stepped into the water together and Tony supported Leo as we went in further.

"Are you ready for this adventure, Leo?"

"Yes." His eyes sparkled as the reflection of the sunlight hit the flowing stream.

"Should I grab a net?"

"A big one." His excitement had him shaking and the weight of his body and the waders almost took Tony down, and Leo along with him.

"Hold steady, Leo, Papa doesn't want to drop you."

While Tony held Leo, I held the pole of the net in Leo's hand with him. He shifted his eyes back and forth in search of movement. Tony "bunny hopped" Leo from side to side, forward and back throughout the stream.

"I see one," Leo shouted with excitement.

"Let's get him, it is a big one!" The three of us worked together as we dipped the net into the water and scooped up a full net.

"I see it moving." The crawfish was making his way out of the net.

"Do you want to grab it out, Leo, or should I get it?"

Without hesitation, "You get it, Papa." We placed it in the bucket, and Leo was satisfied with our accomplishment. "All done," he stated proudly.

Time in music class always brought joy to Leo. Watching him play instruments was such a wonderful experience. He may have lacked rhythm, but he didn't miss a beat. He loved to engage in songs even though his sense of timing was delayed. During choir performances, Leo owned the stage. He was immersed in the songs as his whole body moved in the wheelchair to get the words out. He had his own special way of doing things. He may not have been able to get each word formed, but the ones he did, you heard. This was often the case because his final word of the song was released moments after all the other children, which made his voice stand out.

God is an artist. He creates beautiful masterpieces on the canvas of the sky. It makes me smile when I see all the colors together, reminding me of Leo's love to paint. I used to tape large sections of paper on the floor and let him scooch around on his hands and knees when he was about six, creating beautiful watercolor paintings. It was hard to let go of this love as his limbs began to lose control. This led to hand-over-hand assistance, which frustrated Leo, yet he would push through, aiming to please. The difference between art time at home and art during school involved an occupational therapist.

I was grateful for the therapists that had Leo under their care. I could tell from the start that they had the patience to conquer the task. Leo's fine motor skills were an area that tugged at my heart, watching him struggle, yet never giving up. He had laser focus as he gripped the paint brush, always drawing his face close to the work of art as if he was trying to step into his masterpiece. He had such determination and often pushed through pain and tears just to accomplish and finish alongside the other kids.

His involvement in gym class also brought on a variety of adventures. Leo loved the parachute game where everyone gathered in a circle, holding the edges of a parachute while balls danced on the top, flying in the air until all of them flew off. This was followed by everyone shifting to the center of the parachute while it domed over them, enclosing them beneath the rainbow of colors on the material. Playing kickball with friends in third grade was another activity that brought joy, but some activities brought struggle. The strength in his legs was fading, and time spent utilizing the walker lessened with more time in a wheelchair.

Getting to school was one of Leo's favorite pastimes. He was fortunate to have incredible bus drivers. The love and compassion exuded from these individuals was so heartwarming. The drivers who took on the role of special needs drivers often had more than just a job in mind. Accepting this assignment, they knew it meant building a relationship. This task allowed for a more intimate and personal opportunity. Often the route involved only a few kids, and in Leo's case, just him on the bus. This gave him the attention he needed with all eyes on him. Relationships were built, and friendships sustained from these beautiful encounters.

There was, however, one time where Leo's ride home involved a little more adventure than what we hoped for. On one route home, Leo was assigned a substitute driver while in elementary school. The bus pulled up to our home. I stepped on to help like I always did.

"How was the ride, Leo?"

"I fell over."

"What do you mean you fell over?"

I looked at the bus driver and she appeared surprised. I believe she saw Leo's limitations and assumed he was non-verbal. Sure, he was in a wheelchair for the safety of the ride, but her reaction showed she saw Leo as an object and not a boy.

"What is Leo talking about," I turned to her and asked.

"The wheelchair tipped over on the ride home. I stopped and picked it back up." She expressed her words so nonchalantly.

"How is that even possible?"

"I forgot to strap him in."

"Do you realize how fast you had to be going to make the weight of this chair tip over? And what do you mean you forgot to use the toggle supports?"

"He is okay." She crossed her arms and rolled her eyes.

"I realize that he is okay. What is not okay is your lack of attention to detail and the fact that you weren't even going to mention it to me."

There is so much trust required to release your child into the hands of others. When you combine both the physical and verbal limitations that Leo experienced, it heightens this level of trust even more. Leo's abilities, or lack of abilities, put him in a vulnerable position. He needed to feel safe. He needed to feel secure. I needed to know that he was valued and trust that he was going to be looked out for. So, let's just say that particular bus driver did not maintain this route.

Just like relearning words, we had to go back to the basics for every aspect of his life. Learning to regain his ability to grasp objects had to be presented through a variety of games to keep him from becoming frustrated, taking the focus off of "working" and making it playful. Having Oliver participate in these activities was so crucial. He was a model Leo could see and try to imitate. Leo intently watched as he played, trying to mimic Oliver's actions. Using treats, such as fruit snacks, also became an incentive for Leo to grasp and coordinate his movement to place them into his mouth. We celebrated every task he accomplished.

In the Bible, God saved the Israelites from slavery in Egypt and led them to the promised land. Ironically, our situation could have been viewed opposite to the Israelites. As a family, we were free to come and go as we pleased, and do the things we enjoyed, but Leo's needs changed all of that. His restrictions eventually had us become more withdrawn from daily life and pulled into isolation. This could have been viewed negatively, but thankfully, this transition occurred over multiple years which allowed us the time needed to adjust our mindset and realize that a life that was simple was a life simply worth living.

As our journey wound over the path of Leo's life with peaks and valleys and twists and turns, I watched and learned how Leo remained steadfast in his love for Jesus. Leo didn't only turn to God in times of trouble, he kept Him with him from our initial cry for help. God rescued us in the beginning from the illness. He heard our voices calling to Him and made Leo His own.

We had no idea what we were doing, we learned as we entered each new day. We had to strip away everything we knew and rebuild it from scratch. Just like parenting in general, there was no manuscript to follow and without any similar cases, there was no one to lean on. We had to construct our own plan, and with time ticking away, we tried to compile as much as we could to succeed with the new path laid out before us.

For a period of time, Tony was stuck in a mindset of how can we "fix" this. He said there had to be something they were missing or that we were not seeing. Something that would make Leo return to the little boy that he was. We were desperately searching for something to bring back the reality of all the hopes and dreams we had for him. Those moments when we felt like we had no control over things left us lost and wandering. It could have been easy to become angry and lose sight of the bigger picture happening around us. It was at this moment when that faint source in the distance helped keep us calm and started to move closer to us. Leo knew, but we didn't yet know what was behind it.

Somehow at an early age, Leo learned to remove his thoughts of the challenges of his flesh and rested peacefully in the spirit of the Lord. Leo had a mind that consistently thought about God as providing him with perfect peace throughout his storm. Although he was well aware of the pain his body endured, he didn't typically let it control his mood or his attitude. He was somehow able to breathe through his circumstances and redirect his focus on Jesus. In the process, his pain became secondary to the peaceful nature his spirit was experiencing.

Leo took this separation of flesh and spirit further than most people seem capable of, not because we can't, but because we don't allow our minds to become completely still, letting God settle in. Leo would literally drift, transcending to another place, and be overcome with such calmness. In the state of flesh, Leo was full of limitations; his body lacked normal motion, and from head to toe, his body felt pain. However, in spirit, Leo was free without restriction, and fear had no place to take hold. It was only a matter of time that what was happening within Leo became known to us. We literally watched our son experience the spirit form.

The spirit of God lives in each one of us. With His will, we have the capability to live at peace, knowing that He has our backs and will help us successfully fulfill our purposes. As I let the Spirit direct my thoughts and actions, I gained a sense of freedom. The reality is, we had little control over the direction of our lives without Him. Leo's illness delivered him into a realm of love, and there, he was comforted by the protection of his loyal Master. He found his redemption from the illness, and he held onto his faith and trust to the very end.

Chapter Twelve

COMMEMORATE
THE DAY

With each rotation under the sun and stars, there was cause to celebrate amidst our sorrow. The struggle had been real to get to this point, and while living life as each day rose, we found joy and comfort in the sun. There were days that had Leo on edge with anticipation, days I could barely contain his emotions that were projecting outwardly through involuntary motion. As much as going to school motivated Leo to prepare for his upcoming days, holidays also kept him encouraged for weeks as he counted down to their arrival. As the two intertwined, school projects that focused on the holidays made each feel more special and inviting.

A few days prior to one Easter, while Leo was in third grade, Tony and I gathered around the kitchen table along with Matthew, Trent, Leo, and Oliver, to color eggs. My boys loved to dye eggs each year, resulting in many egg salad sandwiches to follow. We bought kits ranging from glitter to spinning designs, to stickers, in addition to the colors. One favorite method, however, was writing with crayon before dipping the egg in the dye cups to reveal hidden messages. Matthew and Trent loved trying to sneak hidden messages or designs on the egg and then watch Leo's reaction when he pulled the colored egg from the cup.

"What color do you want your first egg to be?" I asked while assembling spoons for the eggs. Plastic cups were centered on the table, revealing the colors of the rainbow.

"Red."

It was always red, but I asked anyway. I pushed Leo up closer to the kitchen table so that his wheelchair slid comfortably underneath. This allowed him to peer over the top of the red cup, almost getting his nose wet. As Tony held his hand, I placed the hardboiled egg upon the spoon. Together, we slowly helped him release it into the cup.

"Is it done yet?"

"Leo, you just put it in. Let's put the timer on for two minutes and check it."

"Okay."

The timer sounds. "Check it."

"Is it red enough?"

"A little longer."

One by one, the eggs were placed in the cups as he anxiously waited and watched them turn colors. Meanwhile, Oliver placed an egg in the cup, and unable to sit still, he busied himself with other activities. He occasionally resurfaced, glanced in the cup, and decided if it was ready to be pulled out. Once finished, we gathered all the colorful eggs and placed them back into the egg carton. Leo smiled with pride as he gazed upon his assortment of eggs. He saw blue ones with stickers and yellow ones with the sun, but what caught his eye most were the perfectly colored red eggs.

A few days later, the excitement continued. Waking on Easter morning, Leo rose earlier than the average day. We turned to look at each other and his glistening brown eyes looked into mine.

"Is it time? Did the Easter Bunny come yet?"

"Let me go look." His body stiffened with excitement as I returned back to the room. "He came!" Laughter released from his belly as his body extended fully like a plank as if he was going to get out of bed without help.

"Let's go!" he yelled. I scooped him into my arms and carried him to the family room while the rest of the family remained asleep.

I sat him upon my lap and asked, "Do you see any?" His eyes began to scan the room and he responded without a word as his body became erect, almost spilling from my lap. "Careful, Leo. Where is it?"

"Right there." His eyes showed what his arms were unable to point out.

The laughter continued throughout the entire search. Since the weather was nice, a few of the eggs were even hidden outside, adding more adventure to the morning. Matthew and Trent helped guide their brothers to the correct spots and gave out high fives when lost eggs were found. The imaginations of my four boys worked well together and I found joy in their bond. When the search was completed, Leo held his basket proudly with the eggs and chocolates spilling over its edges.

As the rains of spring came to an end and summer warmed our bodies, time for socializing was provided with wonderful gatherings until school would return in the fall, continuing Leo's opportunity to be surrounded by kids. These activities enhanced his life. There was an exciting camp for children with special needs and their siblings. It was a beautiful display of interaction between all walks of life. Oftentimes, siblings of special needs kids can feel overlooked, as the demands of their brother or sister need to be met. This unique camp brought them all together, giving children a chance to gather and be free of their limitations.

Camp was staffed with specialized adults who otherwise used their educational background to create modified activities that would be otherwise difficult for these kids to achieve. Children with a variety of obstacles found it possible to fish, horseback ride, rock wall climb, dance, and engage in arts and crafts. All of it was made possible by donations and love from others. These gatherings were beautiful to witness, and I saw families interact, create lasting friendships, and make memories that held a place in Leo's mind for weeks after.

Leo also participated in a yearly vocational bible camp, spending the week singing songs and having breakout sessions with a central focus on love. At the end of the five-day camp, the kids performed for their families. The camp administrators provided each child with a CD consisting of the songs that they practiced during the week. One song, in particular, held the lyrics, "There is only one way to Heaven and Jesus is the way."

We were in the car driving when this one came on and Leo simply responded, "I already knew that." He said it so matter-of-factly, his delivery was precious.

On the day of the performance, Leo couldn't help but be noticed on stage. Not only did his physical presence in a wheelchair contrast with the other children standing in rows, but the love in his heart poured out through the lyrics.

I positioned Leo to the side of the stage. "Are you ready?"

He thrusted his head back in the chair and pushed up on his foot-plates. "Yes."

The music began and his face illuminated the space. He leaned forward and applied weight to his elbows that rested upon his tray. "There is only one way to Heaven, and Jesus is the way." Although he was only able to get out a word here and there, he managed to release keywords in the songs with emphasis, never missing a chance to say, "Jesus."

The crisp air of fall entered Wisconsin, bringing a new set of adventures our way. Outings to the farm were always a staple in our traditions. Baby cows sucked on Leo's knuckles, thinking he was a teat, while he laughed at the sensation of their gums and tongue engulfing his fist. Leo scanned the pumpkin patch as we wound through it on a hayride. Tony and I typically sat him on our laps or wedged on the hay between us. Cuddled close, we watched his head bobble back and forth with every bump.

Going trick-or-treating was a must each year, rendering his bag full of chocolates, one of his favorite treasures in life. No matter the weather, we always found a means to accomplish this beloved activity. Some of his favorite places to trick-or-treat included nursing homes, where he not only received candy, but was able to encounter people up close and be warm while doing it. He also enjoyed "trunk-or-treat" at our local church where church members decorated the trunks of their cars with different themes and lined them up close in the parking spaces to hand out candy. This event was perfect for Leo. It held his attention and provided comfort on the flat smooth surface of the lot.

No matter the location, getting ready for the outing was tiresome, but so worth the enjoyment it brought Leo. It was all about the costume and finding a perfect one that was not only warm, but easy to get on with his restricted flexibility. One of my favorite costumes was one Leo wore from ages twelve to fifteen as a dog. This adult size, cozy, brown fur outfit allowed for easy on and off ability. It provided warmth and allowed Leo to become, for the day, one of his favorite animals. His love of dogs must have been influenced by the dogs our family welcomed into the home.

Strolling through our neighborhood was different for Leo. Those who could run free took shortcuts through the crisp crunchy grass. Having to go up and down each driveway took time, time that his body couldn't withstand. Yet, he powered through. Literally, a few times, when we utilized his battery-operated wheelchair and watched the line of the charged battery disappear quickly with every house situated on top of a hill. Praying it would last the duration as Leo anxiously would say, "Let's go," each time he spotted a porch light on, indicating they were home. We held our breath and prayed that the power in the battery would last, or it was going to be a long, heavy push home.

Thanksgiving brought joy to Leo, especially the years that we hosted, and everyone gathered around Leo's bed during our prayer. This was another moment in time when all Leo wanted was to be a part of something, share in the laughter, and listen to the endless conversations that surrounded him. As his ears took in the social aspects of life, the light of life engulfed the space he was in.

Winter brought out a special sparkle in Leo's eyes. The spirit of Christmas and everything tied to it made his whole being light up with the love of Jesus. Searching for the perfect Christmas tree to cut was something that Leo took very seriously. Back and forth down the wooded lanes, Leo's eye scanned the variety of pine trees.

Tony stopped and asked, "How about this one?"

"Keep going."

Oliver dashed ahead, searching for the direction we should take. "This way," he yelled.

Again, Tony would stop. "Is this a good one?"

"Too little." Endless attempts led to the same answers. Then, finally, "I see it!" A large thirty-foot tree stood in Leo's pathway. It towered over his chair and left an even larger shadow behind it. There were snowflakes nestled in the branches and a few pinecones dangling from it.

"That one might be too big for our home. Let's keep looking." Tony turned the wheelchair around the bend and pushed forward with determination.

Leo stated once again, "I see it."

"That's the one," Tony said. It was the perfect green and stood proudly amongst its brothers and sisters. Its branches were even, and no empty spaces were visible. Before we started cutting, however, Tony asked "Are you sure?"

"Yes."

I propped Leo up by the tree, holding him under his armpits, saw in hand, and together, they attempted the back-and-forth motion. Unable to withstand the pressure for too long, Tony embraced Leo and gently placed his exhausted body back into his chair.

"Should we let Oliver have a try?"

"Yes. Your turn, Oliver."

Grabbing hold of the saw, Oliver finished the final passes of the sawing motion and yelled out, "Timber!"

Leo shouted out into the pine tree forest, "Hurray!"

Despite that his body tensed and tightened in the cold, he loved playing in the snow. He didn't care if it was to make snowballs, build a fort, play with the dogs, or sled down the hill. Those events were all wonderful memories. Sledding was a workout not only to get Leo all bundled up in his proper gear to remain warm, but what comes down must have first started up. Hoping to maintain our footing was just the beginning of getting Leo to the top of the hill. Once at the top, it was easy to see through Leo's expression that it was all worth it.

The lights of the Christmas season matched the light of Leo's heart. Multiple artificial trees surrounded his bed in addition to the one we cut down, as the family room transformed into a winter wonderland. Strings of lights covered the trees, weighing the branches down, while red balls cast beams in all directions. Garland swayed off the banister with more lights intertwined within it. Strings of lights swooped across the mantel and windows, providing a light show of love completely cocooned Leo in a glow.

The one thing that made Leo's face radiant with excitement were visits with Santa. The purest form of his heart surfaced every encounter he had with Santa. Two jolly souls were drawn together during the holidays. Each year we drove to visit a special Santa, and one, also known as Leo's uncle, came to visit Leo in our home.

Every year our town hall hosted cookies with Santa. This special event allowed children to be entertained, while they waited their turn, with a variety of activities and a cookie at the table. One year, I arrived an hour too early. I entered the parking lot, *I wonder where everyone is?* I thought to myself. I parked the van and began to unload Leo from the ramp. There was a chill in the air, and I covered him with a soft red blanket as an extra barrier to the wind. I began to push Leo to the door.

"Let's go see if Santa is here."

"He is." I reached the sidewalk and was greeted by a helper.

"Can I help you?"

"We are here to see Santa," I explained.

"Oh, I am so sorry. Santa won't be here for about an hour."

"I must have messed up the time. Sorry, Leo. We will have to see if your body can make it out again in a little bit." Leo's smile turned to disappointment.

"Hold on, let me go see if Santa arrived early." The helper swiftly went through the doors and moments later returned exclaiming, "I was wrong, Santa is here."

"I knew it," Leo replied.

Discreetly, I made eye contact with the volunteer and whispered, "Thank you."

"Follow me. Let's just give Santa a few minutes to settle in, I think he may need a cookie first."

Leo and I entered the building and waited in the lobby. Suddenly we heard, "Ho, Ho. Ho. I think one of my special friends has arrived. Leo, is that you?"

"Yes, Santa!" Leo's anticipation had him sliding down the seat of his chair.

"Come on in, Santa is waiting for you." Carefully, I scooped Leo from his chair and propped him up on the seat of the sleigh next to Santa.

"Have you been a good boy?"

"Yes." Leo could hardly contain himself.

"What do you want for Christmas, Leo?" I handed Santa a typed list. "Boy, Leo you sure have a lot of items on here. I don't know if Santa can get them all on the sleigh."

"You can. I know you can."

This beautiful exchange of love for the spirit of Christmas sparkled in both of their eyes. The reflection of belief and joy beamed from the blue of Santa's eyes to the deep chocolate brown of Leo's. This kind-hearted man recognized the tremendous effort it took to get Leo to this spot. He saw beyond a boy wanting to visit Santa, and realized the exhaustion involved to make this visit happen. After a conversation with both Santa and Mrs. Claus, they saw an opportunity to make this joyous occasion possible for families with special needs without the stress that sometimes accommodates it.

Santa had a soft spot in his heart for Leo. He was so taken by Leo's spirit, and honored Leo on his sleigh with beautiful angel wings that he attached to the front. What this mishap, on my part, led to was a special day set aside for families with special circumstances known as Leo's Legacy. By appointment only, they allowed families to sign up for a fifteen-minute time slot, providing one-on-one time with Santa. No waiting. No distractions. Just time to fill joy in the hearts of those who may not have the endurance, or the ability, to attend the traditional way.

Then, just weeks after this special visit, Santa appeared at our home, confirming Leo's wish list. My brother-in-law (this time) made this encounter so personal, narrowly escaping being discovered. As the conversation unfolded, hearing Santa's voice made Leo inquisitively tilt his head.

Lying in his bed, "I heard something."

"You did? I didn't hear anything."

A distant jingle began. "I heard it again."

"I heard it this time too, Leo. Do you think it is Santa?"

His whole body erected with excitement. "He's here. It is Santa!"

"Ho, ho, ho. I am looking for Leo."

"I'm here," Leo tried to get the words out through his laughter.

Santa made his approach to Leo's bedside. "Have you been a good boy?"

"Yes."

"I have something for you." He reached into his bag and pulled out a gift and gently placed it on Leo's tummy. "You have to wait until Christmas Day morning to open it."

"Okay," Leo said reluctantly.

Every year, this scenario of exchanged love played out, and each time, it was received with the same level of excitement, fully believing in the spirit of St. Nick. Seeing Santa was something Leo never outgrew. The sound of his laughter filled our home, even on his final Christmas which was just days prior to his death. Santa was faithfully there by his side for the sixteen Christmases he was able to experience.

The Christmas that Leo was getting ready to turn eleven, he received a special gift, but Santa wasn't the one who delivered it. Oliver and I spent a weekend away in northern Wisconsin for a hockey tournament. During some down time, we took a drive to a local farm and discovered basset hound puppies for sale. I have always loved the breed, finding them irresistible with their long ears that drag on the ground.

We spent a couple of hours playing with the litter and engaged in a beautiful conversation with the owner. We shared details about our family and Leo's love for animals. I was able to maintain willpower, and left without purchasing a puppy to call our own. A few weeks later, I received a call. "Is there any chance you would be interested in one of the puppies?"

"As much as I would love to, I just don't feel like I can take on another responsibility."

"Are you sure? We are having trouble finding a home for the runt."

"I really wish I could help you, but my hands are pretty full as it is right now."

A week went by, and the phone rang once again. "We are really in need of some help. My wife and I are supposed to head south for the winter. Would you be willing to foster the puppy until we get back?"

We all know how that turns out, once they are in your home, they are forever in your home. I remained strong, "I am sorry. I really hope you find a home."

The morning of Christmas Eve, the phone rang again. "My wife and I are leaving tomorrow and would love to give this puppy to your family and provide love to your son. Please consider taking us up on this offer."

"I am sorry, it is Christmas Eve, and I just can't commit to that long drive."

"We will meet you. Just name the place."

I looked to Tony, "What should we do? I have turned him down three times."

"It looks like this is meant to be. Take the other boys and go get the puppy."

Lucy, this tiny, tenderhearted basset hound, unexpectedly found her way to our family. Matthew and Oliver took turns holding her in their arms throughout the long drive and quietly walked into our home entering from the garage door.

"Leo, we have a surprise for you," Matthew expressed joyfully.

Oliver ran ahead, "Close your eyes, Leo!"

Leo giggled, only half shutting his eyes, peaking with excitement. "What is it?"

Gently, Matthew placed Lucy onto Leo's bed. "Open them."

"A puppy!" Kisses covered his face as Lucy wiggled her tail with excitement. Quickly, she settled in upon Leo, wrapped around his neck like a scarf. "I love her." The immediate bond Leo and Lucy shared was apparent the moment she entered the door.

In a blink of an eye, seven days later, we went from the excitement of Christmas right into celebrating Leo's birthday. This was an event that brought just as much happiness to Leo as it did to all who attended. Love of life is what you witnessed as you looked at Leo celebrating his special day. For him, it was about the gathering and being surrounded by people who loved him (in addition to chocolate cake and ice cream). Leo's birthday was as much of a holiday in our family as New Year's Day itself. It was almost like part two to the day's party after the ball dropped.

The love for a dollar bill played a major role at his celebrations and stemmed from my dad who innocently said to Leo one day, "You are a nice boy, do you have a dollar?" Little did he know at the time what a monster he created. Leo took that statement, turned it around, used it on so many occasions in his own way, and remarkably, people gave it to him! It went as far as having a one dollar theme at his birthday party where, all on his own, he came up with the concept of charging a one dollar entry fee for those who attended.

Leo's guests were so creative and amazing that they came up with all kinds of ideas to show their love for him through the dollar bill. One of them created a beautiful drawing using the dollars as the leaves, another blew up red balloons with a dollar in each. One guest utilized a Kleenex box with endless dollars tucked within taped together as you pulled them up, another made a belt out of dollars and Leo even received origami figures made from dollar bills. Even in his playful moments, Leo still inspired others with ideas. This birthday celebration expanded his wallet and his safe where he stored his money, this didn't go unnoticed by Oliver.

Following that birthday, Leo had some time in our home with our parish priest. Leo told him the story and the priest replied, "Leo, I believe you are on to something. I will have to try this at church."

"Good," Leo replied, acknowledging his brilliance.

Singing "Happy Birthday" was the highlight of the occasion. At this point in time, Leo was strapped into his stander, a device used to help stretch his legs, with Velcro straps that provided support around his chest and waist to maintain stability. Still hopeful that one day he could find mobility with his walker again, we wished for success with the stander. We positioned him by the kitchen table with his hands on top of it. Although his core was weak, his inner strength flourished, and we witnessed him stand as proudly as he could.

The group began to sing, "Happy birthday to you..." Leo started giggling. "Happy birthday to you ..." By this time, he was laughing with such excitement that he began to sway in his stander. As the group continued, "Happy birthday, dear Leo," the utter love for this song nearly had him tip the whole stander backward as he thrusted his head back with laughter, enjoying all the attention. "Happy birthday to you!"

When it came to the end of the song, Leo attempted to blow out the candles. Between laughing, and his inability to obtain the proper mouth position to actually blow, this took a while. Wax flowed from the candles and saliva flowed from Leo's lips, dripping down his chin. Wanting to step in for the guests' sakes, I asked between his laughs if he wanted assistance.

"Do you want Oliver and your cousins to help you blow them out?"

He tried to catch his breath long enough between giggles and replied, "Yes."

Leo, Oliver, and a few of their cousins sitting near the cake blew in unison. Smoke billowed up to the ceiling, and before the flames were completely extinguished, Leo was ready for more.

"Again!"

There was always a round two of singing the birthday song at every celebration. Each year we did so willingly because each year was one more rotation around the sun. It was one more year that proved we could defy the odds given to us by charts. We saw Leo lose a lot, and then gain back some, and now flourish with what was given to him. It was a gift in itself to hear him speak and to be a part of the air that gravitated toward him with each laugh. A contagious laugh that spilled into the lungs of everyone around him spreading love and the comfort of connection to other people.

After Leo's birthday, Trent's and Matthew's soon followed. It was our family's tradition to get Jimmy cakes for special occasions and each occasion brought reasons to indulge in more treats. Cake elevated Leo's mood with every bite he took. I am confident there is a reason why cake is served at birthdays, having seen how much all of my boys loved consuming it. Then, time sprung ahead followed by spring finally releasing all of the Wisconsin snow from our lawns. Like grass poking upward toward the sun, each day came with possibility and we took advantage of time spent in the light. When the temperature allowed, the boys were quick to play outside once more and reconnect to the land and one another's imaginations.

Once informed he wouldn't likely make it to age three, and at one point seeing Leo blow out a total of ten candles, tripling the expectation, it was hard to see what this accomplishment could look like. Sitting with him and seeing the reflection of candles or Christmas lights in his eyes made each moment special. Life did slow down for us, but living day by day was a way to keep life simple, and to enjoy what was simply beautiful.

Chapter Thirteen

CAUSE TO
CELEBRATE

Like a giant sunflower sprouting from the ground beneath a bird feeder, Leo filled the space around him. In a way, unbeknownst to us, the house was designed to have him at its center. Leo's physical structure was gaining in weight and losing in ability. For his safety, and my own, we decided it would be best to bring in a hospital bed to limit carrying him.

On a typical afternoon, Leo would be sprawled out on his hospital bed positioned near the windows of the living room. Between him and the windows were his beloved pets: his gecko, T-Rex, and his betta fish, Angel, from which the sunlight reflected through the glass enclosures into the room. Blinds displayed lines of the sun over the rock fireplace, second-floor balcony, front entryway, and hallway, reaching all corners of the dwelling. All hallways and walkways led to the living room between couches, antiques, and toys. Positioned at the focal point of the couches stood the bed, and usually Lucy cuddled in the sheets. Gravitating toward Leo, like the Earth to the Sun itself, all guests would walk around him, but always be drawn toward him.

The gentleness of Leo was such a beautiful presence to be around. His loving nature made you feel calm and loved because of his glance, or the efforts put forth to shine a brilliant smile. Outings with him awakened your senses and helped you to see life from a different perspective, while also seeing how others looked upon him. There were so many outings where I felt life from under my steps as the rotation of his wheels spun upon the surfaces we traveled. The smoothness of the concrete with the occasional crack, to the bumpiness of gravel and yards, was, in a way, meditative. With each bump, however, Leo's fragile body shifted, and that movement would not go unnoticed. Even so, Leo wouldn't complain about any discomfort, yet just be content with experiencing the raw beauty of nature. The bumps were just part of the walk, and the walk was a way to connect our own bumpy road to nature and experience life.

Leo's heart was tender. If you leaned in and pressed your ear against his chest you would feel just how tender, but at the same time, its beat was strong. That inner strength was the result of good character, and in his life, he naturally attracted good people toward him. The tenderness came from youth, and imagination from a mind wise beyond his years. His body was young, but his personality was layered with dimensions. He just "got it" and knew how to maneuver through life. He went with the flow, like water in a stream, despite the mountain of limitations placed before him. The stream may have had difficult paths to navigate, but Leo's natural peace kept a smooth flow without appearing to use much effort. His imagination was so vivid, he would get transported into the words expressed and appear to become one of the characters. He loved story time in the classroom. Stories of adventure and stories with animals both brought him extreme pleasure. He also wrote several short stories of his own, each one a labor of love.

These stories involved a great deal of patience on both of our parts, as he expressed each word and I listened intently to maintain his wording. He had so much to say and lacked the ability to get it all out. His eyes shifted back and forth, as if trying to pluck the perfect word from the sky, then slowly releasing it to me in a whisper. This exercise was extremely exhausting for him, yet it held such importance in his life. Although there were moments I released a heavy sigh when Leo mentioned he wanted to add to his story, I now exhale with a sigh of relief that I took the time to share this experience with him.

During his third grade school year, Leo was quite ill and missed a good portion of the year. During this time, his teacher and classmates drew pictures that corresponded with the words Leo wrote, then laminated and bound his writing into a book. When Leo returned to school he was presented with the final results and embraced with hugs. One of his classmates really touched my heart when she expressed to Leo "I forgot how adorable you were." How tender and precious is that wording from a child.

Leo, himself, actually became a comic book hero, Power Boy, when "The Hidden Heroes Project" used his life story to base a superhero character off of him and gave him the superpower of flying. This story captured Leo's inner strength and made it a tale to inspire. In a world where so many people find themselves relating to heroes, it was nice to see Leo given a chance to relate to others. Power Boy was developed based on opportunities that came from our life experiences both at home and in school.

The heroes in Leo's life at this time came in the form of Disney's Mickey Mouse Clubhouse. Leo was captivated by the colors and characters. We sensed an urgency to fulfill Leo's wishes when his health slipped, and with it, a visit from Jesus returned.

During this fragile time, I remember I held Leo on my lap, and he looked right into my eyes and said, "I'm going to miss you."

"Why?"

"I'm going to see Jesus. My body is hurting."

"What do you mean, you are going to see, Jesus?" I sat there, frozen, unable to react, afraid of what the response would be. He kept his focus on me, the intensity of his gaze was an image I can still see and feel.

"Are you nervous about me being gone?"

"I am not nervous, because so far, I have been able to spend wonderful years with you and you have taught me Jesus will take care of you until we meet again." I am not certain if what I replied was right, but at that moment, those were the words that spilled out of me.

My emotions were elevated as I tried to process everything Leo was telling me, and at the same time, Leo was insistent that he also talk to Oliver. "I am going to see Jesus because my body hurts. I am going to miss you, Oliver."

"Will you be back?" Oliver asked innocently.

"I will always be with you."

I tried to console my sick child along with my five-year old son, who probably for the first time, saw the severity of Leo's condition, while also trying to keep my own emotions intact. Not wanting any regrets, our plan to give Leo the world of adventure took flight in June of 2008. Our circumstances led us to the Make-A-Wish Foundation. They were amazing at coordinating Leo's desire to go to Disney. From start to finish, our wish grantors planned a once-in-a-lifetime trip to give our entire family memories to cherish forever.

When the two wish granters arrived at our home, it appeared as if Leo already knew what was coming. Despite Leo's weakened state, he greeted them, "Hi, hi, hi!"

"You must be Leo." A warm smile accompanied this statement.

"Yes." Leo was now almost falling off the couch as his body tightened with excitement.

"So, I hear you want to go to Disney and see Mickey Mouse."

"I do." Leo's eyes sparkled with joy.

Tony and I gathered around Leo, along with Matthew, Trent, and Oliver, and listened to the amazing details of the trip they had in store for us. This well planned and professionally organized trip opened our eyes to the possibilities we could further expose Leo to. It helped educate us on how policies worked for traveling with a wheelchair, both by plane and vehicle options we could use.

We rose early when the day arrived, the dew settling upon the freshly cut grass as the limo pulled into our driveway. The dogs were excited, the birds were chirping, and the sun shone brightly on us all. Tony began to take our luggage to the vehicle with the help of both Matthew and Trent.

Leo exclaimed, "Don't forget my new bag." One of the gifts he received was a personalized carry-on with Lightning McQueen from the movie, *Cars*.

"Don't worry, Leo, Papa put it in the limo."

We drove forty-five minutes to the airport and then enjoyed a smooth flight to Florida. We were greeted, and escorted safely to our hotel, the Disney Caribbean Beach Resort, which was just a quick bus ride to all the main attractions. The grounds were illuminated with festive lights and surrounded by colorful imagery, making Leo's eyes glisten even more. We walked around, discovered the layout of our home away from home, and settled in, knowing we had a big day ahead of us.

Arising early as the sun streamed through the crack of the curtain, we felt the warmth. "Good morning, boys, are you ready for adventure?"

"Let's do this," Matthew expressed.

His eagerness to get started was followed quickly by each of the boys sounding off with excitement. On our first day, we enjoyed the Magic Kingdom with a wonderful breakfast surrounded by multiple characters. At one point, Winnie the Pooh snuck up behind Leo.

"Good morning," Winnie the Pooh whispered.

Leo became startled and tears flowed. "Go away."

I pulled Leo closer to me. "It is okay, sweetheart, they are friendly." Leo didn't seem convinced and looked to Tony. "Papa will protect you."

Hesitation continued to fill the space around us, and Leo was unable to enjoy his food, worrying about who would creep up behind him. Even his beloved Mickey Mouse, along with Minnie, still made him anxious. But then, Tigger came into sight.

Leo's tears turned to laughter. "I love him."

"Are you talking about me?" Tigger made his way closer to Leo, sounding his famous giggle. His orange stripes reflected in Leo's eyes.

"Yes."

Tigger came over and the two of them shared a special moment. The other boys were relieved the crying was over as well, so they could all enjoy the rest of the meal. This encounter with Tigger also brought calmness to Leo long enough to obtain a nice photo. Taking pictures of moments like these was something I always tried to capture.

SeaWorld was, by far, Leo's favorite. His face shined with excitement at the sight of Shamu, the killer whale. As we made our way to our seats, nothing could have erased the permanent smile that stretched across Leo's face. We were just close enough to feel fully engaged, yet far enough from the water to avoid the huge splash as Shamu emerged from the water, coming down with an enormous thump.

"Again, again, again," Leo yelled.

The action maintained his attention throughout the whole show as the dolphins joined in, causing Leo to pivot his head in multiple directions. Seeing this movement amidst his joy may have been a little thing, but it meant a lot to Tony and me. Then, it was off to a boat adventure tour at Animal Kingdom, followed by time at Islands of Adventure and Hollywood Studio. The trip was packed with action and was physically exhausting to Leo, but filled with moments that enhanced his life. Each day, we started off strong, making the most of all the theme parks, and closed the day with a quiet soak in the pool, followed by snuggling in bed. Thoughts of the day swirled in his precious mind as Leo's imagination continued to take him places that his body was unable to keep up with. Given how weak his body was at this point in his life, it was truly astounding the activities he made happen. This led to an opportunity for Leo and me to be on the radio and participate in the Make-A-Wish Radio-A-Thon. We shared our incredible adventure and our story helped raise funds for the cause.

The impact that the Make-A-Wish Foundation had on our family went beyond just the trip. Although Matthew didn't know it at the time, it planted a seed in his heart. He said the expression of Leo's smile was forever an image he held in his mind and he wanted to be a part of making that happen for other kids. He himself became a wish grantor and witnessed firsthand those same beautiful smiles appear on several other children. Make-A-Wish gave our family an experience to treasure, even more so now that Leo is gone. We witnessed the sparkle of pure joy in Leo's eyes, despite the weak and fragile state his body was in.

A few years later, we took what we learned from that amazing adventure and capitalized on Leo's strong condition. Since Tony had been covering the Midwest for business for so many years, he wanted to share the beauty of those locations with the boys. Unfortunately, Matthew and Trent did not attend these memorable adventures with us. At the time, Matthew lived out of state and Trent was away at college tied up with other obligations. But, with Tony's knowledge of the area, and my investigation of activities to conquer with someone in a wheelchair, we managed to plan back-to-back Christmas trips to unforgettable destinations.

Our first escape was to Jackson Hole, Wyoming. So many elements lined up to make this one of the most memorable outings in Leo's lifetime. Considering how rigid Leo's body became in cold climates, we were so fortunate to have temperatures in the mid-20s, as all of our adventures took place outdoors. Our concept for the trip was to partake in excursions that involved movement, allowing us to get Leo positioned, and then letting him enjoy the event.

First, we took a magical sleigh ride into the Elk Refuge. Sitting at the base of the mountain, we were not only surrounded by God's natural beauty, but also more elk than the eye could see. Leo sat upon Tony's lap and took it all in. Around us stood these majestic beasts in the raw element of nature, and that connection brought us all closer together as a family. That, and the frigid winds blowing past us. As the cold weather settled into Leo's bones, we opted for an enclosed gondola ride to the top of a mountain. More incredible views lay before us as we took them in briefly. Leo's body was shivering, so we returned to warmth for the rest of the evening.

Next up was an incredible all-day tour on snowmobiles through the Teton Mountains. Utilizing the specially designed Velcro straps we made, Leo was fastened securely in front of Tony as he straddled the machine. The weight of the helmet was a lot for him to withstand, but his determination persevered.

"Are you ready, Leo?" Tony peered around his shoulder, waiting for a response.

Through the muffling of the shield and face mask, Leo managed to utter, "I am."

With Oliver securely in place in front of me, we began our journey, winding through the beautiful trails of the mountain side. At our midway point, we stopped for lunch and Tony removed the weight of the helmet from Leo's head.

Leo sighed "I made it." His body exhausted, Leo thought he was done.

Tony replied, "Oh, sweetheart, we are only halfway. We are stopping for lunch."

Leo released another heavy sigh. He was such a trooper. This sigh stemmed from fatigue only. His eyes were filled with wonder from everything he experienced, and with that he dug deep into his inner strength, fought exhaustion, gained energy from a nutritional lunch, and made it back to the hotel where he enjoyed rest.

We ended the holiday with an unbelievable experience driving a team of dogs on the Iditarod Dog Tour to Granite Hot Springs. The smiles never left each of the boy's faces, including Tony. Well, perhaps for a brief moment when Tony tipped his sled over along with Oliver, and his face planted into the snow. Tony listened intently to the instructor as he described how to control and manage the team of dogs, yet he tested the limits and discovered quickly at Oliver's expense what happens when you don't follow directions. Meanwhile, Leo and I were safe in the sled driven by the owner.

Once we arrived at the springs, the 105-degree water was a refreshing contrast to the brisk winter temperatures. This was exactly what Leo needed after an action-packed day to ease his body. There were several layers to take off him to change him into swimwear. This process was exhausting, with each article of clothing clinging onto his body, making them difficult to peel off. There was a shanty, about thirty yards away from the water hole with steps that led to reach it. Thankfully, this time I had Tony around for the heavy lifting.

I got into the water quickly, and Tony gently handed Leo off to me. As I submerged him into the water, we were rewarded with his smile and his legs hung free. His neck became more mobile, and his fist clenched a little less. He was free from the confinement of his body as he clung to an innertube under his armpits. Oliver began to adventure around the spring, and he too had freedom. At the base of the mountainside, nestled in the woods, laughter echoed as my boys floated.

The following Christmas brought an equally exciting adventure to Big Sky, Montana. As we settled into the small-town atmosphere, we discovered how easy it was for us to access things, despite the cumbersome wheelchair. Leo was so excited to see another part of the world, allowing his imagination to expand further by having more of an understanding of the ways of life. In so many ways could his beautiful mind be seen, from the way he smiled at you sincerely to the way he used his delicate words. It was easy to settle in as Tony, Leo, Oliver and I were ready for the Christmas magic at Montana's greatest national park.

Without wasting time, we dove right into our adventures. First, we enjoyed a snowmobile ride into Yellowstone State Park. Just like family vacations before, Leo was firmly strapped to Tony. Yet, this time, I was the one who tipped! Once again, Oliver was the passenger. We came to a complete stop to allow a buffalo to cross our path. The buffalo was so large and close that we could hear its breath as it passed by.

"It is a bison," Leo would correct each time a buffalo was mentioned.

As I pulled off the shoulder, the snowmobile slipped, and I ended up on soft snow. Once I accelerated, I lost control and over we went onto our sides with a thud in the snowbank.

"Sorry, Oliver," I quickly said. It was a natural motherly instinct.

"It's okay, Mommy," he replied as his gentle blue eyes gazed at mine through the shield.

"We need to get this turned back over."

My heart was pounding as the mighty beast stayed within close range, staring us down. Thankfully, our guide noticed our situation and one, two, three, we were back on track to see Old Faithful. It was a moment that caused my heart to flutter, but looking back I'm proud of how my boys handled it all.

Tony and I got separated once we reached the site. Tony and Leo scrambled and scurried across the parking lot to find us. Anxiously, Oliver and I waited, hoping they wouldn't arrive too late.

"Where are they, Mommy?" Oliver looked around as if unable to stay still.

"I am not sure."

There I stood. I took Oliver's hand in mine to keep him close in case he got any ideas to take action. But then, as I used my free hand to look past the sun, I saw Tony strutting up, with Leo in tow, toward us.

"I see them. Let's run to help Papa." Standing before the mighty Old Faithful, we waited for our one shot to see it explode.

"Is that it? Well, that was a dud," Tony stated.

"I can't believe our one opportunity to see the power of the water just happened to be the rare occurrence of a dud." I was disappointed, only because of the work involved to get us to that point. "Oh well, on to the next excursion. We have a long ride back."

We took a snow coach tour to the canyon, which was beautiful, and embarked on another dog sled tour. We also took a magical horse-drawn sleigh ride into the mountains. We cozied up under soft warm blankets, bundled in our winter gear. Big fluffy snowflakes floated from the sky, appearing like a snapshot for a postcard. Over the river and through the woods, we arrived at a wonderland with a bonfire burning, and a beautiful dome building with large windows bringing the outside, inside. Although these trips had similar outings, the experiences were unique, adding memories and adventures to remain in Leo's mind.

I don't have any regrets over exposing Leo to robust life experiences. We searched for, and found, opportunities for him to try. I was able to see the world through Leo's eyes and it forever changed me. We found strength in our love for each other to continue on with each new day. We started small and grew more ambitious over time as we gained confidence. We realized there wasn't anything he wasn't able to do if we adapted it in a way to make it safe and comfortable.

Fear left us when we saw the joy that adventure brought to Leo. Leo was my driving force. Leo is my driving force still to this day. He motivated me to live a creative life and to see beyond the surface of things. God's river of flowing water streamed freely through Leo, which taught me how to channel my sorrow into strength. With the lessons he taught me, ever so patiently, I was able to surrender and understand that I was not in control of the events that took place in my life. I do, however, have control over the way that I face them and react – for me, that will be head on and not looking back. Life is experienced by doing things. Doing things together made memories. Memories created a core strength uniting us as a family.

As he advanced through life, and through experiences of love and desire, a hidden challenge remained tucked away. There was one young girl who held his attention for years. To set the record straight, Leo might have had his eye on several ladies, but he desired to spend a lifetime with this special lady most of all. She held a place in his heart to the very end. This was a love that began in second grade and carried on up until his passing. In her presence, Leo felt adored, and in his eyes, she was the only one for him.

All the dollars he accumulated over the years, from birthdays, special occasions, or just given to him because he simply asked, "Do you have a dollar?" were collected and accumulated in a special safe, kept under lock and key. In this special place, they were held for what the future would bring. There was a list of things to accomplish with those special dollars. One of the most mentioned interests of his was a marriage to his bride. He knew he felt love in his heart, even though he was only nine at the time, and he knew happiness could be achieved with her. Leo also mentioned getting a horse farm on a beautiful piece of land near the water. The water brought a tranquility to his day-to-day life, which he knew would be great beneath a house on the hill.

This location was described in great detail with all the specifics mentioned numerous times, including the names of his horses. Leo spent hours over the course of years describing details of these desires. One word at a time, he spoke and I repeated. On rare occasions I would be left without knowing what he was trying to convey. Those moments were hard, yet Leo handled them with grace and patience. A typical sentence that flows from our own mouths in seconds, easily took Leo minutes, if not hours, to fully state.

We spent time cuddling together, recalling the desires he had already expressed, and adding to the story. He enjoyed having his house goals written down and read aloud to him. You could see him "living" it out in his mind as his body remained motionless in bed. His legs may have been still, but at his future house, they were running wild with the horses. The descriptions built a foundation for his imagination to build upon and created visions to inspire all who would hear them.

In a repetitive nature, he gave details about the appearance of each horse as well. He mentioned their structure, color, and personalities often. He had big dreams, but sadly, they never had the time to develop and play out. Time was not in his favor. This may have been true, but with so many thoughts in his mind, it made me happy knowing that some dreams awoke. For instance, he had the opportunity to stage a wedding in our home with his beautiful bride who so lovingly appeased Leo's wishes. As mentioned before, Leo loved this girl with his whole heart and it was big of her heart to engage in the "ceremony" fully committed to the experience.

The sun rose earlier that day. With it, Leo sprang into action with a swift morning routine. He was almost too excited to eat his morning pudding and drink his Gatorade. Lucy sensed the excitement as well and was running all around the room. He giggled and brought my ears more joy than any holiday special. She arrived at our home with a beautiful dress, all prettied up for the day, while Leo was decked out in his shirt and tie. She remained out of his view as anticipation began to swell up inside of Leo. The humming sound of "Here comes the bride," resounded in the background and Leo's body turned from stillness into shudder. As she walked down the aisle, or in this case, the hallway, she came into Leo's view. His smile was so big, you could barely see his eyes as the roundness of his cheeks pressed high. She paused, stood before him, while exerting laughter and words simultaneously.

Leo uttered out, "Hi."

"Hi, Leo," she replied as she climbed up into the hospital bed, to be beside him. Nerves of the moment shook him with glee. The bed shook from the force as well, but she remained undisturbed.

"Shall I begin," I recited as I stood next to the bed. I playfully stated the traditional words given at a ceremony. Leo gazed into her eyes and appeared to be able to see the future without having the time to live it out. I removed the ring that he purchased for her. It was held within a precious dog stuffed animal holder that he wanted it stored in. We opened it and I helped him slide the ring onto her finger.

"You may kiss the bride." These words nearly sent Leo rolling off the bed as she leaned over to give a tender kiss on his full, wet lips.

"I love you, Leo," she whispered.

"I love you too."

They shared a tender moment of innocent love, grade school sweethearts, but to Leo, it was true love and he remained faithful to that love "till death do us part." He may not have had the opportunity to experience an actual wedding day, but to him, it was real.

Later, down the road, elementary school days turned into high school and Leo's limitations took hold of him. His ability to engage in moments together with this special girl slipped out of his grasp. They drifted away physically from each other, but she never drifted out of Leo's heart and mind. Unknowingly, at the time, Leo expressed his love for her to me just weeks before his time came to an end. The thought of "what could be," motivated him to continue to push through, hoping it would become, "what is."

Leo was victorious in his struggles because his mind was set on God and not on things of this world. He celebrated being in, not only the moment, but the moments lived. As his elementary years came to a close, he had an emotional awareness, almost as if he sensed his time of inclusion with peers was ending. On his final day of school as his friends ran freely around the playground enjoying the celebration of the hot dog social, Leo remained confined to his wheelchair, but filled with inner peace.

He was sad to leave his friends. Tears poured from his eyes, as he recognized things were going to change. The fleeting motions of friends swooping in to give him a hug, and then exiting as quickly as they came had Leo's emotions on edge. He was unable to express himself with words, because he wasn't given the time needed. The carefree capricious ways of youth were transforming within him as his character was being built. A character that we were beginning to see more prominently unfold before our eyes.

Chapter Fourteen

MOVED BY STILLNESS

Like a tulip breaking through the frost of Wisconsin's early spring ground, we witnessed Leo break through and bloom. As the fragility of the tulip's bud surpassed the crispness of the evening darkness, Leo's fragile state pushed upward to the light to partake in events that may have been missed if we had taken the easy route. And by easy route, I mean surrendering to the bed without trying to make things possible. What we searched for were ways to find movement in his stillness.

Top Soccer was an amazing opportunity to play soccer with other special needs friends. This organization was coached and aided by students from the high school Leo's older brother, Trent, attended. The volunteers included the girls' soccer team and their head coach. It was a beautiful sight to witness kids with all levels of challenges coming together and being patiently instructed and encouraged by other kids. One of Leo's favorite items was the enormous soccer ball that came up as high as his tray while sitting in his chair. Resting his hand upon the top of the ball, he would lean into it. The head coach once told me that this event helped strengthen the unity of his team and he contributed their endless successful state wins to the bonding and giving experience the Top Soccer organization provided them.

Each session started by pairing up with a buddy.

"I got you, Leo," the young, pretty girl expressed as she grew closer.

"Hurray!" Leo honestly didn't need to reply with words, his body language showed his approval. Scattered across the open gym, mini soccer goals bordered the area. Each of the helpers, along with their special child, ran drills mimicking soccer plays. It often took two helpers to work with Leo. One to maneuver the chair, and the other to help guide the ball.

They started midcourt, and began to ease the ball along with Leo's footplate from his chair. Zig-zagging back and forth, they approached the net. Leo pushed down on his foot plates, trying to extend his leg to make contact with the ball, but couldn't. His bottom lifted from the seat with force, desperately wanting to get up and run, but he couldn't. His eyes remained focused, never taking them off the ball ... well, except for brief moments to look at the cute girls. They began their approach to the net, turned Leo to the side, and with a swift motion, used his footplate to make contact, sending the ball steadily, almost in slow motion, to the net opening. Goal! Leo arched his back, thrusting his head into the headrest, and laughter echoed.

Hockey blood ran deep in our family. Each of my boys played one form or another, and Leo was determined to also show what he could do. As we watched Oliver out on the ice, I asked, "Do you want to give it a try?"

"Yes."

I approached the coach. "Is it okay if Leo joins you on the ice for some drills?"

"Of course." He skated over to Leo and asked, "Should we get some equipment on you?"

He responded with a resounding, "Yes!"

We rolled out onto the ice in his wheelchair. He beamed with pride doing something his brothers so passionately loved. Sitting in his chair, fully geared up, with a helmet and a hockey stick duct taped to his chair, Leo took part in drills and out-smiled all of the other kids when a team photo was taken. It didn't matter to Leo if an event lasted one minute or one day, participating and being included gave him endless satisfaction.

Leo and Oliver also loved driving their motorized cars around in the driveway. Unable to steer, we set the steering wheel all the way to one direction which caused it to go in a circle.

Oliver yelled, "I am going to get you." Leo burst into laughter, which caused him to turn the wheel and push the gas pedal all the way down, veering in the direction of the garage door.

"Look out," I yelled as I ran to control Leo's car. This activity involved our complete attention, not knowing when a possible accident could occur.

Leo also loved visits to the lakes, seeing new life as baby ducks made their grand entrance into the world. The new life brought more energy, and that positivity drew Leo and me to it. It was fun to see them waddle up to us in anticipation of treats. With a bag of old bread on his wheelchair tray, we would slowly approach them so as to not scare them back into the water.

"Can I feed them?"

"Let me help you get the bread out of the bag." I took a few slices, broke them into pieces, and laid them on his tray top. "Are you ready?"

"Yes." With a swiping motion, Leo took the back of his hand and pushed the bread pieces off the side of his tray. Like a wiper washing away the fog of morning's breath, his arm brushed the snacks away with purpose and success. With his limited range of motion, it meant a lot to see his determination to share goodness with nature and other life.

"Can you see them?"

"No." I guided his wheelchair backward, until the ducks came into view. "I see them."

Summer also included taking rides on the ATV through the woods and visiting deer at a preserve center close to our home. As Tony drove, with Leo securely Velcro strapped to him, Leo yelled out, "Floor it!" followed by laughter. Sometimes his hand would slide to the accelerator and cause them to increase speed until Tony was able to unlatch his firm grip. Together, they would wind through the dense trails of the woods, searching for nature as the leaves blew from the summer breeze.

Leo also enjoyed fishing with his dad. He would intently watch and tell Tony what to do. "Put the worm on." Grabbing a worm out of the container, Tony held it up.

"Are you sure you don't want to help?"

"I am sure."

Leo kept his eye on the bobber and when it disappeared, he yelled out, "It's down!" Tony reeled it in and as it came out of the water, the line swung toward Leo's face with the fish hanging from the hook.

"Too close," Leo said.

Tony reached for the line and pulled it away. "I got it."

Leo loved the experience, but was more of a distant lover of fish, enjoying the peaceful movement of them *in* the water more than them *out* of it.

Leo never grew tired of watching fireworks and held a strong opinion about the quality of the show. Tony displayed many shows from our backyard when Leo's health took a turn in his middle school and high school days, so he was unable to make the drive to local shows. Tony worked hard, getting everything set for the night, and from one year to the next, he went from being the hero as Leo exclaimed, "These are awesome," to the following year, "These are awful."

Leo was fortunate to have an uncle with a pontoon boat, but more importantly, one that allowed him to be the captain. One summer, this role left us stalled in the middle of the lake.

"Do you want to drive, Leo?"

"Yes."

Leo sat on his uncle's lap and yelled, "Floor it!" He grabbed a hold of the throttle and leaned into it, pushing it all the way forward. Leo seemed completely unfazed by his actions, as we waited for the engine to cool so we could make our way back to shore.

Outings were more manageable in the warm months with a wheelchair since we didn't need to fight the elements of bad weather. Warm days were also more forgiving to the tension in his body. We were so fortunate to live in a location accessible to many parks, trails, and trees in nature. Going to the park brought Leo a lot of laughter as he wanted to try everything from swings to slides to the monkey bars. It was exhausting, but we finished them all together. As I look back on my days with him, I hold no regrets, because we lived life to the fullest.

We exposed Leo to everything. There wasn't an opportunity that we didn't at least attempt to make work for him and his physical limits, because his mind had no limits. From things as simple as playing at the park to attending school, we explored every angle to adapt to his needs. These situations often took multiple adults to make them work, but even if it was a task as brief as one time across the monkey bars, guiding his hand from one rung to the next, watching the expression on Leo's face was worth the effort put into it.

Leo was always up for trying amazing adventures. When adaptive water and snow skiing were presented as opportunities, Leo was up for the challenge. These adventures were led by special people dedicating not only their time, but their resources to make the experiences happen. The engineering behind these events is brilliant. Creating a ski that can help support an individual with limited core strength, crafting it so it can click on to the lift safely, and then providing a skilled skier to assist in taking the special needs child down the hill is such a heart touching moment.

Sometimes it wasn't only Leo's expressions that made an experience worth doing. I clearly remember the look on Tony's face when we took Leo downhill skiing. Now I know that some of you may be thinking, you live in Wisconsin, what kind of ski hills could you possibly have? With that thought aside, I need you to keep in mind the physical ability of Leo. Leo didn't have control over any aspect of his body. He was 100% reliant on our care and needed complete support for all parts of his body. Although he could somewhat manage to hold his head upright, that was only for short periods of time and was almost always supported by either a pillow, a wheelchair headrest, or our loving embrace. So, you can imagine Tony's fear as he watched Leo be secured into a tiny seat on skis.

He was completely beside himself as we made our way to the chairlift with the assistance of the helper. He looked at me and expressed, "Are they taking him to the top?" I thought to myself, *Where else would he be going?* Tony was under the assumption that the bunny hill was the destination.

I reassured him, "Leo is going to be fine. They have years of experience doing these special outings."

The instructors lined up in position as the chair lift swung up from behind them, "Get ready Leo," I yelled out from a distance.

And just like that, Leo was locked into position, lifted, and on his way up. "I can't believe this," Tony exclaimed as anxiety overtook him and he scanned the hill waiting for something horrible to happen. It must have felt like an eternity to him as he waited and watched.

Then, before he could see Leo, he heard him. Laughter and giggles filled the slopes. As his helper guided him from side to side, another helper snowboarded down backwards to capture every precious moment. Other skiers passed on both sides, but the attention was all on the zig-zagging boy who could not stop giggling from the rush. Tony exhaled a sigh of relief when Leo arrived before us at the base of the hill.

Without hesitation, Leo exclaimed, "Again!"

The next morning, Leo woke up and said, slowly, one word at a time, "I can't wait until next time. I loved it. I am going to make it down eight times. Daddy was a nervous nelly."

"He sure was," I laughed.

As a family, we also had the chance to attend a one-day picnic camp that offered kids with special needs an opportunity to shoot a rifle. This experience took a great deal of patience and preparation to make it successful for Leo, but it was worth it to see the reward of his reaction. With Oliver by my side, we rolled Leo up to the line and waited our turn. Oliver crept down by Leo's side to be eye level with him.

"Are you excited, Leo?"

"I am," he said with his body shaking a bit.

"I will help you, brother."

"Thank you."

"It is our turn next, Leo." I peered over his shoulder and noticed his eyes wide with excitement. With the shooting target about 25 yards away, I positioned Leo's wheelchair into place. The volunteer approached us with a smile.

"How are we doing today?"

"Good!" Leo shouted.

"Well, let's get you all set up." He maneuvered the tripod while both

Oliver and Leo watched closely. "Just a few final tweaks and everything will be lined up." The helper gently placed the gun and positioned Leo's finger to engage the trigger.

"How does that feel, Leo?"

The excitement made Leo lose his voice, and as the volunteer released the safety for Leo, all his focus and attention transferred into the muscles needed to bend his finger back. Boom! The bullet exited and after the shock of his entire body being jolted, he let go of all his tension with laughter.

"I did it!"

Not wanting to be left out of any of the excitement, Oliver turned to me, "Is it my turn now?" I looked back over my shoulder and saw the line of those waiting to engage in the experience. Although I wanted to be respectful of their time, I also knew the importance of Oliver's involvement being more than just "Leo's helper." While Leo's body appeared to still be shaking from the effects of the kickback, I quietly asked the volunteer, "Would it be possible for my other son to have a turn?"

"Of course. That is exactly what this day is all about. What is your name, son?"

"Oliver."

"Have you ever shot a rifle before?"

"No. Just a BB gun and a pellet gun."

As the volunteer out in the field switched the target sheet, the volunteer beside us, instructed Oliver. Looking at Leo, the volunteer asked, "Do you think Oliver can outshoot you?"

"No," Leo replied quickly, "I am the older brother."

"What do you think Oliver?"

"Let me shoot and we will find out."

The volunteer positioned Oliver, supported the rifle on the tripod, and told him, "Take a deep breath. When you're ready, pull the trigger." Oliver looked so tiny as he held the gun in his hands. He looked down the barrel, took a deep breath, exhaled, and fired. Jolted by the backfire, he regained his footing.

"I did it, Leo!"

"Good job, Oliver."

"Who had a better shot?" Oliver patiently waited as they retrieved his target.

"Wow! Sign this kid up for target shooting. Look at that bullseye." Both boys left the area chattering away at each other about how much they enjoyed the experience.

We made our way to the petting zoo area and the calmness of the animals helped release the tension that Leo's body held from the aftershock of the gunfire. Oliver gravitated to a box of newborn kittens while I helped Leo stroke the side of a baby bison resting in the grass.

"Can we have one, Mommy?" Oliver held a gray and white tiger-striped kitten with four white paws.

"Can we, Momma?" Leo obviously saw an opening to take advantage of a two-on-one situation. The kitten remained in Oliver's arms, biting his fingers playfully.

"Oh boy, do we really need a kitten?" Thinking of all the responsibilities that waited for me at home, I wasn't sure this was another one I wanted to take on. "They are pretty little. I am not sure they are ready to leave their momma just yet. Let's go ask."

Oliver didn't waste any time as he sprinted to the owner. "Are the kittens ready to go home yet?"

"Not yet, they have about two more weeks to be with their momma."

"Then can we have one?" Oliver's inquisitive eyes peered long and hard, waiting for the answer. He was determined to make a new friend.

"Yes, if that is okay with your mom."

Needless to say, a few weeks later, we headed to the farm and that is how Ernie, our newest addition to the family, came to be. Now there were twelve paws tapping away on the wooden floors with their nails, but those were twelve footsteps making sounds for Leo to listen to from his hospital bed. All to satisfy his yearning to be with life.

Leo also experienced a special needs basketball game with some local talent from a nearby university team. The team hosted an event at his school. I was not prepared, or properly dressed for this event. We sat in the stands, watching when suddenly we were asked to join and be part of the game.

"Do you want to play?"

Leo attempted to roll to the court on his own from the motion his body exhibited. "Yes."

"I don't know what I am getting myself into, but for you, Leo, anything."

Leo giggled as we raced up and down the court alongside the players. Leo received the ball midcourt as the ball was passed to me. I gently placed it on his lap. His arms pulled in, unable to extend. Carefully, I adjusted his wrist from the dropped position it was in and opened his fingers to extend them across the top of the ball. We ran fast to the basket. I helped him hold the ball, we released it into the air. Not even close. My ego was a bit embarrassed; I could feel myself become flushed, or perhaps it was the exhaustion of running. I desperately wanted to make a basket with Leo.

He received another attempt. A bounce pass came our way. I rested the ball on Leo's lap once again. "Are you ready, sweetheart?"

"Yes."

"Let's do this." We rolled under the hoop. Once again, hand over hand I assisted in his launch. The ball seemed to move in slow motion. "Please go in," I whispered. Swoosh! The sound we had been waiting for. The crowd roared with excitement.

"I did it!"

"You sure did, Leo."

There came a point where we did have to let go of some special things that Leo desperately wanted to cling to. Leo's pain was just too much and was interfering with all levels of learning, to the point where the bus ride was the only part of the day that Leo could withstand. This led us to incorporate homeschooling into Leo's schedule during his middle and high school years. His body struggled to tolerate the wheelchair and learning from his bed provided him with the ability to focus more on the lesson being taught, and less on the discomfort. It really was a family affair as all the pets gathered around Leo's bed to partake in the session. This once, or sometimes twice, a week structure gave Leo the ability to still be involved in school, but as this way of life took hold, his connection with classmates diminished.

As things wound down for his school days, it was the love of bus rides that maintained his attendance. His desire to hear the sound of the bus coming down the hill in front of our home gave him the strength to get strapped into his wheelchair and endure the pain. From kindergarten to high school, Leo responded the same way to the sight and sound of the bus. Anxiety filled his body and he stiffened in his chair to the point it appeared he would slide right down, like a two-by-four plank of wood trying to rest upon a wooden chair. Oftentimes, he arrived at school, and almost immediately needed to return home. This may seem unnecessary to you, but to Leo, it was a great accomplishment.

As the ability to be mobile turned into more moments of stillness, we were able to see even more clearly that Leo was able to connect the two worlds and remove the separation that many feel. Jesus moved into our hearts. He was literally dwelling in our home. In his stillness, the encounters became more frequent. I so desperately wanted to hear and see what he knew. When I witnessed the peace that overcame Leo, I wanted that too, but it wasn't for me, not in that moment anyway.

As Leo was still, his focus gazed intently above on numerous occasions, concentrating on what was being said to him. There were times when Leo verbalized his side of the conversation out loud as it occurred, and I often wondered what was being said on the other side. There was a calmness that engulfed the room, stillness as if even the air wasn't moving. A presence was with us, but I couldn't see with my eyes the same way Leo saw.

Leo asked in a complete, full, clear sentence, "Is everything ready for me?"

I held my breath as I waited for Leo to tell me the reply. He stared at the ceiling and listened actively to the message.

"Jesus said yes." I tried to ignore Leo's stare and his awareness that Jesus was present. It became very apparent that neither of them were going to allow me to ignore them.

The lights flickered in the house, and I felt a shift within me. There was no question at this moment that Leo and I were not the only ones in the room. At almost the same moment, Tony was up north, having his own encounter. He was trying to sort through his thoughts as to why Jesus was coming so often. After having his own conversation with God, and asking that when the time came, please let it be pain-free for Leo, he proceeded to put his boots on and go outside to call home. Somehow, way up north, hours from home, one of Leo's plastic Easter eggs was lodged in the toe of Tony's hunting boot. He reached in to grab it and realized he, too, was not alone.

This awareness of presence happened one other time, and I wasn't alone with Leo, for which I was grateful. While in Madison with Leo, I visited with his healer, Ray, and an amazing woman who joined our sessions for the last few years. The visit caused a great deal of distress for Leo. He was uncomfortable and felt pain from the maneuvering of his body that Ray was enabling to help with alignment. A transformation occurred while in the room and all of us witnessed it. Leo's state of mind went from cries to quietude, and he gazed at the ceiling while a softness covered his face, enhancing a glow. The three of us looked at one another and we felt it too, someone or something else was in the room with us.

Ray looked at Leo and said, "Is someone here?"

Leo's eyes met his and he gently replied, "Jesus is here, I asked Him to come."

What we all experienced in that moment was a calming energy that settled into our bones and changed the weight of the air in the room. This encounter left us feeling peaceful. I imagine this was what Leo experienced on a regular basis. What a gift to open up and willingly seek God into your heart so that He can rest there with you. Leo's illness delivered him into a realm of love, and there, he was comforted by the protection of his loyal Master.

Leo's purity and ability to open up with Ray's sessions connected his physical failures to spirited possibilities. The precious gifts we valued in Leo were strengthened by Ray's hands and Jesus' encounters. Leo's health still had its ups and downs, but the illness no longer defined him or our family. In each unwavering gaze Leo shared with the space above, he found peace amongst the pain and purpose in truth.

Chapter Fifteen

LEO FEEDS OUR SOULS

Leo's words were precious, and taking the time to understand him taught Tony and me patience. Although his movements were restricted, he still found ways to communicate and displayed admiration when his arms and legs moved. It took concentration for Leo to extend his arm and reach over for a snack, but when the good days blessed his movement, he made it possible. I saw the intense focus in his eyes as his mind thought the thought, waiting for his body to respond. Within reach, yet feeling out of reach, as his body struggled to grasp the snack upon his tray. The slow extension of his elbow, which was held so constricted, appeared to be in need of oil like the tin man from the Wizard of Oz.

Some days shone with a brighter sun, allowing him to speak with more clarity and be in control of his swallowing and blinking and laughter. In moments like these, Jesus made us think often about not only what He would accomplish in Leo, but also what we could accomplish with him despite his challenges. God gave us the strength and the mindset to provide every opportunity possible to Leo.

The little things brought joy. A love for life sprinkled over us with appreciation for every moment of each day. Leo's strength returned for pockets of the day, and in those moments, we tried to pack in as much as possible. Whether shopping or walking at the park, many people looked at Leo's circumstances and felt pity for him. Even if it was obvious to me how strangers reacted to the hand dealt, it didn't faze Leo. Although moments of sadness consumed our family, we tried to look through the lens of God's love to see the blessings hidden within. When seeing through a scope of clarity, it became clear that God loved us so much. There is raw beauty within each breath of life and each step taken forward. I felt God's embrace as He comforted me daily, encouraging me to keep going. There may not be anything special about Tony and me, yet God saw we were the perfect instruments to use for His plan. He set the music in our hearts to match the love He felt for Leo. God kept time, while we learned without any prior lessons how to be a family with special needs.

God used Leo as an example of what it meant to honor your mother and father. Leo looked upon us with nothing but love in his eyes. I would often let time pass when his eyes focused on mine, allowing him to see how much he meant to me within. Leo was influenced by our actions, and even though he suffered daily from pain, his focus remained on God. He was humble and coachable, and he sat at the foot of Jesus and let the Teacher teach him the lessons to be learned. In return, Leo became a beacon of hope and an example of love. This was ultimately one of the lessons God was trying to convey when things looked grim and impossible to feed the number of individuals who gathered. Jesus provided a solution, feeding 5,000 people with only five loaves of bread and two fish. (Matthew 14:15-21)

Leo often became our teacher, but he humbly played that role, seeking no reward. An inner drive motivated him to share his insight, seeking nothing back. He didn't need much to be happy besides what he already had around him. For everything that he did have, he was thankful. From the moment of Leo's birth, throughout his life, and until death, he was steadfast in his love for the place he showed no fear of obtaining. Leo's adoration for God spilled over into the way he adored me as his mother. He was selfless in his ways, even in moments of complete discomfort. With the realization that his time with us was possibly coming to an end, he became more concerned about our wellbeing.

"Will you be okay, Momma?" Leo asked me with his innocent face.

"Yes, honey, you have no need to worry about me." I felt the intention in his words in the gaze he directed my way.

"Are you sure?"

"Because I love you so much, and because of what you have shown me, I know Jesus will take care of you until we can be together again."

"Good." A sigh of relief, seeing that I understood.

Leo was elevated above his circumstances because of his constant communication with Jesus. He was able to take what appeared as a hopeless situation, a life without movement, and turn it into a hopeful lesson for others. As people spent time with Leo and experienced opportunities to observe our lives, they began to quickly see there were more blessings in our situation than there were hardships. This perspective wasn't obtained overnight, and the struggles were long and painful. One of the toughest things I witnessed as a parent was observing one of my children suffering. Especially when there was nothing I could do to fix it or alleviate it altogether.

As time passed, and learning from experience became part of our days, we figured out Leo's limitations and how to work around them, yet also with them. I watched God lay a cross on Leo that seemed unbearable to manage for such a young child. As I witnessed this, I simultaneously saw God strengthen Leo through faith by providing the ability to endure the pain. He kept Leo's soul peaceful and calm in his difficult times.

What was even more amazing about these moments was that when Leo spoke his words, they could be difficult to understand; but when he described conversations and visions with Jesus, the words flowed more fluently. Jesus had a message to send, needed it to be understood, and Leo was the instrument He used. I found myself so captivated, hanging on to every word that came out of his mouth, wanting to make sure I remembered it exactly how Leo described. Some of the words he used were simple terms, but not common in his daily vocabulary.

When he was strong, we made opportunities happen. Hippotherapy was one of those things we capitalized on. We left the original arena where Leo was introduced to the horses and were blessed with more private sessions at his therapist's home. The drives to the countryside were exciting for Leo, Oliver, and me. Leo knew he was going to be free in the pasture with majestic creatures. Arriving at the stable and seeing the horses run along the fences, I saw Leo's excitement begin to build. He tensed up with glee and shouted above the sound from the radio what he was going to do.

"I want to ride Chelsea!"

This gentle horse was a beautiful shade of gray, but a bit tall for Leo's physical therapist to safely maneuver Leo. Leo sighed with understanding, recalculated his thoughts, and smiled before speaking again. As I pushed Leo past more stalls, he would attentively search. The dim lighting reflected in his eyes and beamed with excitement.

"Where is Scout?"

I leaned in close to his ear and whispered, "He is coming, Leo, keep looking."

Meanwhile, Oliver bolted up and down the barn, searching for the kittens. "I found one, Mommy." He held the kitten tightly in his arms as he rushed toward us.

"Can I pet him?" Leo asked.

Oliver gently brought the kitten closer to Leo as he extended his hand only inches forward. His love for his brother had him share the good parts of life without hesitation. A pure connection between brothers at such a young age often made me proud.

"You can hold this one, brother; I am going to go find another one." Oliver gently placed the kitten on Leo's lap and scurried off and disappeared behind the haystacks. As Leo continued his search for Scout, the rolling motion of his chair startled the kitten, and it lept from his lap, launching itself onto a bale of hay.

"I found him! Can I give him a carrot?"

Another beaming smile from Leo reminded me once again these outings were good for the soul. I gently placed a carrot in the palm of his hand and assisted him by turning his chair sideways so that his limited mobility could extend through the stall opening.

"Keep your hand flat, Leo. We don't want him to nibble your fingers instead of the carrot."

Leo tensed up with anticipation of being bitten. Scout was removed from his stall and, as he was being saddled, Leo asked, "Can I brush him?"

A brush was handed over and Leo's gentle touch grasped the handle.

Sliding the brush over his confined palm, hand over hand, we stroked the side of the horse.

"Are you ready, Leo?" I lifted him from his chair and with the help of the therapist, we carefully straddled his legs around the wide girth of the pony. Another helper led the horse while the therapist and I securely held Leo, making the impossible possible.

"Yeah, yeah, yeah," Leo exclaimed.

I walked on one side and his therapist on the other. Leo held the reins and the horse began to stride at a comfortable pace, engaging Leo's core, aiding to strengthen it. The body I came to know so intimately over the years would balance on the back of Scout and create the image of adventure. With soft clicks of hooves resonating beneath us, I saw my son shining with innocence and faith.

His smile grew wide. "Hi, Scout. Hi, buddy. I am doing it, Momma!" Then, out of nowhere, Oliver appeared from the barn, holding yet another kitten. His little adventures usually resulted in surprises like this.

"Can I have a turn?" Oliver asked, hoping to have the spotlight on himself for a moment.

"When Leo is all finished," the therapist replied, admiring his charming blue eyes.

Leo approached everything in life with the mindset of, *If you let me be a part of the journey, I will do my best to overcome the pain my body is suffering, just so I can be with you.* He never wanted to be left out and had an amazing ability to mask the pain. Leo's mind was much stronger than his body and his spiritual presence outweighed them both, honestly, best described from supernatural powers being present.

As the warm weather of summer continued, it allowed for more outings. Time at the public swimming pool was by far one of his favorites. It was an exhausting excursion to prepare for and get to; but almost daily, we headed to the pool. As we entered the narrow doorway and through the locker room, we were led to a large pool. Cradling Leo in my arms, we made our way to the zero-entry area and slowly walked in.

As my legs submerged into the water, I asked Leo, "Are you ready?" The water hit his bottom as it swooped over his shorts.

"It's cold." He tried to arch his back, pulling his bottom up out of the water.

"Let's go under quickly so you get used to it."

"I am not ready."

"One, two, three."

The cool water enveloped his body and goosebumps covered his skin. At last, his body was free of the weight that held him still. I grasped him under his armpits as he began to kick his legs and, for the moment, he was able to run free. He felt different in the water. Like a feather drifting in the stream.

Leo, of course, made an impact on other kids while we were at the pool. It didn't matter if he was a toddler or a teenager, it always seemed as though we would be surrounded by them. Playing games with a variety of toys in the pool stirred up attention and we would have wonderful children who wanted to play with us, as well as a few sneaky ones who hoped to slip off with one of our toys while we weren't looking. All of this occurred while their moms stretched out comfortably on lawn chairs, bathing in the sun. Initially, I was irritated to a certain degree, but I quickly realized they were the ones who would possibly have regret by missing precious moments with their children.

Leo and I often spent time in the deep end of the pool watching kids go down the water slide and off the diving board. Keeping true to wanting him to experience all life had to offer, I asked him, "Do you want to try the slide?"

Without hesitation, "Yes."

I waved for one of the lifeguards to come over. "Leo would like to go down the slide. Can we make that happen?"

The lifeguard gazed down and immediately replied, "Definitely."

We exited the pool and made our way to the long winding endless tower of stairs. I took a deep breath and began my climb. Halfway up, I paused, looking around, and saw half a dozen lifeguards seated on their towers.

I said to Leo, "Mommy can do this, but it sure would be nice if one of those strong lifeguards would use their muscles to help."

"You got this, Momma." The excitement in his face gave me the extra push I needed to continue. Once we made it to the top, the lifeguard positioned there offered help.

I laughed out loud and replied, "I got it from here. Maybe I could have used you for the enormous staircase!" He smirked back at me as I stepped into the frame of the slide and straddled Leo.

Holding him close to my body, I said, "Are you ready, Leo?"

"Let's go!"

Winding down the slide, his laughter filled the tube which echoed across the pool. Splash! We hit the water, and both went under briefly. Resurfacing, Leo gurgled some water from his mouth and shouted out, "Again!" Exhausted, but determined to fulfill his desire, we started the adventure over. The steps may have been hard to take, but the ride was worth the journey.

The following week, I reached out to the manager of the pool and arranged for two lifeguards to help me let Leo experience the exhilaration of jumping off the diving board. Leo, of course, held the hearts of many of the lifeguards, so it wasn't difficult to find a few volunteers. Carefully, I held him on my hip and made my way up the ladder. I walked Leo out to the edge of the board. People from all areas of the pool watched attentively. I grabbed him just a little tighter. We got to the edge. My heart plunged from the height.

"Do you want to bounce up and down?"

"Yes." He giggled and stiffened his body which caused me to do a balance check.

"Careful, Momma doesn't want to drop you before you are ready."

"I am ready."

"I am not sure that I am." I released him from my grasp into the loving arms of two lifeguards waiting in the water. Clapping and cheers sprung from all directions of the pool. Another successful attempt of looking past fear and letting opportunity conquer.

As a family, we decided early on that each day we were gifted with Leo's life, we wanted to make him happy and put a smile on his face. We knew having joyful days helped keep our spirits strong. The days we allowed pity to consume us were the days that were long and seemed to have no end. An endless spiral into doubt and fear brought an uneasy silence to the house. We realized we had no control over the outcome, and it was better to lay our burden at the foot of the cross and lean on God for help.

Leo seemed to have wisdom beyond his years. When I looked into his eyes, they were endless pools of deep chocolate brown, a depth that had no end, capped off with long, lush eyelashes that stretched out from his lids, able to touch his round full cheeks with every blink. They were made for him but admired by the females in his life. Although his eyes were dark in color, they held a light that twinkled with love as if you could see the spark of God living within.

It often appeared that Leo wasn't alone when he gazed back at me. A divine presence illuminated from within him, casting light outwardly through the sparkle in his eyes. This presence gifted him with insight, which led to beautiful things that he made us aware of in the years that followed. He fed our souls and helped transform us into better people.

If his eyes weren't the first thing that caught your attention, then for sure you wouldn't have looked past his captivating smile. His love for life filled the space that was exposed as his lips separated and his teeth gave way, instinctively making you want to smile back.

Leo lifted our spirits and gave us hope. He showed us we really do have control over being happy. Our circumstances may not have always been easy, but we decided to have joy in our days. That didn't mean every moment was filled with laughter, but we did find peace at the center of our troubles and knew God was holding us and guiding us.

There were so many factors in finding happiness, and for me, the magnetic force I needed began with God. Once I surrendered and put my trust in Him, circumstances seemed to be managed from a different perspective. I felt strength bolster my soul and a resolve to push through my days, which at times, could have easily conquered me. Instead, with the love of God, I was able to overcome them. More importantly, I did it with a joyful heart. Something shifted within me; my mind became more focused on my purpose and less on my problems.

When we witness pain and struggle daily, it can become the thing that breaks us, or it can hopefully be the thing that makes us stronger. Watching Leo smile and laugh, despite the chronic pain that consumed his body, gave me insight to true happiness. It stemmed from the pure love of Jesus and keeping my eyes and thoughts centered around Him and His teachings. Jesus willingly went to the Cross and took on our sins to help purify our souls. That thought alone brought peace to my day. Then, I took that image, witnessed it on a daily basis, and saw the love God has for His children. Leo lay before me, with all motor functions stripped from his reality. He had no control over anything in his own life. It was this visualization that brought to light the gift of belief. Despite his circumstances, Leo had nothing but love in his heart and love for God. What more could I ask for to feed my soul?

Happiness isn't something that comes easily. It is something I consciously must choose, not just once, but moment by moment. Every situation that arose gave me an opportunity to choose: do I choose frustration and anger, or do I realize that God is beside me in everything that occurs in my life? God ultimately wanted me to succeed. He didn't want me to fail. Often, our own fear and self-doubt lead us to not succeed (trust me when I tell you, I have had my share of self-doubt). Fear is like a weight, holding us down, when it is only an emotion that holds no power. Release it. Let it go. "The Lord is my light and my salvation; whom shall I fear? The Lord is the stronghold of my life; of whom shall I be afraid?" (Psalm 27:1)

God invested in me. He saw in me the thing I couldn't see in myself and patiently waited for me to catch up to His ways. Some may think I have been handed more than what any one individual should have to take on. There were times along the way when I would have agreed. What I see now is God broke me, and then built me back up. He blessed my life with hardships to enable me to have empathy and relationships with others. He didn't give me more than I deserved or more than I could handle. He shaped me to be exactly what He needed so I would have a willing heart to assume His plan.

A plan unfolded, but as Leo's condition continued to deteriorate over time, we became more and more withdrawn from the outside world. This scenario presented two different worlds to me. On one side, we were very secluded from the everyday business of people's lives, and therefore often excluded from things that occurred. As Leo's pain increased and his mobility declined, we were often left with only each other's company. I asked myself in the quiet moments within the living room, *Is this truly my life? Was my main purpose to be a caretaker to my terminally ill son?* So much self-doubt started to close in on me as I questioned my worth as a wife, mother, daughter, sister, and friend. I was limited in fulfilling any of the other roles in my life and often had to decline invitations. Eventually, the invites just stopped coming because people knew my answer would be no.

I felt very isolated and alone. Even amongst my immediate family, life continued, as Leo and I remained still. Tony needed to work and travel and continued with the things in life that needed to be cared for. My other three boys still needed to proceed with their lives. There were moments I felt angry that no one else's life seemed to be on hold, the way mine was. In the stillness, God opened my eyes to the gift He placed before me and rebuilt my faith. The enemy no longer had control.

God empowered me with strength and belief. He gave me eyes, to truly see for the first time, life and the purpose of it. He gave me hope, and the ability to look beyond circumstances to see life was more than the business of the day. Life is God and God alone. He used Leo as the tool to steal my heart. He gave me the most precious gift, the gift of a son. In a similar way, he used Leo just like His son, as a human vessel of the purity of His love. God took every possible chance He could to show me a sign of His never-ending love. He poured it into Leo, and Leo patiently showed me the way to God. Together, we created joy out of sorrow, as Leo showed me love can conquer all, even when you are up against a giant.

Chapter Sixteen

LEO AGAINST HIS GIANT

Some scenes from the Bible are easy to visualize. For instance, on an occasion where the people needed a hero, soldiers waited for their champion to approach. A young man who stood for something they believed in. Something to fight for. A chant echoed in the distance, followed by footsteps and quivering boots. An approach seen by all and felt by those nearest. Now encompassed by shadow, the young man stood taller and looked to the sky. The odds stacked against him, hope scarce in the winds, yet the young man remained steadfast in his faith. Using the resources given to him, he placed five stones in his hand, grabbed his sling and prepared to conquer evil. A chance to defy the odds built courage amongst men.

Similar to the biblical story of David and Goliath, Leo was up against his own giant: illness. Leo, like David, was weak and small, and his illness was strong and mighty, like Goliath, trying to destroy him. However, with God's love, Leo triumphed and found peace in what appeared to be a no-win situation. Leo, too, was a boy after God's own heart. Pure and full of love, he always kept his eyes fixed on Jesus and wanted to do what pleased Him. Because of the faith Leo had in his Master, he was victorious. Sure, he might not have beaten the illness, but he didn't let it define who he was. Others may have seen him as a boy with limited abilities, but Jesus saw Leo with endless opportunities to show God's grace and love, proving appearance has nothing to do with faith propelling you when you trust in God. "God uses the weak." (Corinthians 1:27)

So many times, Leo's illness tried to beat him down and deplete our family of hope, to steal our joy in life. Time and time again, Leo made progress and prevailed, only to have gains stripped away once again. Considering Leo was only two when his whole world turned upside down, it would be unfair of me to assume he fully understood what was happening within him. I saw fear overtake him, and I saw it slowly fade away. Leo was rebuilt and broken down so many times, relearning skills only to have them detracted away. Yet, he endured the struggle and attempted to accomplish tasks to the best of his ability. God was always the rock in Leo's life. Together, they took his sling and his five smooth stones and fought for his life. Even though every day was a struggle, Leo continued to experience God's grace and mercy, and had faith that He would not forsake him, but that He would remain by his side.

Over the years, I watched Leo regain the ability to do simple tasks. I witnessed countless occupational and physical therapy sessions, where he struggled to grasp a spoon and tried to bring food to his mouth to sustain his life. I watched him try to regain his footing with the assistance of a walker and saw the pride on his face when he could accomplish what was asked of him. I also saw him fail, and those moments tugged at my heart. All I wanted to do was accomplish it for him. Leo's up and down journey went on for years. It was a ride that threw us all from one side to the other, with each twist and turn.

As Leo's body transitioned and his movement declined, his muscle tone was severely impacted. The fibrous tissue that held the joints in their sockets weakened, making Leo more delicate, so handling him became a concern. As a result, Leo's shoulder and hip dislocated on several occasions. It didn't always occur based on the way he was handled, sometimes it just happened on its own. Our visits to the healer aided in this situation, manipulating them back into place.

On one occasion, Leo was in a great deal of pain when he dislocated his left hip. The slightest movement caused him to whimper and changing his diaper took extreme precautions. I could hear it pop every time he was moved, and it began to swell and hold fluid.

"Leo, why don't you ask Jesus for help?"

"A true angel cannot ask for help for themselves."

"Should I pray for you to be healed?"

"Yes." His innocent chocolate brown eyes spoke to me beyond the "yes".

There were no longer spikes of improvement. Sadly, things just remained steady. Then, to completely derail us, there was only a steady decline. The gains Leo faithfully worked to accomplish could not outweigh the gains the illness made on him. It appeared from the outsiders' perspective that Leo was losing the battle, but the inner battle of his faith prevailed.

How can you trust God during difficult times when you don't have answers and you are consumed with pain? Leo's life was a composition of years of uncertainty. We did not have any answers. We were left to find our own way, and we found it through God. In Job 1:21–22, Job said, "Naked I came from my mother's womb, and naked I shall return there. The Lord gave and the Lord has taken away. Blessed be the name of the Lord." Through all this, Job did not sin, nor did he blame God. To have this mindset takes so much wisdom, trust, and faith, and Leo had it all. Like Job, Leo did not look to blame. He did not ask, "Why me?" He seemed to accept his circumstances with grace, and grew fonder of God while his faith grew deeper. Leo had an understanding and a connection to God that most of us will never truly experience in our lifetimes. It was built on acceptance and trust in God's plan. Leo seemed to understand he was being used for something bigger than himself, that he was a stepping stone—a stone that would sling a plan into action from the lives of those he impacted.

Leo continued to persevere. As his faith grew, the power of the illness began to shrink. What began as a battle in the small frame of a two-year-old boy going up against an illness that didn't follow any guidelines and made up the rules as it went along, turned into a boy of faith striking his opponent to the ground. "There is no fear in love; but perfect love casts out fear, because fear involves punishment, and the one who fears is not perfected in love." (1John 4:18) Leo's faith rose above the control of the illness, and with his pure love for Jesus, fear was removed from his eyes and replaced with trust.

I continued to see this trust grow deeper as the years passed by. We regained control of our lives and the abnormal became our new normal.

Our days were still filled with challenges, but they just became a part of our lives. We knew obstacles were going to present themselves, but we chose to face them and found our voices. We had to accept some things as they were and then advocate for others that needed to be changed. We started to realize the circumstances that were worth fighting for, like fighting for Leo's right to have equipment and services necessary for him to thrive and flourish. It was amazing how many times he was denied equipment, or the length of time it took to receive the items necessary for his development. Those moments were the brief exposures to the reality of the world, making us appreciate what we were in control of making better.

Despite the fact he was 100% dependent on our care, he did not qualify for in-home nursing because he didn't require a respirator, ventilator, or IV. The things that were extremely effective for his progress: hippotherapy, massages, and visits with his healer, were all items not covered by insurance. This was startling to hear at first. How could these services meant to improve the quality of life be denied by the insurance that should be looking to give the same? This was just another awakening to the darkness of what drives society that we tried to not be consumed by. It made Tony and me reflect further on our choices and what we could do to navigate the uncertainties.

There may have been many dominos stacked up against us, but there were a lot of warriors on our side of the battle too. One of the most prominent came from services that were provided often at little to no cost. Katy's Kloset was an organization that brought a great deal of relief to our lives. They provided a free service to borrow medical equipment that they had in their inventory for any length of time. These items were donated by previous users who either outgrew them or were no longer in need of them. Access to these items bridged gaps, especially during times when several months were necessary to prepare a specialized item, such as a wheelchair, to suit Leo's particular needs. They had numerous volunteers giving their time to assist in finding what was needed, such as a walker, wheelchair, bath equipment, or diapers (to name a few). There were many workers over the years who got to know Leo and had their hearts warmed by his presence. The handyman was wonderful at making what was in stock fit Leo's needs until his own personal item was ready. They did such an amazing job meeting Leo's needs, that over the course of his life, we only had to request one wheelchair from our insurance company.

Another source in Leo's battle facing his illness, Goliath, was a grant that he received from our county. The funding provided from this program helped our family on several occasions. Over the course of Leo's illness, it helped ease the cost for items such as a wheelchair accessible van, an adaptive jogging stroller, and remodeling our shower to make it safe for Leo to get in and out by using a bath chair on wheels. This program made our life easier and enabled us to take Leo into the world. Without a means of utilizing his wheelchair, we would have been homebound more years than we already were.

Our victory over the illness also could not have been won without the family and friends who put on their armor to fight with us. Over the years, we were provided with emotional support through an email update I put out monthly. This allowed loved ones to stay informed on Leo's progress and any changes in his health, but more importantly, it inspired others to get out and live their lives. When people heard and saw the experiences Leo was exposed to, it brought us all together. In times when things were especially difficult, loved ones provided for us and helped drive the other boys to things they needed to attend. Helpers became informed on all the ins and outs of our life. If you were the one to drive Oliver to an event, for example, he let all the details unfold!

For several years, my sister and her family hosted an annual rummage sale. This was not your typical rummage. It brought a community together and it benefited the lives of so many people in so many ways. First, it allowed people to clean out their homes and free themselves from items that were weighing them down. This led to carloads of items that filled my sister's garage and driveway. Nothing was priced at this event; it was strictly a donation only rummage.

People took what they needed and gave what they could. This loving act ultimately ended up with such a beautiful balance of giving and receiving. Some over-gave, which compensated for others who had little to give but were also in need. People had an outlet for helping in a situation that often, they felt helpless about. Many times, loved ones don't know how to help and those in need don't always know what to ask for or how to ask for it. This event not only helped us gain funds to put towards items Leo needed, but it also helped those in the community who needed items at a small cost. It built charitable skills for my sister's family and for all those who helped make each year a success.

Leo's strength didn't always allow him to attend this special event, but for the years he was able to, he shined like the sun. He assumed the role of foreman. He sat amid the items and gave instruction to those who helped. On the days of the actual sale, he sat in an oversized recliner next to the check-out area and kept a close eye on the money. As people approached, his warm smile drew them in and most likely aided in their wallets being opened wide.

"Hi," he would greet them as the sun reflected off his eyes.

"Is this sale for you?" many of the shoppers would inquire.

"Yes," Leo responded, beaming with pride.

The good moments outweighed the bad. It might have been a strenuous effort to take down the giant blocking the path, but when we were thrown into a battle, it helped to have God on our side. "The Lord is my strength and my shield; my heart trusts in Him, and I am helped; therefore, my heart exults, and with my song I shall thank Him." (Psalms 28:7) It also helped to have a supportive team of love and positivity surrounding us. We took refuge in those who came to us and found shelter in the arms of the Lord, both in times of joy and sorrow.

Most likely, people are always going to have a difference of opinion, but wouldn't it be beautiful if we all agreed to believe in God? Imagine the peace that would surround us. Our walk in life is filled with so much uncertainty. As we stepped into each new day, we had many choices in front of us, and those decisions led us into opportunities as well as some disappointments. The one thing I am certain of, and never disappointed in, is God and His love for us. God is our faithful and loyal friend. The One I can always count on. Leo recognized this. Leo believed it, and as his witness, I too believed.

I feel it is only natural to have questions, to wonder what life is about and where the path leads. Each day opens and closes with new experiences and new opportunities to make choices. There are choices which can be influenced by external factors, resulting in an overwhelming anxiety that creeps its way in and steers us in the wrong direction. There are other choices that build character and faith. Faith is a lifelong journey of discovery and trust. At some point, a hurdle will cause a stumble and fall while following the wrong signs. Those who pick themselves back up and follow the light will shine with prosperity and clear consciousness.

God will always be there to pick us back up. During the crushing moments of defeat or fear on the horizon, God will be there. When silence is overwhelming and the sounds of the world appear to be distant, God will fill your heart with music. Each day, I remember to be open to life's possibilities, and to God's love. When allowing Him in, I am filled with His love, and then love is what I am able to extend. Love can conquer fear.

The shadow of darkness tried to linger over us, but Leo's light burned bright. He lit the hearts of others, illuminating a glow of love around us. We are all in this world together, so there will come times when we need to help guide one another. We are meant to live together, to live like one in a unit of God's love. We should be warriors and walk boldly with confidence because God is our shield. We ought to wear His armor proudly. Keep your eyes open, look for signs. Be still and hear the voice of God. Speak to Him and let Him guide your steps. If a shadow looms over your steps, look within, and then step into the light with your head up.

Chapter Seventeen

BREATH
OF A WHISPER

I leaned over the rail of Leo's bed and whispered in his ear. The tingling sensation of my breath sent goosebumps down his neck and across his full cheeks. His body quivered from the stimulation, and a smile covered his face from the secret we shared. My time with Leo taught me how to also lean into God's breath and hear the whisper of His truth. It was sometimes hard to detect, as the enemy sent distractions into my life and tried to steal my attention away from my loving Father. It was this same breath He used to breathe life into me, and the name He revealed to Moses when he had the nerve to ask God what His name was, *Yahweh*, which actually mimics the sound we make while breathing when we inhale and exhale. (Exodus 3:13)

Leo and I often exchanged "pretend" secrets and giggled when Tony asked, "What are you two whispering about?" It was a playful game that we shared, passing the time, when time sometimes seemed to stand still. Then, there were moments when Leo had a real message to share.

Looking at me with eyes full of wisdom, Leo whispered, "I have a secret."

"You do? What is it?" I whispered back playfully and leaned in closer.

"I have a secret life."

Leo expressed the words with such authority it left me in awe. I leaned back in my chair to examine him. His body softened, and his intentions were pure. It was as if this was a secret he had been holding in, but it was something I should have known all along. Then, he drew a deep breath and continued to share.

"I am an angel."

Then he beamed at me, displaying his beautiful smile and the room grew brighter. It was a smile sourced from joy rooted further than those of a great oak tree could reach. His smile was a glimpse into his soul, and that sneak peak within was always welcomed. His secret was rare in that it wasn't revealing what was hiding in the dark, but rather, shining light on what was there all along. I believe this was how Leo best described the other life he lived serving God in the spirit realm.

The way Leo carried himself always seemed years ahead of his time, his expressions and words moved the hearts of those who sat beside him. When he shared that he was an angel, after all our family endured, I knew that he was telling the truth. I knew that his innocence resonated a message that this world needed to hear. He told me his truth to shine light on the foundation of faith from which our lives could be built.

Prior to this sturdy footing, some secrets held a spell over me, a power I needed to reclaim. Guilt and shame weighed me down and I slowly gave way to the darkness, and it led me to believe I was bad, and not worth saving. No matter how much I tried to cover up my wrongdoing, there was no way to hide it from God. He knew my heart and He saw me for what I was. It was a long battle to find peace within myself, but that inner peace did come with some sacrifice along the way.

Many events took place behind closed doors. Changes within my life that most never saw. The struggles in our daily life were not the areas I chose to focus on. I preferred to highlight the moments that brought us joy and provided inspiration and hope to others. The reality was there were tough days, ones that not only changed Leo's life, but also all of those who shared a home with him.

Leo required the majority of my attention during the years he suffered. This affected my time with Tony. Little by little, our relationship was stripped and reshaped into something we didn't recognize. We somehow managed to become almost strangers. Each of us attended to the needs of the family, but did them separately. Distancing our own needs and desires, but somehow strengthening our love for each other.

Tony and I were both climbing the mountain of uncertainty, scaling it at different speeds and with separate strength, but both willing to wait for the other one to catch up.

Tony was relocated to another bedroom as I cared for Leo, leaving us with less intimate time together. Although we managed to find time, it became less of a desire to the point where there was little desire left. We moved to another phase in our relationship that, ironically, left sex behind. This situation played with my mind, and I often felt as though Tony didn't look at me any longer with longing in his eyes. We adapted to our new relationship, but that was part of the problem; we accepted the change. As our routine continued, we had less time together and what we became was "together, but apart". We were okay with doing our own thing and, as a result, distance had space to settle in.

When I felt like I had few things in my life that I could control, I began to control whatever I could. My body image became a control for me. If I'm being completely honest, I had a difficult time looking at myself and liking the reflection looking back at me. I held so much disappointment internally, it was hard to love what I saw externally. Like many women who struggled with body image after childbirth, I wasn't taking care of myself because someone else needed to be cared for. I saw the changes in my body, and an image I had in my mind I couldn't recapture.

Yet, after the birth of my third and fourth sons, I started to finally come into myself. I tried hard to not compare my body to the women who surrounded me, but the reality was, we live in a world where beauty and body image is prevalent. I realized I could take control over some things, and some things I needed to let go. Although my sons had impacted parts of my body from nursing and care, others still made me feel beautiful. There is beauty in women beyond that of the features for which most are judged.

It was at this point I entered the office of a plastic surgeon. I wanted to make a change in an area I knew no diet or exercise was ever going to help. I arrived at the medical building, and after completing the necessary paperwork, I was guided down a hall and escorted into an exam room. I sat anxiously upon the table and waited. The doctor extended his hand and greeted me promptly as he entered the room. I felt my inner body temperature rise as I thought to myself, *Why did he have to be good looking?*

"Hi, how are you doing today?" He shut the door behind him and sat across from me.

"Good, thank you." The words spilled out of me yet, my posturing indicated that I was uncomfortable.

"How can I help?"

My voice quivered as I replied, "I'm hoping you can help me rebuild some of my confidence."

"What did you have in mind?"

"Perhaps you could fill these flat tires with air," I replied, glancing my eyes down at my chest.

He chuckled politely before responding, "Let's take a look."

My straight posture slunk down in embarrassment while guiding my shirt over my head. Meanwhile, my mind raced with thoughts that I must have taken him back with my blunt comparison, but my breasts literally looked like they had the life sucked out of them. My humor and honesty were a combination of truth and humiliation. Did other women who bore children and nursed them have breasts that looked like this? I felt like my chest was made up of excess skin with a nipple hanging off the end. I simply wanted back what was initially given.

After my consultation, I decided to move forward with the breast augmentation procedure. I knew this decision involved more than just me. I had to consider how I was going to care for Leo while I healed. I knew there was a five-to-ten-pound weight limit for six weeks, and with Leo in need of full care, I was going to have to be creative in how I moved him in times that I was alone. That said, Leo was so patient with me during those weeks of stillness and recognized my limitations during the recovery. During this time, there were some creative ways I had to adapt (like changing him with the assistance of my teeth), but his understanding made the time go by easier.

Once again, I regretted a decision I made in a time when I didn't fully know God. If I had the choice now, I would not have moved forward with this procedure. God created me in His image, and He perfected me the way He wanted me to be, and I altered that creation. I didn't accept myself the way He accepted me, and as a result, my body has now suffered side effects that possibly stemmed from the surgery. Breast Implant Illness, (BII) has been linked to a multitude of side effects that women are experiencing. BII is not a formal diagnosis at this time, yet the symptoms are real, affecting the immune system and hormone production along with fatigue, brain fog, breathing problems, hair loss, depression and several others.

All that aside, Tony and I had work to do. For two teens who so passionately took any, and all, opportunities to be intimate with each other, our relationship stalled like river currents approaching a dam. Our minds were filled with an overwhelming number of details (essentially in survival mode). So much time passed that I couldn't clearly state how long it had been since we were intimate. I actually enjoyed sex and the closeness it brought to our relationship, but I also appreciate the fact that Tony and I still intimately valued each other. We didn't use sex as a tool to poke at each other or make the other one feel less than. Our relationship is now the friendship we began with, enhanced by all the years of love, experiences, triumphs, and heartbreaks. It is at a level where we see the bigger picture, the picture that was revealed by Leo's secret and spilled over into our hearts—that to live is to live for God.

Our brokenness, with all our sharp edges, somehow fit together like a gear with the occasional wound that punctured the other from the rough edges of our pasts which had not soothed and healed. These rigid emotions caused the gear of happiness to pause and jam up. It wasn't until we paused along with it, and allowed love to find its place in our hearts, that the gear smoothed the edge of our wounded hearts and proceeded in unity with each other.

Working together as two was efficient, but adding a third gear, God, into our marriage not only provided a balance, but also allowed some of the pressure to be taken off of us. I believe we were meant to rely on God, to have Him shape and mold us by bringing Him into the circle of our challenges and our victories. God created a new heart within me from the shattered pieces that fell and, with His help, my heart learned to heal and grow. I now wake each morning and I look to Him, and in Him, I find my way.

We all have gifts within us, gifts God Himself selected for us to uncover and use in our lifetimes. On occasion, I found myself comparing my life to others, wondering why mine seemed to have so many thistles and weeds while others seemed to live in lush green pastures. I struggled with seeing myself as just a wife and mother while watching so many people climb the ladder to success. Thankfully, through my years of isolation, God whispered in my ear to open my heart to see that caretaking, and inspiring others to overcome their struggles, was my gift! He humbled my mind and opened my eyes to discover how powerful simplicity in life can be, a message my dad also tried to convey.

It was through my struggles that I gained the compassion needed to comfort others. For many years that comfort was provided by others witnessing my actions. Time away from Leo was difficult, so making time to help others was limited. Yet, outsiders looking in were able to see the love that was exchanged between Leo and me, and by getting a glimpse into these moments, they were able to see God display His love. This lesson taught me that unless we have endured some form of pain or trouble and reacted with compassion, how could we have the ability to feel and understand someone else's hardship, and provide them with the support they need?

God is forever my Shepherd. Whenever I felt weighed down by the wool of my life, I learned to rely on Him to shear away my sins, strip away my pain, and provide Him the space to come into my heart to get me back on my feet, finally walking in His ways. Sometimes His love comes in the form of a whisper, guiding me. Other times, it is found in the smile of a stranger. For me, God's love was packaged in the form of a child who showed me how to shed myself of the overbearing weight of trying to live life without His help. In a sense, God forced me to rest by removing me from the commotion of everyday life, giving my heart the time it needed to grow in His love.

As I walked along a smoother path, I easily became robotic in my thinking. It was when God put a hurdle in my way that I stumbled for a moment, and it helped me to refocus my thoughts back on Him, asking for guidance. If I chose to go about it alone, I felt overwhelmed, lost like the sheep that falls in the water and can't find its footing because the weight of the wool, or the world, held him down. It is so easy to get swept away in the rushing water. It is a conscious choice to choose God each day and find joy, so I lean on Him in times of trouble.

By allowing Jesus to be One with him, Leo obtained serenity in his life. In a world that was consumed with pain, he was consoled by love and found peace. It was then, through Leo's peace, that I was able to find my own inner light, begin to have a deeper relationship develop with God, and feel my spark turn into a flame.

As the years went by, Leo's body steadily declined and his faith rapidly increased. As intertwined beings, I was allowed to come along for the ride. I found myself experiencing some of his aches and pains. His capability to be empathetic had him taking on my emotions as well. Leo looked into my eyes with such deep intensity, picking up on the slightest feeling I tried to contain. My heart was filled with so much emotion as I helplessly watched physical life fade away from all I hoped and desired for Leo; at times, it was too hard to hold that inside.

As I cared for Leo twenty-four hours a day, there was little opportunity to have a good cry and not let him pick up on it. My happiness weighed heavily on his heart, and he looked at me with the same tenderness I adored him with. What replaced the physical decline was a spiritual growth that demonstrated complete trust in God's plan. Leo's faith showed he had no doubt in his mind that God gave him the special gift of insight, and his mission was to provide hope in what appeared as a hopeless situation.

These intimate years together, the ones when I often questioned why Leo was homebound, when he could benefit so many more people by being out in the community for them to bear witness to his story, are the same years that God planted the seed of my mission. Just as the Apostle Paul found his purpose while in prison and wrote many books of the New Testament, I also found my peace and joy with God while "imprisoned" in the walls of my home.

There is still a lot of brokenness. Tony and I need time to rediscover each other and find our way back to the love that originally united us. There were many times when it seemed it would just be easier to have a fresh start and leave the pain from the past behind. The truth is, Tony is my forever love. We took a vow that stated in good times and in bad, and we have experienced them both. We have had one challenge after another blocking and rerouting our path, but we have also faced them together and overcame them.

We can never really know what our loved ones are experiencing; what they are thinking. Only God knows exactly where our hearts lie. More often than not, problems exist because of a lack of communication or a misunderstanding of one another. When we add such a stressful situation on top of an already existing pile of daily tasks that need to get done, we often lose sight of what the other person in our relationship brought to the table. At times, Tony and I each felt like our portion of the job was the more exhausting one. I felt my self-worth being questioned multiple times as he pointed out he made the money, making me feel like what I did all day was not valuable. I cherished that I was afforded the opportunity to care for my children and I valued that Tony's job made that possible.

Tony's job had him traveling and he missed out on a lot of day-to-day activities. I believe he felt underappreciated and left out at times. I was so wrapped up in my own chores, that I didn't tell him (as often as I should have) how much I appreciated the things he provided and the sacrifices he made. There's a fine line in a relationship where you are comfortable with each other without taking the other for granted. When we began to make assumptions, we needed to take a step back and reassure each other that we valued our relationship, communicating it in a loving way.

Statistics may show that many marriages end following the death of a child. I don't want to be a statistic. Although I understand the reasons why it may come to that, what I don't understand is why you wouldn't want the one person who ties you to the lost child to be the one who supports you through it. Who in your life can better understand the pain, suffering, and emotions experienced more than the spouse who helped create that child? There isn't a way to escape loss, but with the help of God, you can heal it.

Chapter Eighteen

RAINBOW BOOTCAMP

When everything seemed out of control, we found stillness in our storm from the trust in God. We learned how to "walk on water" and do the impossible because we knew God was by our sides. We were able to obtain this level of peace over time, as we watched Leo's transformation, and he guided us on our rocky boat.

It was evident Leo was never alone. I witnessed moments, sometimes the length of an afternoon nap, and other times after a full night of sleep, but in all cases the transformation was undeniable. I watched as his rigid frame softened and his mind drifted off and connected with Jesus, as if removing his soul from the body containing its relentless agony. His lips that he always held so tightly in almost a perfect straight line, became puckered and full. The tension in his face loosened and was replaced with an angelic white glow. He lay still, but was visibly miles away, yet the repetition of his rhythmic breaths were seen and heard. At last, after relinquishing his movement, his frame found relief from the constant pain, and he was finally free.

As my bedtime buddy, I loved the way my mornings began. The darkness parted as the sun began to ascend. Slowly, it pushed its way through the east curtain, casting a ray of light upon Leo. As my eyes opened, I turned my head to the left, allowing them to come into focus. There, peering back at me were two wide open big, brown eyes.

Leo sweetly whispered, "Hi, how did I do?"

He was genuinely concerned that the "work" he did while he slept disrupted me. Now that I have had time to reflect on his life, I realize why he posed this question. The intensity of his time between two realms had him spiritually moving, yet, next to me, his body remained still.

"I am so tired," Leo added as my blue eyes locked onto him.

"How can that be? You just slept all night long." The intensity of his stare elevated.

"I have a lot of work to do at night helping people and training other angels." Leo then welcomed even more light into the room with a smile, "Training is hard."

I lay there taking it all in. The level of intimacy elevated to a higher dimension. What was initially disclosed as Leo's conversations with Jesus now became interactive. He was "working" with Him.

"What makes training hard?"

"Because there are other angels training. Jesus trains me, and then I have to train them."

When I think about Leo's morning question, I can't help but wonder how intense was this "training" which caused him to be concerned about keeping me awake at night? This word, "training", became fascinating to me. What did that entail? I envisioned Leo standing beside Jesus, receiving instruction from Him. What an incredible image formed in my thoughts, to work so closely with Jesus, and even more unmistakably beautiful, knowing it was playing out for Leo.

One day back in December of 2013, as we got ready for bed, Leo mentioned to me, "I am going to be training to become a Master Angel like Jesus. You cannot be living to be a Master. I need to find a grave and have a funeral and live in Heaven before that can happen."

"When will that be?" My heart sank, not wanting to hear his response.

"Not for a long, long time."

Training continued throughout his life—while awake and while sleeping. Leo was very obedient to God. Within that same week, Leo continued to mention his training to me as we snuggled under the blankets.

"I have more training to do. I get nervous when other angels are watching my sessions with Jesus because I am a special angel."

"What makes you special?" My anticipation for his answer drew me in closer so I wouldn't miss a single word.

"The gift within me." A slight pause as he gathered the strength to continue with his message. The air from the room breathed into his lungs and exhaled when he was ready to speak once more. "Jesus is the Master Angel of the secret method."

"What is the secret method?" My curiosity heightened hoping to learn more.

"I can't tell you."

Like a teaser trailer for a movie waiting to be released, I found myself eager to watch the projection in its entirety, but understood Leo couldn't give it to me just yet. Instead of pressing to get the answers, I just continued to observe him. Training definitely influenced Leo. It became a serious presence that brought spirituality into our bedroom and our lives. It brought questions, but it also delivered answers.

Leo continued to captivate me. As we lingered in bed, I noticed the clock ticking. An hour had passed by since we began this intimate beautiful conversation, then Leo had more to share.

"Although Jesus' wings appear white, they actually have every color within them."

"That sounds so beautiful." I closed my eyes and tried to envision what he saw.

"It is hard to earn additional colors."

"How do you earn them?" The fascination of his words swirled in my mind as I tried to discreetly type his exact words into my note section on my phone.

"Time with Jesus. Right now, I only have red, but I am working on earning more colors."

These conversations continued for many months. The clarity of his words and the level of his description was more than his average vocabulary. As the sun would rise, Leo would wake and describe the color he had trained for. As I looked back on my notes, I began to see a pattern. Leo was earning colors in the order of the rainbow. It started with red, then added orange, yellow, and green. Each time he earned a new one, I began to see his actions reflect the teachings he received.

Then, on the night he earned blue, he said, "Jesus is passing the colors down to me for the work I have to do."

"Can you tell me what that is?" My heart began to race as my mind tried to catch up.

"You will see." In my mind I thought, how long would I have to wait for this revelation?

Then, after many months passed by, I held Leo in my arms and rolled him from his side to his back. Gently, I adjusted all the pillows needed to support his body. I leaned over to kiss him, and told him goodnight. He then said to me, "Tonight, I have to earn purple. It is the hardest color to get. I have to do a lot of training to get it."

"I guess we better get some sleep then." I turned off the light, and in its place, a beautiful lightshow of stars and moons scattered across the ceiling. When the light show finished, I remained awake in the dark, yet light filled me. The visions Leo described were breathtaking, and before we both drifted off to sleep, my mind found peace.

It wasn't long after that, the reply of "You will see," was finally revealed to me. All the training that Leo had prepared for during the previous ten years came into play. The rainbow of God's love that He bestowed upon Leo was actually God's gracious gift of redemption for not only him, but for those who would soon need his help. The visual image of Leo training with his Master left me in awe. It is how I still envision him today. The only difference, Leo now stands on a higher platform, in the midst of God.

Moments like this helped us remain quiet in our storm. Because inside the darkness, where we couldn't physically see the changes occurring within him, we saw the light of God shining outward from the seed He planted inside of Leo's soul. Just like taking a pumpkin seed, which Leo loved to grow every year, and placing it in the damp dark dirt, it pushed its way to the surface, looking for the light to guide its way. Leo, too, had a dark beginning full of struggle that could have pushed us deeper into the darkness, but through him, we saw the light of Jesus shine. The seed God planted in Leo was one of hope and one of love. He had a particular calling, a gift from God. Even though he was 100% dependent on care from others, he somehow managed to relay God's message to all those willing to listen.

Like water flowing through a creek bed, trickling around rocks and pebbles, we never knew which direction the water of life was going to flow or what rocks it would hit. What we did know was our path wasn't going to be straight and smooth. Leo's time with us wasn't going to be easy sailing. We were going to hit boulders and rough spots, and sometimes be swept away, drowning in despair. Like most things in life, I didn't realize how important an experience was until after it had already occurred. And through our adversity, we saw the love of God in our son's face.

For so many years we floundered in the water without any life source offered to help us. We discovered ways to make things work on our own. It felt overwhelming at times to know where to direct our energy and attention. Leo's body seemed to be constantly changing and I battled with myself, wondering if some of the pain was worth the reward. I was uncertain if the discomfort Leo endured by using such things as wrist splints, orthotic foot supports, and a back brace, were worth it, considering his life span seemed to be without answer.

When it was initially expressed how little time Leo potentially had with us, was it really going to matter if his wrist stayed straight? Or if his ankles were bent, considering he lost the ability to bear weight on his frame and walk? Leo's body was described to us as being like an electrical wire without the casing. Every nerve ending was exposed, and prior to getting him on all the right medications, which took years to orchestrate, this left him in so much pain. When he was touched, or even if the wind blew too hard, pain covered his face. Our storm was never ending, causing us to lose our sense of direction from time to time, but Leo's soul was peaceful because he channeled his energy. He focused on Jesus, and knew he was being used for a purpose.

I, too, was in need of some peace, a sign of direction, a symbol of trust, an escape to reset my mind. As a result, I booked a long weekend away to attend a conference in California with a friend. This was my first extended period of time away from Leo. I knew it was a risk to take this chance, but it also felt right to pursue something for me. After all, Leo was twelve at the time and it had been ten years of continuous caregiving. After checking into the hotel and grabbing a bite to eat, I reviewed the program and finalized my decisions for which sessions to view. Several inspirational speakers spoke on a variety of topics. One, in particular, grabbed my attention.

I felt a warm energy settle in my body while listening to her words. The speaker spoke about angels and the symbolization of feathers and their colors and how they appear in places you wouldn't expect. The timing of this seminar was no coincidence. It was a "God-incidence", fitting so perfectly as the visions of Leo's conversations with Jesus also become more prominent in our home. The fact that Leo explained how he needed to earn his colors just before I attended this seminar was astounding. I was so captivated by what the speaker said that I took it all in like a bird gathering materials for her nest.

My footsteps were light as I walked down the hallway with my friend to our room that night. Thoughts raced around in my mind, and I saw Leo's beaming smile through them all. Smiling to myself, I swiped the room card and closed the door behind us. We engaged in conversation while I placed my belongings on the nightstand and checked the time. As I began to change into something more comfortable, I noticed an object and examined it closer. A beautiful free-flowing gray feather was stuck in the inseam of my nightshirt! I gasped and experienced a fleeting rush from witnessing my first sign. I didn't know it then, but that feather became more significant with time and helped me transition with clarity. I have come to realize that in my moment of turbulence, gray feathers symbolize peace and tranquility to encourage hope when the path ahead is windswept.

Feeling refreshed, and brought to a new level of belief, Leo continued to fill my heart after returning to his side. Reflecting on what I heard at the conference, and what I witnessed throughout Leo's training, it was as if the kaleidoscope aligned in a way to see all the colors of God's light, much like Jesus' wings. The inward love of Jesus poured outward from Leo's soul.

Red was the original color Leo obtained in his training. He disclosed this when he was quite young, and with that I saw Leo's passion and courage (which the color represents). As the training increased and new colors were obtained, I witnessed Leo's character building with it. Leo remained optimistic despite challenging odds, holding on to positive energy (as orange is described), and spreading that hope to friends and family. Yellow provided Leo with mental alertness. In the moments his body failed him, he found joy in the experiences we shared together. The layers of Leo's spirituality just kept building as more colors were added and Leo's ability to be used for greater purposes were eventually revealed.

Green brought healing, not necessarily for Leo, but it would soon be discovered who that gift was for, and blue gave inspiration and spiritual connection. But it was purple, the one Leo mentioned was the hardest to obtain, that made the arch of the rainbow complete. It became clear to me why Leo worked from the center outward. God must be our center and from there we can reach the outer limits of life. Universal consciousness and heightened spiritual growth were obtained from purple, and I witnessed these beautiful gifts play an active role in Leo's life with God's perfect timing and mysterious ways.

There was one light source, and typically three simple words, that began each of his conversations with Jesus. His powerful proclamation either started with "I see Jesus," or "Jesus is here." Leo's very first verbalizations of Jesus were initiated with "I see Jesus." As the encounters became more regular and frequent, it transitioned into "Jesus is here," as if there was a degree of difference in their relationship. No longer was Leo just saying, "I saw Him." Their level of intimacy became like someone announcing when the doorbell rang, their friend had arrived. For Leo, that friend was Jesus.

Jesus came to Leo on a nightly basis for a while. Leo would announce, "Guess who's here?" I would then pause the TV momentarily while Leo had a discussion with Jesus. The pattern was somewhat similar. Leo stared up at the ceiling, a smile came over his face and his conversation began. Sometimes, Leo intently looked, with laser focus, steadily fixed on a certain spot.

He did on occasion drift from this pattern and recite his side of the conversation as it was occurring. He used words like, "Okay, I understand," and even "See ya," like he was talking to his best friend. There were also a few times Leo seemed uncertain as to why Jesus hadn't arrived yet and yelled out, "Where is He?" Most encounters of these visions and conversations would end with Leo sharing his experience, but one time, he did ask me, "Why do you need to know?"

"Momma was just curious."

"Some things I can't tell you."

"I understand." I really did come to understand that Leo didn't have the freedom to tell me everything.

"Some things you are not ready to know."

As this pattern continued, Oliver's awareness of the situation heightened. Night after night, as these pauses took place, Oliver patiently waited. Until one evening, he was engrossed in a particular show on TV and Leo announced, "Guess who's here?" I paused the show.

"Come on, He's here again?" Oliver protested.

"Be patient, sweetheart. You won't miss anything."

"But it is right at a good part!" Oliver sat with his arms crossed in disappointment.

"And the part will still be there when we hit play."

"Okay, see ya," Leo sounded off, ending the conversation with Jesus. Nothing, not even God, apparently was worth the interruption of a favorite show being halted to Oliver.

These intimate aspects of Leo's day had me on high alert. I felt the need to be on my best behavior all the time because God was literally in my house. The funny thing was it didn't require these talks to make that real. He was here, in my home. He never leaves our sides. "Be strong and steadfast; have no fear or dread of them, for it is the Lord your God, who marches with you; He will never fail you or forsake you" (Deuteronomy 31:16)

I was able to obtain inner peace because Leo showed me and taught me the love of God. Witnessing all the moments of, "I see Jesus" and "Jesus is here," gave me a glimpse into what awaits all of us after our walk of life comes to an end. Leo held my hand and took me along on his journey. Through it, I deepened my faith and enhanced my trust in God.

What a beautiful gift I was able to experience! This gift stemmed from hardship, but instead of hardening my heart, it softened it, and allowed love to grow.

Leo was the force in my life that gave me purpose. He was a simple soul who showed me the simplicity in life. He motivated me to live without regret and to channel my sorrow into strength. With each lesson he taught me, I learned to surrender and understand I was not in control of the events that took place in my life, but I did have control over the way I chose to face them. Looking back over all the obstacles and challenges we faced in our days, I recognize they made us stronger mentally, emotionally, and spiritually. We didn't try to seek absence from our problems, we welcomed them and trusted there was a purpose behind them. We saw how one boy's positive approach to life left a rippling effect of love trickling steadily from one person to the next, all because he believed.

Chapter Nineteen

LEO BUILT OUR FAMILY ARK

As I looked to the sky, clouds swirled together to form larger and darker beings. In the distance, the patterning sound of drops falling to the earth marched nearer. A storm was building, both above me and around me, and the storm of life came quickly. As the uncertainty of Leo's ever-changing body continued to take form, we were often thrown upon the rocks like a ship wrecked at sea. Just when we believed we had found our way, a wave would thrust upon us and change our course. As we sat amid our wreckage, we could have remained broken. However, it quickly became obvious that Leo was going to be the rudder, directing our way. Leo had the gift of inner peace and he let us all climb aboard his ark, where he kept us safe during this storm of life, as we witnessed his faith.

Leo embraced the same type of faith I imagine Noah demonstrated in the Bible. Both heard the call of God's request, and both listened and followed His instructions. The ark Leo built was not made of gopher wood like that of Noah's. It was made of hope, trust, belief, and love. Yet, like Noah's Ark, it was strong, sturdy, and weathered the intense storms we face daily. Thankfully, Leo was my life jacket, anchor, sail, and compass, protecting my heart and navigating me with his light.

It is difficult to make sense of hardship, especially when the agony of suffering pounds against you, making you weaker. Maintaining faith in those moments, and trusting God to use them to better you, might not always be easy to accept, and even more difficult to be grateful for. I am not able to fully explain, but an inner peace came over me, and strength replaced the weakness. Once I surrendered to God and allowed Him to guide my steps, my unknown course became known. He remained in the eye of the storm and brought peace with it, even when days ahead looked grim. I then discovered that the promise of eternal life was my key to peace. "For God so loved the world, that he gave his only Son, that whoever believes in him should not perish but have eternal life. For God did not send his Son into the world to condemn the world, but in order that the world might be saved through him." (John 3:16-17)

Hope filled Leo's soul. His struggles crashed against his fragile body over and over in life, just like the waves of the ocean meeting the shore, but he never took his eyes off Jesus. Leo's ark was assembled by the losses and challenges he tackled and faced over the years. It was raised from its foundation by the excursions and memories created with loved ones when his body was able. He wanted to experience all of life's adventures with his family and his friends, and made every attempt to connect with life and his surroundings, wherever that may be. He wanted inclusion and often asked, "Can I come?" His mind was so full of life, and all he wanted was to be a part of the experience.

Even in moments that were the most unbearable, when the pain escalated to a level that his medications couldn't mask, his hope held firm, but his question was different. This time, he stated, "Can I go?" He was directing this question to Jesus. Leo knew at a very young age that meeting Jesus in Heaven meant he would no longer have pain. Yet his hope remained. In those days, when the pain was too much, and no form of medication helped as it seeped its way through every crevice of his body,

Leo looked to the sky and cried out to his Savior, "Can I go?"

"Where do you want to go?"

"I am talking to Jesus."

"But where do you want to go?"

"To Heaven." It appeared Leo didn't fear death. His concerns were in leaving us behind. "Will you be okay?"

"My heart will be broken. I will miss you being by my side. But you have shown me the true meaning of faith. Your belief has become my belief. Plus, I know you will still watch over me, right?"

"Yes, Momma." Such wisdom and compassion stemmed from his trials in life and, through it all, he remained a loyal servant of God.

It appeared the presence of God was within reach. I watched my son ask for the one thing that would make most parents fall to their knees and weep. Although my heart was in agony at the realization of what this request held for my family, my heart also ached from the daily pain I watched Leo experience. My love for Leo reached the ultimate level of love; a love so pure, I would rather see a life without Leo by my side. To know he would break free from the cross he bore and walk beside his Father in Heaven. I was willing to let him go, versus continuing to witness days remaining with me in pain. At that moment, when Leo begged for the pain to come to an end, I too wanted that for him. I understood the request of "Can I go?" was not one of wanting to leave me, but one of wanting the pain to leave him.

Leo had an immeasurable amount of trust in God. Here was a young boy who had his life drastically changed at age two, learned how to adapt to his struggles, and found the gift of the Holy Spirit. He was patient and kind, even though his body was incapable of the actions that his mind thought. He literally was a soul trapped in a body, but because of this stillness, he was able to hear God and listen intently. Like Noah, Leo consistently followed God's will and enjoyed a close relationship with Him. The trust he had in God was what I imagine kept him calm and sane while not being able to move on his own. Like the depths of the ocean, his faith ran so deep that he had complete trust, knowing God knew what was best for his life.

The belief of Jesus that we witnessed in Leo's eyes as he remained still on his back was evident. As Leo interacted with Jesus, it was undeniable that he clearly saw God. Despite his circumstances, Leo was always left in the position of looking up to God. When witnessing Leo's face time and time again as he gazed above toward his ray of light, the ark we rode together became more intentional. There may have been a stillness to his body, but behind those warm brown eyes raced a mind that chased after his Master to navigate the waters.

The love Leo felt in his heart for Jesus was beyond any type of love I have witnessed in my lifetime. As the Bible states, Noah was a pleasure to the Lord. I saw this same adoration in the interactions Leo had with

Jesus. The purity of his facial expressions as he gazed upward gave me a small glimpse into the beauty of God's love, and I am certain God smiled upon Leo, saying, "My loyal servant, I am happy with you."

With all of us safely aboard Leo's ark, the storm took hold of our family and began to wipe out some of our old and bad habits. It let light shine through, and this light was Leo's faith. As we watched him love God, we felt a shift in our own mindsets. It took over 100 years to build the ark and Noah built it big enough for others to be saved, but sadly, they didn't trust him or have faith in his process. It took almost 17 years for God to work through Leo to teach us lessons, lessons we were willing to learn. I am so grateful that many people came aboard Leo's ark. They saw his love and took shelter aboard his faith. I often teased Leo and told him, "I need more time with you, Mommy is a slow learner." My hope was to gain additional moments with him. This comment always made him smile.

My earlier years in life, I described myself as an unpruned Christian, exposed to the basics in Catholic belief, but not practicing what it meant to be a good follower of God. My guilt, shame, and lack of self-worth kept me from growing, and without Leo's insight, I was potentially going to wither up and become completely separated from God. "Every branch in Me that does not bear fruit, He takes away, and every branch that bears fruit, He prunes it so that it may bear more fruit." (John 15:2) I had the potential to be a good branch, stemming from the solid rooted trunk of God's love, but I was weighed down by things that didn't really matter. I wasted energy on comparing my life to others, not valuing myself nor my potential to achieve the gifts God instilled in me. My branch was heavy and unkempt and in desperate need of being lifted by God's love.

It wasn't until my life abruptly changed and caused me to surrender to God that I allowed His spiritual blessings to flow through me along with the discipline to build an understanding for the holy word. Then, through the adversity, my branch began to feel lighter. This moment of surrender shifted my eyes from the storm swirling around me and allowed them to settle upon Leo's view. I was able to look through his eyes, take the focus off our turmoil, and see Jesus on the cross willing to sacrifice everything to save us. It was the moment that shifted my fear to trust.

It is said that Scripture is alive—the Living Word—and I am in awe of how it always seems to be written for me and for whatever I am feeling at any given moment. God speaks to us; we just need to actually listen. Sometimes His communication is in the form of Scripture, but even moreso, He speaks to us through all that surrounds us. I used to think things happened merely by coincidence. But now, as I grow deeper in my faith, I realize they are orchestrated by our Maker with intention.

It is much like the things that used to make me sad when they didn't work out, or the relationships that drifted apart and eventually ended. I used to view these as failures and disappointments, seeing them as things that were my fault. Now, after viewing life through the eyes of Leo, I can see them as God's way of pruning my branches in order to elevate me to the next level of my spiritual walk with Him. As I continued to let go and put more trust in Him, I literally felt the weight of my life struggles being lifted. As those worries and doubts shed their hold on me, I found it easier to hold my head high and raise my arms up to praise the One who held steady by my side and intertwined Himself within me.

There are many things in life we must let go of, things or situations that don't work out as expected and should be left behind. It is never easy to allow the process of change to set in, and it is extremely difficult to let go of those we love. I never imagined I could look at loss as a gain, but that is exactly what Leo did for my life. For every loved one I have lost, I have gained strength from another angel watching over me. Loved ones never leave us, but instead become a part of us that we can carry on our adventures, and they often carry us in times of sorrow, until we are reunited once again.

I have experienced my share of loss and some of it has come at me like a crashing wave, pushing me back under before I could regain my breath. From 2014 to early 2021, eight loved ones close to my heart all lost their battles to illnesses, cancer claiming seven of them. They all seemed to come without warning, and just as I began to process the reality of the situation, the next one was diagnosed or came to the end of their fight. Leo, of course, began his fight years prior to the others since he started at age two. His situation seemed to prepare me for what would challenge my strength and my faith. His gift of communicating with Jesus brought my mind to a level of belief that didn't exist prior to his diagnosis. Leo's ability to slowly reveal and teach me the love of God showed me suffering could be looked at from a perspective of beauty, and through our pain and heartache, Jesus never leaves our side.

I know God worked in my life. The old me who lived in the shadows would have turned to destructive choices as I suffered loss after loss. The new me, who held Jesus in her heart, was lifted. He carried my burden. He held me close. He saw me through my troubles, basking in His light. My past no longer held power over me. My shadow stayed with me, but it never became part of me again. It casts around me in all directions, yet never upon me. Finding God allowed me to stand in the light, the light that reflected from His love. God kept me centered in the eye of the storm when that same storm sought to knock me off my feet and blow me away into chaos.

The preparation Leo so patiently and lovingly demonstrated gave me the ability to breathe and not let grief consume me. Since my initial loss of a sister at a young age, I witnessed numerous family members struggle with illness and perish. My brother, Glenn, was the first to be diagnosed with lung cancer. Ironically, he lived a healthy lifestyle, ate well, and never smoked. He carried his cross with such dignity and courage, and his faith grew stronger and deeper along the way. He did the hard work and put his trust in God.

With enthusiasm in his voice, he mentioned to me, "Leo is a sign."

"That sounds beautiful. What is he a sign of?"

"An example of the faith I want to follow."

As his words hit my ears, my body was overcome with warmth. "Thank you for expressing that."

"That special boy has really influenced me." The two of them had a beautiful connection and Leo looked at his Uncle Glenn with such peace. Leo saw my brother's belief, and he knew Glenn was going to a place of undeniable beauty. It was moments like this that made Leo's cross to bear more manageable.

Over the years while observing Leo's actions, I came to see that Leo operated in two realms; the physical and the spiritual. Leo had the gift of translation. Translation happens when a person's spirit travels for purposes of intercession, leaving their body behind (there are examples of this in the Bible). Whether he was dreaming when this happened, I don't know, but it happened to Leo during my brother's illness. In fact, on several occasions, Leo woke up in the morning and expressed the aftermath of his travels.

"I am so tired," Leo expressed, once again, as the sun trickled through the blinds.

"You must be so busy at night, Leo."

"It is all the training I do." Leo paused and took a breath, "I have been training with Jesus, it is my job to help train other angels."

"Even though you have told me about training before, I love when you tell me stories about this, it makes me smile thinking of you running or in this case, flying free."

I know for certain on one occasion, he was indeed performing God's miracles. My brother observed Leo over the years, witnessed his faithful acceptance of his path, and applied it to his own. He said to me, "Leo taught me how to accept with grace."

"I love that he did that for you."

"I can face my end-of-life situation with hope because of the visions that Leo shared with us."

"That warms my heart. It helps to ease my pain, knowing that Leo's suffering has purpose."

On multiple occasions, I witnessed Leo during an out of body experience. Leo's body would naturally be held in a rigid state as the contrast muscle groups fought one another. Then there were those moments when Leo transcended to another place. His mind drifted to a state of ecstasy. His body transformed, softening, and peace overcame his frame. A glow of purity changed the appearance of his face, and all imperfections were removed. He remained a body with limited movement, but shined with a limitless spirit.

My brother's illness escalated quickly with the need to proceed with chemotherapy treatment. The doctors found that it would be best for his situation to have a port placed in his chest to administer medication. While in the shower, my brother passed out which caused him to crash to the ground. The sound of the fall had my sister-in-law rushing to his side. He was unconscious and she quickly called for the ambulance. When my brother came to, she was able to get him to his feet and onto the bed. When the paramedics arrived, they thoroughly checked him over and proceeded to take him to the hospital. It was discovered that Glenn had a severe septic infection stemming from where the port had been placed.

After stabilizing his condition, they sent him home with a regimen to follow and hoped that the infection would heal. Although this was startling to both of them, my sister-in-law was a registered hospice nurse and more than equipped to handle the long road ahead of them. Yet, God stepped in as well and used a precious vessel that He had utilized before. As my brother peacefully slept that evening, he had a dream. He later awoke, so lifted by the experience he saw in his dream, that he turned immediately to his wife to share what he saw.

"You won't believe it!" he exclaimed with excitement to her. "I had a beautiful dream. Leo came to me. A hummingbird hovered over me, the most amazing sight! Everything about the bird was normal, except that the face was that of Leo."

She held him in a tight embrace, "Oh, sweetheart, that is incredible."

Meanwhile, back at my home, while getting Leo ready for bed the previous night, he turned to me and expressed, "I have a secret life. I am an angel." This comment that Leo expressed with such conviction didn't surprise me. Up to this point, he shared so many spiritual comments and moments with us, so all I felt was belief. As he continued, he said, "I am going to help Uncle Glenn. I am going to hover over him and then come back here. Jesus told me to, it is my job."

Glenn called me as soon as Leo and I woke that morning and shared his dream with us. I turned to Leo, who was beaming. His smile brought a light into the room unlike anything the sun could bring through the blinds. I expressed to Glenn what Leo told me the night before and we spent a moment in silence, taking in what had just occurred.

Leo then stated, "I check on a lot of people." It left us all in awe; the fact that Leo's gift of intercession took him into realms most people don't experience until the afterlife. Leo was determined to be used by God to help answer prayers, in spite of his lack of physical abilities.

Remarkably, my brother's port healed. This was the intervention of God using Leo as a vessel to aid in the support of one of His precious children, my brother. Glenn was able to move forward and live the remainder of his life the best he could, but one thing strengthened by this event even more was his faith. He lived his days for God. He was an example of a peacemaker by his actions and message. He accepted Jesus as his Redeemer and Lord and showed others how they could have peace in times of struggle.

After my brother passed away, I remember snuggling in bed with Leo as he began to describe Glenn's angel wings.

"I can see Uncle Glenn in Heaven." Peace overcame me as Leo spoke these words.

"Can you share anything with me?"

"He has his angel wings." I closed my eyes and tried to envision what Leo saw.

I pulled Leo closer and asked, "What do they look like?"

A gentle smile came across Leo's face. "Uncle Glenn's wings are green like the grass."

"They sound beautiful," I closed my eyes again, this time seeing through the lens Leo provided.

"They are." A smile settled on Leo's face as if he recognized, mission complete.

The color seemed so fitting for my brother. Green symbolizes prosperity, money, nature, animals and plants, and spirits, along with forgiveness. Glenn was passionate about the outdoors and gardening. He spent years employed by Milwaukee Transport Services, Inc.

God continued to thread the connection of His love to us. The following summer, as Leo and I sat amongst the flower gardens surrounding our home, I noticed a recurring flutter out of the corner of my eye. A hummingbird came daily and visited flowers in a similar pattern. Once this was brought to my awareness, I decided to sit amid his pattern with Leo on my lap. Together, we held a flower in our hands and waited. It wasn't long before our hummingbird friend arrived, staying true to his pattern. We experienced a tender moment while the tiny bird, one that appeared to have special needs, as his beak was shorter than normal, came near. This was a very distinct characteristic which is why I could tell him apart from the others that came to feed. As it approached our spot and drank the nectar from the flowers in our hands, we heard the power of its wings and felt the vibrations. This moment allowed me to feel the force of the spiritual realm upon us.

We encountered multiple intimate moments with this beautiful creature; times when the hummingbird redirected his pattern to hover briefly above Leo while he lay in his lounge chair. It was as if replaying the hovering moment that healed my brother. I was even fortunate to have my own intimate moment when this tireless bird paused to rest upon my knee as I sat on the front porch step. This was my very own tender moment when I felt my brother at my side.

Leo's illness felt like a great flood at times. Hardship and change came at us so quickly, along with so many questions and much uncertainty. It felt like we were being pulled underwater, unable to breathe. With every new concern about Leo's condition, we were left with a new unanswered solution. We treaded water and grew tired, yet Leo weathered his storm and cast a light in the midst of his cloud. Like a sturdy light house, standing strong at the shore, Leo calmed the souls of many. Amongst the crashing waves, he spread his light in all directions and guided others home.

While witnessing how Leo cared after the members of his ark, I felt myself grow in faith and security. The planks of Leo's ark were secure and strong and nailed in place with the nails that held Jesus to His cross. The feeling of the unknown could have pulled us downward quickly. Yet, God spread a rainbow of His love over the sky, and showed us He would not destroy us in this storm, but rather build a sturdy ship of faith, allowing us to feel Leo's love well after he was no longer visible to us. We had strength in numbers because our strength came from one another. This connection was formed by belief and love, and was unshaken by the winds of the storms in the world. It was shown through the warmth of a sunny day, the kiss of the wind, and the promise of His love in every sunrise and sunset.

Chapter Twenty

THE HEAT OF LOVE

An angel scurried, flapping its wings purposefully to make its presence known. The rapid motion released a feather, and it descended from the sky, drifting, seeking a soul in need. As I walked, peace filled the space around me. Nothing within my sight, only stillness. I planned to walk a certain direction but then a nudging tug pulled me, and I stepped off course. Just as I pressed my foot upon the crispness of the earth, my eyes drifted from the open field as if being pulled by love to look down.

A tiny white feather clung to the top of an unharvested wheat stalk. The stillness shifted and the wind began to pick up, whispering, *I love you*. The feather released from the grain as I reached out, managing to grasp it between my fingertips and draw it in, as I held it close to my heart. My angel heard my cries. My angel said, "I walk alongside you."

There really was a unique force within Leo. He had the ability to be by my side and watch over many others at the same time. He had a peacefulness about him so that even through pain, I saw calmness. Leo provided hope in his visions with his words, especially during times of struggle. There was an evening I was away and Tony prepared Leo for bed. He noticed Leo intently staring over his right shoulder.

Tony looked behind him to see what held his gaze and asked, "What are you looking at?"

"An angel."

Tony asked, "Is there only one?"

Leo proceeded to pivot his head in several directions, indicating where other angels were located, and stated, "They are white." Leo's stillness and untainted belief in God allowed him to see naturally what I believe we all can.

Then, while I was getting ready for bed on August 27, 2013, I noticed Leo intently looking at the ceiling. After a few moments passed by, I scooped him up from his hospital bed in the family room to carry him to the bedroom. Once we arrived in the other room, and I had him all tucked in, I noticed his gaze shift to the direction of one side of the room.

"Jesus followed us here," he stated.

"He did?" I looked over my shoulder thinking I would see Him as well.

"Yes."

"How did He get in here? Through the wall?"

Leo smiled. "I have a special assignment tonight. I have to see Grandpa."

"Is Grandpa okay?"

He shifted his eyes to me and said, "I need sleep now." This conversation didn't alarm me until about a month later, when my dad received news from his doctor that he had liver cancer. It appeared Leo knew about my dad's illness before my dad ever discovered the news.

My dad was diagnosed only months after my brother was told of his own cancer diagnosis. While years of enjoying a good cold beer may have contributed to my dad's health situation, he actually had been sober for several years leading up to this news. Although my dad would have preferred not to be sick, he too took on cancer with a fight. He knew what surrounded him was a life worth living.

I asked Leo, "Will Grandpa have an angel watching over him?"

"I have a double job. To watch over Grandpa and Uncle Glenn until I can find a new angel to help Uncle Glenn. Grandpa will be full time."

"Grandpa can be a lot of work," I laughed.

"Trust me, I know," Leo released with a heavy sigh.

I began to think back and reflect on their beautiful relationship. My dad's heart was so wounded by Leo's diagnosis. The reality of how precious time was really set in for him, and this made me recall a tender moment I witnessed between the two of them.

While visiting my parents one afternoon, we went for a brief walk with my dad, and stopped at the foot of the enormous pile of fieldstone that consumed a large portion of their yard. My dad spent years selling stone to people for all types of projects for indoor or outdoor use.

As the two of them sat there, Leo in his wheelchair and my father upon a large boulder, I saw Leo looking at my dad's arm with curiosity. There on his wrist was a simple silver watch with a stretchy band fitting snugly. Leo kept gazing as the sunlight hit upon the silver, casting a reflection into his eyes. Meanwhile, my dad continued with his story, unaware of Leo's distraction. Then the moment came when my dad realized Leo was more interested in his watch and less intrigued by what he was telling him.

My dad removed the watch from his wrist, held it in his hand and asked, "Do you want to try it on?"

Leo's body stiffened and he replied, "Yes."

My Dad gently slid it over Leo's fingers until it settled upon his wrist, dangling and emphasizing the difference in size between them. Leo absolutely lit up and that was the beginning of what would occur for years to come.

"Can I keep it?" His brown eyes glistened with hope as they met my dad's startling blue eyes.

"Oh, sweetheart, that is Grandpa's special watch. How about we get you your own?"

Leo wasn't completely convinced with that response from me, but after a moment, he replied, "Okay." He seemed to hope that my dad would become distracted and forget that his watch was still placed around his wrist as they continued with their discussion.

Leo loved discovering new watches, and although he tried to persuade my father each time we came to visit to release his watches to him, his own collection grew over the years, totaling sixteen watches.

My dad reversed the roles one time when we were visiting, saying,

"That is a nice watch you are wearing, Leo, can I have it?"

Without hesitation, "No."

My dad chuckled, "I see how it is."

This conversation led to years of desire to wear a watch on his wrist each day. Even though he wasn't able to actually read it or identify the minutes and hours passing by, it was an accessory that made him feel good. He took a great deal of pride in selecting a watch to purchase from the store (or should I say pick out and have me buy). We made frequent trips to the store to search for the next new watch. Some had a clock face on them as wide as his wrist. His favorite were the digital ones because they came with an alarm.

As soon as we would come home from the store Leo would say to Tony, "Set it, Papa."

Tony would grab the watch from Leo's tray, "Let's see here. What kind of watch did you find?"

"A big one, with red on the face." His smile beamed as big as the face of the watch.

"Does it have an alarm?"

"Yes. Please set it for my med time." Leo was very particular about pairing his watches to match the outfit selected for him each day, and having the wristband or face of the watch match his shirt. He did have style, that was for sure.

Once again, there was a depth of soul connection that occurred between Leo and my dad. Words didn't need to be spoken when they looked at each other, as if there was a magnetic force. Their foreheads drew together, and the two of them remained still as their hearts, souls, and minds spoke to each other without a word.

It appeared Leo never did find another angel to replace his loyalty to my brother. The time that my dad and brother were ill overlapped and in addition, Leo was also concerned about my uncle and my aunt.

"I have five jobs to do."

"You do. What are they?" I asked inquisitively.

"I still need to watch over Uncle Glenn, even though Grandpa is a lot of work."

I couldn't help but laugh at how serious Leo stated this. "Okay, that is two jobs."

"I also need to watch over Uncle Doug and Aunt Betty."

"Really, Uncle Doug?" I was confused by this statement. My aunt was struggling with her own battle of cancer, and when she died, Leo displayed a beautiful smile as he described her wings as blue, and outlined in purple, yet nothing had been revealed about my uncle having health concerns.

Leo then answered, "Yes, he needs help."

I sat there and pondered what this could be. Maybe it was just help with strength for all that was happening around us. There was a long delay. An hour later I tucked Leo into bed and asked, "Leo, you said you had five jobs. What is number five?"

"Number five is you." My heart pounded quickly. *What is wrong with me?* I closed my eyes and calmed my breathing. Then a whisper of a voice in my mind told me, *Nothing is wrong, Leo is working to protect your heart. His job is to make sure you feel loved amid all your turmoil.* It wasn't long after this conversation that we received the news that my uncle was also about to face his own battle with cancer.

I remember the first encounter after my dad received his diagnosis. Leo was beaming with a smile. "Are you ready to go to Heaven?"

"Not just yet, there are a few things I still would like to do and take care of." Leo's eyes remained locked on my dad's. He continued by asking Leo, "Can you help me with that?" Leo gazed with warmth and love in his eyes and responded with only a smile.

My dad did have time, and he was gifted with opportunities to follow through on some of the things he wanted to sort out. God helped him through that time, but I also believe my dad saw life through the eyes of Leo.

He experienced a great deal of hardship in his lifetime. He served in the Korean War, left behind his new wife, and missed being present for their firstborn child. Money was tight, raising a family of fifteen children and supporting that role on a single blue-collar income which allowed my mom to remain home to care for us. I imagine it caused a great deal of stress, but it was rarely revealed to us kids. My parents faced the loss of so many loved ones as they aged, in addition to the two children who died before them. Yet, my mother remained strong as she pushed forward in life. She stood at the kitchen sink and looked out the back window, cleaning dishes as if she was trying to wipe away her heartache. There was never a shortage of dishes to clean with a family of our size and it appeared she was always in front of the sink, wiping away her sorrow in the bucket of soapy water. I know my mom wept, but she was a private lady and refrained from letting us see her struggle.

My dad, on the other hand, wore his emotions on his sleeve. The loss was more than he could bear. He walked his sorrow out down the lane, through the wooded areas of our family farm. What pain couldn't be alleviated by seeking the refuge of his favorite tree stump and praying there was drowned out by the beer can until the pain subsided. Despite this choice, my dad was full of love and within time, realized the pain couldn't be erased from the numbness of alcohol. He got sober and found new ways to heal his grief. Some of his choices over the years may have unfortunately led to his own illness of liver cancer, but my dad's heart continued to soften, and his faith continued to grow.

The spiritual connection between Leo and my dad surrounded everyone with peace as they sat with each other. Their relationship was beautiful, and at times, more than my dad could handle. His heart ached for what he perceived was a loss of life for Leo when his illness struck him, and he quickly found himself slipping into a state of depression. It sent him back into his painful process of losing Patty, but my dad proceeded with medication instead of alcohol to support his aching heart. This gave him the time needed to process and finally see that, although Leo had a change of lifestyle, it was a positive life-altering opportunity for all of those who surrounded him to witness God's grace and God's love.

With each passing year, I witnessed the relationship of my father and my son blossom into something special. They held such high regard for each other. A man who was my teacher for so many years, someone I looked up to and cherished as my father, looked up to my son; disregarding the normal way of life in which a child learns from their elders. My dad knew that Leo was actually a disciple of God showing him the way.

There was a Christmas where Leo and I made a craft for my father. It was an angel made from tissue paper with a photo of Leo's face adhered to the angel's face. When my dad opened it up, he said, "Thank you, Leo, for taking care of me and for being my angel."

Leo replied, "I am not your only angel anymore, Jesus is too."

The next day, I said to Leo, "Boy, Grandpa must really be a lot to handle."

"Grandpa needed the Master. Jesus is the Master Angel. I am working to be just like Him, but Grandpa needs more help."

"Is Grandpa okay?"

"You will know soon." This comment weighed heavily on my heart as I remained in the "unknown" and Leo in the "known".

I then witnessed exactly what Leo was talking about. I saw God use Leo in the most beautiful way. I believe Leo had permission from God to take physical suffering from a patient who wasn't going to be healed, but could experience some respite during his time of transition. I witnessed this beautiful sacrifice firsthand, as Leo took on my father's suffering during his last days of life.

On October 29th, 2015, nine days prior to my dad's last breath, I took Leo to visit him. Leo was very persistent about going and equally persistent about staying.

"I need to see Grandpa."

"Are you sure? You have had a few tough days."

"I need to be there to see Jesus when He comes to see Grandpa."

"Okay. I will get you ready to go." I was not about to interfere with an "angel in training".

Leo sat on my lap in a chair next to my dad. He intently kept his eyes fixed on him, and continued smiling at him. The light in the room was dim, yet Leo was radiant, as the string of Christmas tree lights hanging outside the picture window reflected in his eyes.

"I love you, Grandpa." So much tenderness poured into these words.

"I love you too, Leo."

"Don't worry, Grandpa. Jesus is by your side." The wisdom and insight of Leo's presence released a quietness into the room as he leaned himself forward to press a kiss upon my dad's forehead.

When we got home, Leo spiked a fever. I gave him some medication, cooled him down with a damp cloth, cuddled in bed with him, and slept. The next morning, the fever remained.

I looked at Leo and asked, "Are you okay?"

"I helped Grandpa. I took away his fever and pain so he can go to Heaven."

"Did Jesus say it is time?" A penetrating ache filled my chest.

"Soon."

Leo's fever remained between 100 and 104.5 degrees for the next eight days. I wanted to take Leo to the hospital, but he was very adamant to remain home and kept saying, "I am okay."

"Honey, your fever is so high."

"I am just helping Grandpa."

"I am worried about you." My elevation of concern increased.

"Jesus is with me."

I trusted him for a few more days, but became extremely anxious. For my own peace of mind, I followed through with a doctor visit. Leo showed no signs of any other issues other than the fever. The doctor supported our decision to observe him from home to avoid interfering with the work that Leo was doing for his grandpa. She simply requested that we notify her if any significant changes occurred. The days that followed, we continued to watch Leo take on the suffering of his grandpa to allow peace to fill his final days. As this transpired, my husband stopped at my parents' home.

Afterward, when he arrived home, he told Leo, "There are a lot of people worried about you. This fever needs to break so you are okay."

Leo simply replied, "I will be, once Grandpa goes to Heaven."

The days continued to pass, and Leo's condition remained the same. We received a phone call from my sister who was by my dad's bedside. She stated, "Dad is seeing angels coming to the window at night."

Leo yelled out, "Yeah, Grandpa believes!" The same Christmas lights that shined light into the room as the reflection danced off Leo's eyes, had angels appear in them. Multiple faces formed within each bulb, none alike, but all present at the same time. Whatever inner battles my dad was sorting through, he finally made peace with them.

The following day, my mom sat by my father. She expressed her love for him and told him it was okay to go. Leo responded, "Finally, Grandma," almost irritated that it took her so long.

Leo held that fever, along with God's guidance, and gave my dad the time he needed to sort out any questions, concerns, and thoughts that were unsettled and unfinished in his life. He gave my mom the time she needed to accept the process of letting go of the love of her life. Leo suffered, to ease their suffering. My dad passed away on November 7th. Leo's fever diminished and no further signs of concern remained that same day.

A few days later, Leo said to me, "I am sorry I couldn't save Grandpa. Jesus said it was his time. He was ready for Grandpa's soul."

"You loved Grandpa so much, sweetheart. I know you did everything that you could. You gave Grandpa exactly what he needed; time."

"Last night, I saw Grandpa with his son. They were playing with a red ball with Mylo and another dog. Aunt Patty was there too."

"What a beautiful vision, Leo. Thank you for sharing, I can't wait to tell Grandma."

Ironically, when my brother Glenn died, he was holding a red tension ball in his hand, which neither Leo, nor I, knew about. I thought it was so interesting that Leo referred to my brother Glenn as my dad's son, but he used my sister Patty's name. So much of my dad's final days mirrored the daily life of Leo. Lying still in a hospital bed, in the middle of a family room, struggling to verbalize his thoughts, trying to breathe life into every breath. It was more than that though; I saw the same belief in my dad's eyes that appeared in Leo's.

Leo once again gazed into the heavenly realm and began to describe what he saw.

"Grandpa made it!" Pure joy spread throughout his body.

"That is wonderful news." I could almost see my dad in Heaven through the reflection of Leo's eyes.

"Grandpa's wings are yellow with green around the edges."

"All of these descriptions are so beautiful, Leo."

"The colors in Heaven are so vivid." Leo maintained his focus upward as if nothing earthly was obstructing his view.

"I can only imagine." Through my own weak eyes, I began to see the brilliance of the color of life in Heaven through Leo's expressions.

A few months after my father passed, Leo and I attended a mass with my mom that was dedicated to my dad. Sitting in the church pew, Leo blurted out, "Grandpa says, yes." This statement was made just after silent prayer time.

I asked, "What did Grandpa say yes to?"

Without hesitation, Leo replied, "That I can have his watch."

When mass ended, Leo asked my mom, "Can I have Grandpa's watch? He said yes during church."

Days later, my mother presented it to Leo. "I know Grandpa would want you to have this." Leo smiled as my mom slid it carefully onto his wrist. Then tears poured down his face. "It is too big." The watch swung loosely on Leo's wrist.

"Don't worry honey, we can get it adjusted by taking out a few links."

"Thank you."

Leo wore my father's watch with honor, and after having several links removed, it encircled Leo's wrist with the same snug love that wrapped around my dad for years. This simple item brought such pleasure to Leo's days, stemming from a relationship that began with time spent with a loved one, discussing the importance of time.

Leo provided calmness through God's grace to my dad as his days drew to an end, but I also know it was their bond, which had grown over all those years, that brought that level of commitment. This beautiful love formed from the moment Leo rested in my dad's arms, to the first lick of sherbet from his cone, through the many stories shared on the couch, all the way up to the end where they became reunited in God's kingdom. There is a purpose in all things, and the relevance of Leo in the life of my father played out beautifully, but it didn't end there. Leo continued his communication with my dad beyond their time here together. He showed me that my dad still watched over me.

Chapter Twenty-One

NOT ALONE IN THE FIRE

The reflection of the flame flickered in Leo's eyes as we sat around the fire. We told campfire stories as he stretched out on his lounge chair. Instead of the traditional scary ones, we reminisced and celebrated Leo's victories. Every victory was worth celebrating! This ranged from hearing his gentle words on a good day to successfully finishing a Gatorade bottle on a difficult one. A victory was waking up. Another, by some miracle, to dress and be able to load up the van for a family outing. But the most celebrated of all were Leo's birthdays—years given to us beyond what was expected. All were causes to be joyous and thankful.

As the crackling fire began to roar, it reminded me of sparks reflecting from candles sitting upon his birthday cake that were so challenging for Leo to blow out; yet he never gave up. His determination elevated our way of seeing life. We were no longer living life waiting to die. Rather, we were alive yearning to live. A diagnosis is only a statement of what might be. Everyone who had ever been a part of Leo's life was welcomed into our home to celebrate. The walls were bulging with people, flowing in and out of our home in an open house format. They took turns approaching Leo, and had a moment in time with this special gift that God bestowed upon all of us.

When the doctors told us to have no hope, that Leo most likely would not see his third birthday, they casted us aside like being thrown into the fiery furnace. God saved us from the heat of destruction, brought hope back, and grew our faith. I openly admit I learned of these three men: Shadrach, Meschach, and Abednego, while watching an episode of *Veggie Tales* with my older two sons. Just like they were taken from their home as children (Daniel 3), Leo was also snatched from his childhood. Satan may have tried to take his happiness, or ours as parents, but we refused to bow down to any other idol. Once again, God rescued us from the furnace of self-destruction and pity.

The journey with Leo was a path less traveled. His condition had doctors uncertain, which then left *us* with uncertainty. We traveled without a map, often taking wrong turns and sometimes drifting further and further from a solution, but we quickly realized the only solution we could trust was God. This became evident when his medical files were sent to various experts around the world. Their findings all had one thing in common; uncertainty. God, however, knew exactly what was to come and the reason behind it.

When my life turned upside down and I lost my direction, I could have lost sight of what was important. I could have found myself digging a deeper hole of self-pity; feeling lost, alone, and depressed. Somehow, in that moment of change, God saved me. Although I did feel overwhelmed and everything happened very quickly, it appeared my beautiful, perfect little boy seemed to have slipped away. What was actually happening was a transformation of life.

As I mentioned earlier, all too often when someone gazes upon an individual with special needs, the first thing they may feel is pity. Although those are genuine emotions for the circumstances, the reality is that a beautiful soul, connected to God, may lie within. For the Bible states God does some of His greatest work in those that lie still in sick beds. I personally have witnessed, from a front row seat, this very statement in Leo.

There was a period of time where his body was motionless, there was only involuntary movement, but his mind was spinning continuously in thought with his beautiful relationship to God. The rigidness that enveloped Leo's body softened, and a radiant glow dusted his face when he connected with Jesus. The tension that consumed his lips made way and released, which allowed Leo's mouth to move more freely. He then formed words that typically were more difficult to convey. An angelic smile covered his face, and his eyes sparkled with the love he held inside for Jesus. It was these magical moments that have not only deepened my faith, but have also given me the strength to conquer my own challenges in life. My prayers shifted from wanting my life to be easier, to praying for the strength and grace to endure the life I had.

Leo opened my eyes to the true beauty of the world. My eyes then saw the gift of love another individual could give you. He stimulated my senses, and truly helped me to see all the colors contained within nature. I noticed all the shades of green covering a single tree, along with the color wheel of plants that were in sight around it. Life came into focus from the endless vivid colors surrounding me. I saw the love before me.

I began to listen more intently to the sounds around me. I heard the call of birds singing and heard God speaking to me through them. I felt the flow of water hitting the rocks along its bumpy path, but sensed God smoothing it out before me. When the gentle breeze graced upon my skin, it stimulated every tiny hair that covered my body, and then I realized, it is God reaching out to me. I was awakened by the physical touch of the senses of life.

Leo also enhanced my awareness of taste. He showed me the value of food, and how it was designed to nourish our bodies. After witnessing him lose the ability to swallow, and having to be fed by a feeding tube for a year, I had a new appreciation for the flavors of even the simplest of foods. I was consciously aware of the gift of being able to eat. He brought together the bread of nourishment, along with the bread of life. He enabled me to see how different they were from each other, yet both were needed to sustain a healthy way of living. Leo continues to instill in me to live in the moment, trying my best not to anticipate what the next moment may bring. Leo was the one who took that feeling of being cast aside into the furnace, and transformed it into burning our own fire within us, to overcome our heat of destruction.

This fiery furnace burned in Leo's soul, and he hungered for time with Jesus. He had the wisdom to recognize spiritual signals and continued to look up, searching for the love of Jesus. Even in human form, Leo was the soul. He was 100% connected to the spiritual realm. This intimate time provided the peace that Leo's mind needed to withstand the hardship he physically endured, and this transformation appeared not only to light Leo's soul within, but also gave him an outer glow that drew others to him.

I am unable to claim that Leo lived a life free of all sin. I can state, however, that he was pure, and the sins he had were either influenced by us, or quickly retracted by him in a state of remorse. While Leo was preparing for his sacraments of first reconciliation and first communion, we set up a special meeting with our priest to do a trial run. Normally, a parent would not sit in on these special moments. The object of this trial was to make sure both Leo and the priest felt comfortable with each other, and confirm he was able to understand the words Leo expressed.

The priest entered our home and with a gentleness in his voice, "Hello, Leo."

"Hi." Leo grinned from ear to ear.

"Do you know why I am here today?" He pulled up a chair and sat at Leo's side.

"To talk about Jesus."

"More about how you can talk to Jesus."

"I already do." Leo smiled and waited for more to be offered.

"Let's get started then. In the name of the Father and of the Son and of the Holy Spirit."

"Amen," Leo replied without a cue from the priest.

"So, Leo. I am going to state a series of questions. You just respond with what is in your heart. Okay?"

"Okay." Leo continued to remain calm stretched out across the sheets of his bed.

"May the Lord be in your heart and help you confess your sins. This is an opportunity for you to talk about your sins and for anything that you want to ask forgiveness from God. So, Leo, do you have any sins?"

Leo replied without hesitation and without any struggle of his words. "No, but my brother Oliver does."

I looked at Father and he stated, "Well, that very well may be true." I thought, *Way to throw your brother under the bus.* I looked at the priest and said, "Trust me, he has a few." Yet, as the priest looked deeper into

Leo's eyes, all he could see was purity.

Leo, despite all his overwhelming pain and obstacles, was never bitter. He didn't hold onto grudges or retain anger. There were times in our family's playful manner, we would have Leo engage in being sassy. One of the habits formed from this was swearing. When he lost the ability to speak, we were desperate for ways to stimulate a response. This sort of backfired on us. When he used these specific words, they came out loud and clear. However, at the slight mention of me saying, "Leo, would Jesus be happy with that?"

"I am sorry, Jesus," Leo replied instantly. There were no circumstances in which Leo didn't want to please Jesus, and put Him first.

Maybe there were a few times Leo liked to put himself first. Leo loved attention, and during occasions that he wasn't getting it, he found a way. There were many times when friends of mine gathered in our home. Leo usually loved being involved in the girl talk, unless it began to completely take my attention away from him. He would find ways to interject, and if that didn't work, he made his presence known.

This behavior wasn't limited to only me. There was a particular moment that comes to mind when Leo was trying to get Tony's attention. We were all in the family room. Leo was watching a show on TV while Tony was engrossed in a hunting magazine.

Multiple times, Leo said, "Hey, Daddy." When Tony failed to answer, Leo continued with "Hey, Tony." Disappointed, and frustrated by the fact Tony still didn't respond, he followed it up with a very loud and well pronounced, "Hey, jackass!" This ultimately got Tony's attention.

Startled by Leo's outburst, Tony abruptly stood from his seated position and went to Leo's side. We all laughed as we realized which word was actually effective to obtain Tony's attention. It had me reflecting back to the outing in the grocery store and realizing how impactful my choice of words had been on Leo.

God's strength remained with us throughout all the years of Leo's illness. Although there were times when it became increasingly difficult to try to find the silver lining of happiness in our flames, Leo was steadfast in his love for Jesus, and he guided our way. While Leo was continuing his battle, I was also faced with many additional obstacles and heartache within my family.

There hasn't been a lot of illness-free existence in my family. Yet, somehow, I found myself in the eye of the storm where it is calm. With all the pain swirling fiercely around me, God held my hand. He continues to guide me to find optimistic hope amongst all of the heartache. The simplest sound of a cardinal singing calms my soul, as if I believe he is singing just for me. As the glow of red casts itself across the sky during a sunrise or sunset, I envision Leo spreading his wings, and soaring above me, protecting me.

Leo's gentle nature soothed the burn in my heart and over time, I too found peace. In the stillness of the day, I can feel a gentle breeze blow, and I am elevated to a positive perspective and reminded God holds my hand tightly. I believe grieving is a never-ending process. Events will occur to either bring joy as a reminder or sadness of the loss experienced. Yes, time can heal, but when you truly love someone a piece of you goes missing along with them. Nothing but the love of God can give you the strength to face another day without them by your side.

I am forever grateful to God for placing Leo in my life and providing me with the visual insight to witness His love; to see His work through the journey of a boy with special needs, and allow me to see with my own eyes the miracles we hear about. His purity and love for Jesus opened my heart and allowed emotions to flow through my soul like nothing I have ever experienced before. I sit in awe as I reflect on how gracious Leo was to accept his condition and how willing he was to serve God. Despite the pain he endured, he wore a smile on his face when any discussion of Jesus or Heaven came into play. Even when those he loved dearly were encountering their final days, Leo expressed happiness for what they were soon going to be exposed to. What an amazing gift to have such an intimate relationship with Jesus and to devote your life to Him never seeking anything more than His love!

Over the years, I believe it is only natural to think, *Why do I have so many more issues than others*? What I have concluded for my own purpose, is God sees potential in me. I am worth investing in. He wants to show me He believes in me, and that I should believe in myself. I approach it like a coach who works you harder than your teammates. It isn't because they don't like you, or don't believe you have what it takes, rather it is the complete opposite. They see what you are made of and what you have to offer.

God sees my special set of gifts—of course He does—He gave them to me! I believe my life is meant to touch the lives of others. God is working through me to do great things. He has turned up the heat in the furnace. He is waiting to see if I will trust that He is there with me and allow Him to do great things. Or will I flee and escape the heat? God knows that answer. The rest of us will just have to wait and see.

Leo stayed in the furnace and Jesus remained by his side to the end. He was in the furnace with Leo and ultimately raised him up. God released him from the weight of his cross, bringing him into the Kingdom of Heaven. I believe Leo knew this was the final plan all along. It took a lifetime of experiences to create the story of his life. Each one built on top of the other to create the young man that Leo became. Somewhere along the way, I, too, experienced God. Through the eyes of my terminally ill son, I witnessed inner light and it transformed me.

Chapter Twenty-Two

IN THE GARDEN WITH GOD

Water pushed through the crevice, breaking the ground. The flow strengthened as the dirt gave way, unable to be contained. The flow of Leo's spiritual growth reacted much in the same way as his body broke down and his faith gained strength. As Leo entered his teen years, he could only withstand short adventures and when we did manage those, the toll it took on him seemed to outweigh the pleasure. As a result, we chose to create a place of serenity in our own yard. We pieced together the things that brought Leo pleasure as well as things that allowed his body to relax. Leo desired to see the world, but it became time to bring the world to him.

As this realization became a reality, I was reminded of how his life paralleled the four gardens represented in the Bible. As humans, we go from being created, to being redeemed in life, to walking in victory, and finally joining Jesus in Heaven. Life was created in the Garden of Eden and Leo brought life back to me. I needed to discover a way to create a space to break down the walls that enclosed us and bring new life to him.

Our isolation was but a mere shadow of how Jesus suffered in The Garden of Gethsemane, yet it did leave us disconnected. We found victory in the Garden of Golgotha, as my vision went into motion, and I knew Leo would find true peace once he reached his final resting place in the ultimate garden, The Garden of Eternal Life. "Take My yoke upon you and learn from Me, for I am gentle and lowly in heart, and you will find rest for your souls." (Matthew 11:29)

In the book of Genesis, God sent rain to grow the shrubs and life on Earth which had otherwise been unfinished ground. He found that there was no one to work the ground, however, so man was created out of dust. When surrounded by the beauty of what God created, it becomes clear that nature is a space to connect with the roots of what makes us human. It was time for us to prune our bushes and allow the love that Leo had for nature and animals to flourish. Frequently, on days when opportunities were out of the question, we found ourselves watching documentaries about nature, animals (mostly big cats from Africa), or we spent some time outdoors in the sunlight.

Leo started a rock collection early on in his childhood, one that began from his conversation with Grandpa as they talked about life and watches amongst the fieldstone pile. Yet, most of his rocks were accumulated during our walks, from the paths where my feet stepped, and his wheels rolled. As we pressed through the beauty that surrounded us, Leo looked high and low, to his left and to his right. Even as his body began to have less strength and more limited range of motion, his eyes shifted with intention and he didn't miss a thing. He spotted rocks, and then instructed me to grab them for him. This same method was also applied to gathering leaves, which we pressed and put into a binder; if they so happened to catch his attention. The leaves remained a treasure he kept in his book, but for the rocks, Leo had a bigger plan.

The sound of flowing water brought serenity not only to Leo's mind, but also to his body and soul. Additionally, the warmth of a fire kept his rigid frame from becoming too stiff to remain upright in his chair. It occurred to me how to bring all these pleasures together: I reached out to a local waterscape company and began the process of bringing life to our vision of a water feature. As Leo and I worked together with the design consultant, it quickly became apparent that this project was going to extend further than a work relationship; it was going to become a friendship.

Leo and I greeted the consultant with excitement on the fifty-foot front porch that welcomed the entrance to our home. As he wound around the bend of our sidewalk, Leo drew him in with the warmth of his smile and the purity of his eyes.

"Hi," Leo stated, leaning forward on his wheelchair tray as if he was trying to reach him before he reached us.

"Well, hello. You must be Leo."

"Yes," he sounded off quickly, before he could say anything else.

"How are you doing today?"

Leo's eyes glistened in the sun as it parted between the trees, "Good."

The consultant looked at Leo intently and was captivated by him. He paused briefly as peace transcended the space between them. "So, I hear from your mom that you would like to install a pond."

"Yeah, yeah, yeah!" Leo's excitement lifted his bottom from the seat as he pushed on his foot plates and caused his tummy to press into the tray.

"Let me hear your ideas, and then I will tell you mine."

Leo turned to me and waited with anticipation. I began to express how we wanted the waterfall to flow into the stream ending in a pool of water. He took in my words, and then our vision grew. As the weeks progressed, we began to see what at first only existed in our minds start to come alive. When the heavy equipment arrived at our home, Leo was thrilled to be outside watching the scoops of soil lifted, removed, and eventually formed into the shape of a stream which led to a hole that became our pond. Leo observed carefully, and watched with amazement, as our front yard became transformed. Once the liner was cut and measured, allowing each boulder to be placed into position, it formed the borders of the waterflow.

Leo quickly became the foreman on the job and added insight and input. Remarkably, given his limited physical abilities and eyesight, he noticed details and took a great deal of interest in how the final project was going to be fulfilled. His excitement continued to build over the duration of the project, and his limbs stiffened with excitement as the hose was placed in what only appeared to be a hole, but gradually transformed into a pond. The final touches were added, and gravel was sprinkled around, masking any exposed liner.

Leo called out the workers on more than one occasion, saying, "You missed a spot."

"Where, Leo?"

"Right there." Unable to point it out, Leo's eyes focused on an area.

"Right here?"

"Over." His eyes continued to shift to the right.

"Here?"

"Yes." Leo nodded his head with approval. The guys took a short break and Leo yelled out, "Get back to work."

They were all startled by his loud voice. "You are the boss, Leo."

Once everything met Leo's approval, water plants were added which enhanced the beauty, but something was still missing. All the rocks Leo collected over the years needed to be strategically placed in just the right spots. I held one up.

"Where should this one go?"

"Over there." Leo shifted his head to the left and leaned over the arm support to direct his placement. Every motion was purposeful and intentional.

"Right here?"

Leo nodded. I rolled Leo along the flow of the structure and took out one rock at a time. Oliver eventually joined in to help us.

"How about this one, brother?" Oliver darted off with enthusiasm as Leo instructed us, and together, we placed his collection. He was so proud of having his rock collection added to complete the space. In only a week's time, the appearance of our front yard walkway was transformed like a river flowing through heaven itself.

And still there was something missing. Another one of Leo's loves still needed to be purchased to fully complete the project. For years, Leo had a fish tank next to his bedside. He was so attentive to his fish, and always made sure their needs were met (by telling us what to do, of course). To bring the pond alive, we needed to select koi fish that would call our pond home. As we loaded Leo up in his wheelchair and drove to the store to choose just the perfect fish, Leo inhaled and prepared to speak.

He shouted out, "Fourteen."

"Fourteen, what?"

"Fish."

"Leo, I am not sure our pond is big enough for fourteen fish."

"It is."

Fourteen was a high number of fish for the actual space we had, but we also knew there was a chance we would lose some and, at the same time, we knew we weren't going to convince Leo of any other option.

We really made the aquatic store employee work for his picks; Leo had in mind certain colors and specific fish as he peered into the tank. This task was done with a huge smile on the worker's face, wanting nothing but the best for Leo. Finally satisfied with his selections, we headed home and released the fish into our pond which elated Leo with laughter.

"Do you want to sit in the water, Leo?" One of the special features of the pond was a sitting rock where Leo could sit upon my lap and have his feet hang into the water.

"Yes," he expressed with hesitation.

I stepped into the shelf of the pond and sat upon the rock. Tony scooped Leo into his arms and placed him into mine. Leo showed mixed emotions of excitement and fear as the fish swam around us. Never taking his eyes off the water, he squirmed.

"Too close." Leo wanted to retract his feet, but was unable.

"What is too close?"

"The fish." He pressed his head into my shoulder as if that would remove him from the water.

"But I thought you liked fish." I peered around his head to meet his eyes.

"They are going to get me."

"Even if they nibble on your toes, Leo, it will tickle."

"Get out."

"But we just got in. I promise it will be okay. Relax and just watch them swim."

"Are you sure?"

"Yes. I will protect you." We sat there together, amazed by the way the project all came together. The beautiful waterfall flowed into the twenty-foot stream that wrapped around a firepit which ended in a twenty-five-foot pond. Although this was not typical for a location of a pond, from the road in front of our home you would never know it is there, until you walk up the sidewalk and are greeted by paradise.

Each year, the garden of water brought delight and serenity to Leo's days. He loved peering into the pond to watch the silent movement of the koi as they swam. He giggled when it was time to feed them. I tossed a handful of fish pellets into the water, which caused them to thrash around, entangled with one another. We even had a few over the years that were jumpers, and occasionally we were lucky enough to be in position to see as it happened. The pond also welcomed other critters like frogs and dragonflies and butterflies. This combination didn't always work out well for the dragonflies and butterflies, but it was pretty amazing to watch nature in survival mode as we witnessed a frog gain its reward from its patience.

The water feature grew over the years and so did the fish. What started as a pond became multiple streams and waterfalls adding to the beauty and tranquility of the space we called home. Expanding our outdoor living space allowed Leo to take in different views. It also added additional sounds to block out noise so he could peacefully drift off to sleep while stretched out on a lounge chair to enjoy an afternoon nap.

Daily from summer through fall, Leo and I sat amongst nature and allowed God to settle in our thoughts. I watched as Leo's body relaxed and his eyes grew heavy, and before I knew it, he was asleep. I oftentimes had to fight the urge to sleep as well; the sound was so meditative. When Leo drifted off to sleep, I maintained the flower beds and worked on my writing. Some of my most insightful thoughts presented themselves during this time of tranquility. I felt most connected to God in my times of silence by Leo's bedside.

Ironically, Leo didn't always maintain a deep sleep. He appeared to consciously be aware of certain sounds. The slightest creak of my chair awoke his big, brown eyes. He would gaze over at me as if saying, "Where do you think you are going?" One of the other more prominent sounds was the passing of a school bus. Boy, oh boy, could Leo detect those! He had such a love for riding the bus that it could rouse him out of a deep slumber when they hit the gas to accelerate uphill.

The love that filled Leo's soul had no limits. He had the same amount of compassion for a spider that lived next to his outdoor lounge chair as he did for his faithful and loyal basset hound that lay by his side. He had inner peace, and it was a peace he was willing to share. There was a summer in his middle school days when he befriended a spider. He named her Charlotte, for his love of the movie. "Now the Lord God had formed out of the ground all the wild animals and all the birds in the sky. He brought them to the man to see what he would name them; and whatever the man called each living creature, that was its name." (Genesis 2:19)

Each day, as we spent time on the porch, he scanned the window frame and the fieldstone on our home in search of her. His head, which had limited range of motion while lying down, remained still, but his eyes shifted rapidly back and forth in search of his friend. Leo rarely engaged during his middle school years, and his encounters with peers diminished. Without a friend in sight, Leo turned his tender love to a spider, which brought me joy and sadness simultaneously.

With so much pure love to give, it left an ache in my heart that he didn't have a social network outside of his family to offer his love to. I, of course, soaked up as much of his love as he was willing to share. His love was endless, like a deep pool of water. Even a critter, like a spider that most of us wouldn't give a second thought to or would most likely squash, Leo extended his heart to. What an amazing feeling it was to be on the receiving end of his love. How pure your soul must be to love at that capacity. To not have any hatred, jealousy, or wicked thoughts. To only be filled with love and joy. It was through his peace that I found peace. Leo gave me the gift of stillness, which allowed me to also relax in our garden.

There were some beautiful moments that occurred during naps outdoors. Moments when it was obvious Leo's body was physically present, but spiritually, he was elsewhere. In these moments, his body completely softened and all the rigidness that held his tiny frame released. The tension that pierced his lips faded away and a glow of purity spread across his face. Mowers droned from the neighbors' lawns. Horns honked on vehicles passing by. Even a school bus braking down the hill would not awaken him from the deep work he attended to.

When he awoke, reentering the garden oasis that caused him to drift away, he stated, "I was training with Jesus." For a body that held so much pain, so many spasms, and uncontrolled tension, Leo transcended away in these moments and found peace in the presence of Jesus. In our garden, he walked with God, and he learned from the Master the lessons that needed to be shared. It was in these moments, in the stillness of the garden, I learned that you don't have to move to be moved by God.

Chapter Twenty-Three

LEO IN THE LIONS' DEN

Being alone can be an unsettling feeling. There's a silence that stirs in the mind. There is a difference between being alone and loneliness. Leo and I were used to spans of time when we only had each other's company, but when friendships began to fade away and acquaintances stopped coming by, the space felt empty. The void bubbled up a bitter sensation, and at times I felt trapped in our isolation, yet we needed to power through.

In the Bible, Daniel was moving forward in life trying to make the most out of what he was given. In his circumstance, however, he was betrayed and thrown into a den from which he could not escape. To his surprise, he was met with the eyes of predators around him waiting to devour him at any sign of weakness. He remained strong and steadfast in his faith, but still he was abandoned and left without others to communicate with. At times, I wonder if it was more difficult for him to accept that he was with lions or rather, that he was alone with his thoughts in a time he thought he had friends and support.

Leo formed a strong pride with friends and cousins in his early years. When he was walking around before his initial diagnosis, he constantly sought out ways to make people laugh. He found ways to occupy his time, like watching ants crawl into their hole or feeding ducks with his family. Then, at the age of two when he was thrown into his den unexpectedly, we were left with questions and an illness waiting to devour him at first chance. At least Leo had an inner circle who remained with him in the darkness. I stood beside him, ready to defend him every chance I could, and I know there were others in my immediate family who were prepared to do the same.

Unable to be mobile, Leo remained in the den. But for him, it was our blue, two-story home. There were things to do, but there were also limitations prohibiting us from branching out beyond the usual shows, games, and activities that brought Leo joy. These ways to engage him at home so that he didn't feel alone, were reliant on the people who went out of their way to be there with him. Everyone reacts to hardships differently and the unknown can be scary, but those who chose to remain with him made all the difference in the world.

Leo held onto his special people with the highest regard for their value. When they entered his heart, they remained there and were locked in. When Leo experienced an adventure, it was replayed over and over in his mind. His limitations didn't allow him to go on daily outings, so he cherished every opportunity that came his way. I witnessed an amazing foundation of friendships over Leo's years. It was beautiful to watch children embrace their time with Leo. A handful of kids imprinted their marks on Leo's heart, and I would like to believe he did the same for them. These early encounters of friendship stayed with him to the very end. He referenced their names and asked about them. This often broke my heart with the realization they were no longer around.

On gloomy days, it felt like there was a void blocking the flow of connection. When it is so easy to remain untouched by events that don't directly involve you, a darkness can engulf others who directly are. I am proud of how many of Leo's cousins stepped up to the challenges presented by the uncertainty of Leo's health. Just children themselves, they made time in their days for him, when they could have been at home on the couch, or out at a friend's house playing video games. On a day Leo was positioned to watch TV, unexpected visitors brought light through the doorway like the sun beaming through the entrance to a cave.

A knock at the door, followed by the doorbell. Snapped out of his den, Leo would light up with excitement at who the visitor could be. On this occasion, it was his cousins checking in with some love and desserts.

"Hello, Leo! It is so good to see you!"

"Hi," Leo replied. "Come over here!" His eyes stayed focused on the hallway.

"Okay, I'm coming, I just need to take my shoes off first!" He smiled when they came into sight.

Leo completely shut out the sounds of the room around him and focused on the guest who came his way. Then, he took a good look at them and immersed in the joy that came with being with someone he adored.

"What do you have for me?" Nothing got by Leo. If he saw someone holding onto an object, he assumed it must be for him.

"We brought you some of your favorites! Chocolate chip cookies and some Hershey kisses, too. Just baked these today and they're still warm."

"Yumm!" He opened his mouth and waited for a bite to be placed in it.

And just like that, a gathering of people would seat themselves around Leo and fill the space with energy and chocolate. These ongoing visits were appreciated and welcomed, but with time, people changed and life continued to move forward for others. Leo remained in the den. I remained there with him.

During Leo's early onset, we were involved in a variety of groups that provided us with activities outside of the home. These playgroup friends, Leo's pride of lions, became not only entertainment for both Leo and Oliver, but they also provided me with new friendships with the other moms. Our outings expanded from organized events to social gatherings on our own. We had one another over to our homes, went to the parks, and for walks together. When Leo's health changes occurred, it left these groups broken. The added intensity of Leo's condition changed the dynamics of the gatherings and seemed to make them uncertain and uncomfortable. Things were more challenging, and for that reason I slowly saw them pull away during a time when Leo and I really needed self-assurance and love. Yet as others stepped away, Jesus walked in, and I found a friend in Him.

Leo's world was turned upside down and at the same time, so was the family that united us. The faces he knew and the smiles he came to know were stripped away from him the same way his body functions were stripped away. The sparkle in his eyes grew dim; everything that was familiar to him was gnawed at by the jaws of the lion and he lay motionless, looking for a way to be saved. He needed security. He needed a source he could rely on.

Over the years, it sometimes felt like a dark cloud hovered over my family. There were moments when the sun tried to break through, yet the cloud swirled and became larger. One thing after another seemed to go wrong and it became difficult to find positive meaning in a layer of overcast issues. It was moments like this when I needed to pause and center myself in God's loving presence and cry out to Him for help. The swirl of self-pity tried to overtake me, so I quickly had to get my thoughts back on track to be able to maneuver through my obstacles. Leo's unswerving dedication to God guided our steps and helped us find the good in the situation before us.

Sometimes in life people enter another's world without much thought. An encounter with someone can be a brief exchange, or at other times, it blossoms into a lasting friendship. We are not always aware of the impact our presence has on another individual and oftentimes, we take it for granted. I believe it is so important to realize the value in one another, especially when you are entering the heart of a special needs child.

Leo was often surrounded by the love of so many, especially in the times when things looked extremely grim, like the initial first year. Then there were stretches of time where it felt like we had been forgotten. It wasn't a question of what we were up to—people knew where we were—at home. Yet, days went by, and weeks turned into months, and it left Leo and me alone. I honestly don't hold any judgment; resentment is not what I am trying to express. I am openly just trying to show the nature of human life.

We often don't see the opportunities before us until it is too late. What I came to see is that when someone is struggling and in need, they most likely will not ask for help. In addition, they will most likely not reply "yes" when asked, "Is there anything I can do for you?" Without overstepping, I believe it is best to just "do" instead of asking. If for a moment you can put yourself into their shoes, the clarity of the need may become obvious.

Matthew expressed to me that this same revelation struck him as well. After graduating from college, he pursued a life of adventure, seeking out ways to make a difference and make a name for himself. In these efforts he remained present, constantly evolving to become the best version of himself. That reflection, however, took place in a different state since his journey led him outside Wisconsin. He moved to Colorado to join the founding corps of City Year in Denver. With Leo's limited abilities to endure long outings, we managed to escape his den and seek out the missing member of his pride. Leo was ten and able to experience things from a wheelchair as long as he had someone to help him, and as long as the length of time in the chair was under an hour. Even though it was just a trip to the airport, it was an outing he treasured.

Leo sat proudly near baggage claim, holding a sign with Matthew's name on it, eagerly waiting for his brother to arrive. It had been months since he moved out and he was excited to see his brother. When he eventually did see Matthew, his body arched from joyous spasms, and he yelled out his brother's name for all to hear.

"Matthew! Matthew! Over here!"

"Leo, it's so nice to see you, brother!"

Leo leaned forward on his tray as if that would make Matthew draw nearer faster. "Nice to see you too."

"I missed you so much, thank you for coming to get me." Matthew wrapped both of his arms tenderly around his precious brother.

"I love you, big brother," Leo expressed as Matthew's face came back into view.

"I love you too, Leo. Very much."

They embraced. A brief moment as passersby went about their days, but to them, it was a connection that needed to be reformed. Two pieces of metal beams welded back together by faith, family, and physical touch. In a world where it is so easy to access others via media, it was clear that a brotherly bond experienced right there before my eyes could not be matched by what any text or call could achieve. This tender moment nearly made us forget where we stood, until our bubble popped with the reminder to retrieve Matthew's luggage from baggage claim number three.

"Is that it over there?"

"Where?"

"Right over there!"

"Oh, shoot." Matthew took off in slow motion, pretending to fall onto the carousel to grab his bag. This made Leo's laughter spill out from the depths of his body until he almost slid out of his chair. Matthew's playful heart welcomed any and all opportunities to make Leo laugh. Leo spoke of their week together several times after Matthew's plane departed for his life's journey to continue on.

Feeling abandoned, alone, and isolated from the outside world, is a hard situation to be in. When life is going smoothly, it is wonderful to praise God and express your blessings from Him, but true character comes to surface in times of struggle; in times of uncertainty. It was in those moments I witnessed my son Leo rise above the circumstances and rejoice with love in his heart for a God he stayed true to all the years of his life. He didn't moan, thinking to himself constantly about when it was going to be over, or focus on the things he missed out on. Leo instead was thrown in the den, looked to God, and rose to the occasion. Leo was selected to be an angel "...because he was found blameless before him." (Daniel 6:22) An example of pure trust and pure love.

Leo's life changes with his health not only impacted his way of life, but it also changed the lives of all of us living with him. Each of us took on a new way of living and definitely a new way of seeing life. Unlike Daniel, we were fortunate to have one another while in the lions' den, but it affected each of us differently, and as a result, we handled it in our own ways. The uncertainty of Leo's day really did help equip us for living in the moment. We had to be present in time, we had no answers, no direction, and no idea what lay ahead for us.

God was with us in those dark days, shining the light in our hearts to keep us strong and focused. Ultimately, we were saved because our love for God kept our minds in a good place. Knowing it wasn't so much what you are doing or how you are doing things, but rather spending your time pleasing God is what matters, and Leo loved pleasing God. I am forever grateful for these moments of isolation. They allowed me to grow in my faith and my own relationship with God. They also gave me countless moments of one-on-one time with my son—my son who saved me.

It is ironic that Leo's name means *brave as a lion*. Out of all the boy names in the world, this is the one we bestowed upon him. Leo lived up to his name. He looked the illness in the eye, stood firm, and demonstrated a level of strength that showed he was not fighting alone. He emerged from the darkness of his den, found the light of God, and was proud to proclaim he knew Him. Leo showed the world around him that even during your lowest moments in life, you are never alone. You can conquer the struggles before you with Jesus by your side.

A lion is only as strong as its pride. On his own, a lion may be lost or forbidden to join others. As much as you might think you are stronger on your own, there is also strength in numbers. To have to face difficulties head-on by yourself may take time, and lead to an outcome that wasn't expected or desired. But together, with the right members who encourage growth and support needs, a lion can take down an elephant and overcome the odds. To resist the urge to be content in our quiet, blue house, we needed to think like a pride and make Leo stronger by expanding our horizons. There were times he had the strength to leave the den, and on those days, his pride gave him opportunities to shine.

Chapter Twenty-Four

THE BATTLE WITH TIME

Tick, tick, tick … the silence of the morning revealed the rhythm of the clock as the pendulum swung. Stillness filled the air while I tried to emerge from the confinement of the bed, where my eyes had found rest from the night before with Leo by my side. I stepped carefully out onto the wooden floor, which creaked as I pressed the ball of my foot upon it. I held my breath in hopes that Leo would remain asleep. I looked down at him while he dwelled in peaceful slumber, knowing it would only be a matter of time before the rigorous routine looped once more.

We were in survival mode, and with that we established a survival routine. Exhaustion filled every crevice of my being, for what had been explained to be a sprint, had turned into a long-distance marathon. On occasion, when my body craved an uninterrupted night of rest, Leo would sleep with Tony. Initially, Leo resisted and separation anxiety took hold of him, yet secretly, I believe he loved those intimate moments with his dad.

The scenario was almost always the same. As bedtime drew closer, Tony would say, "It's daddy's night."

Leo would turn to me in hopes that it wasn't true. "What time can we call Momma?"

"Nine o'clock."

"Ummm…" Leo wasn't sure that he liked that response.

"Earlier?" Tony attempted to bargain with Leo.

"Yah."

"How about eight o'clock?"

I tucked both into bed and said, "Goodnight," as I left the room. I am sure the discussion continued after my departure before Leo allowed himself to settle in for the night. As the sun streamed through the window, Leo would know it was morning. Tony shared the details of how this always played out. Leo's eyes would open, and although Tony's eyes remained closed, he felt the penetration of Leo's stare beside him.

Leo said, "What time?"

"Give me ten minutes, Papa is still sleeping." Tony kept his eyes closed, hoping to gain more sleep. Then ten minutes would pass by.

"Is it time?"

"It's eight. It's time." Leo's body quivered with excitement.

"Oh, Mother." Leo called out in a soft voice.

"You can say it louder than that."

"Oh, Mother." Leo expressed louder, but still no response.

"Try yelling, Oh, Diane!"

"Oh, Diane!" Leo's legs straightened, and his body shook as he heard my footsteps approach the door.

"It worked. She's coming." As I opened the door, he giggled with anticipation and found peace as I crawled into the bed beside him.

"Papa snores awful," his nose crinkled as he released the words with emphasis.

"Trust me, I know."

Leo was now a teenage boy, usually an age of exploration and independence, but for him, only dependence. The dark clouds brought by times of withdrawal from social gatherings were outshined by the light casted from within Leo. We remained strong as we marched around in circles. A lifetime of no resolution, only reliance on God.

Each day presented a new chance to provide Leo with opportunities to see and do more within the walls of our home and the acre lot it sat upon. Tony and I continued to take one day at a time, but realized the importance of time itself as we watched the limitations of his body take hold. We also knew that the only thing that was going to keep us from accomplishing something was fear. Fear can bubble up and wash away the sand of a beach leaving just earth. That then makes one wonder if that is still a beach at all, or just another patch of land. Tony and I knew we'd much rather be playing with our son in the sand than remain complacent in front of a TV. Extraordinary events occurred, even in the midst of the ordinary, so we believed outings could present moments that opened up Leo to the world.

The average day Leo and I shared together (when he became completely bed-bound) was simple. It was spent meeting his basic needs, which took time and patience, but gave us the foundation to expose Leo to adventures that would have slipped by if we weren't willing to try. Time was a blur of emotions, like needs rising with the tide and fading away with the night. Life became simplified. Doctors appointments and therapy visits had ceased to exist, and we were left with medications to administer as well as quiet moments in the day.

So, as the morning sunlight would shine through the window, I would try to capitalize on the stillness that remained at my side. Delaying the tasks of the day ahead of me, I would ask,

"Do you want to snuggle?"

"Yes." He giggled with excitement. His body stiffened, followed quickly by coiling up as I would carefully turn him on to his right side. Gently, I rested his head upon the soft spot of my chest and pulled him toward me. In this tender position, he was comforted by the beat of my heart. Thoughts would race through his mind. Leo had such little control over things in life. His routine was something he could "control" and he often worried, swirling the daily tasks in his mind, hoping I wouldn't forget to attend to one of them. He would get stuck on an idea and repeat it over and over until the issue was taken care of. This often caused snuggle time to be cut short so his mind could find rest.

Then, it was a few steps out of the bedroom door into the living room. For a tall person, this could be done in ten strides; for me, it was more like twenty. This pathway was one I often took with Leo, holding him close to my heart and protecting his frail body from the ground. Once transferred into his hospital bed, with sheets decorated with animated friends from his favorite shows and movies, Leo would settle in and fit into the pillows I carefully adjusted. After several moments, he would be positioned how he liked.

Leo would then ask, "What is the month, day of the week, and date?" He was obsessed with his calendar which hung beside his bed. Moments of simplicity is what our life became.

"Let me take a look."

"I need a sticker." He carefully studied the square on the calendar then turned his gaze to the page of stickers. "I want that one."

Each month had a theme, and among the month, a pattern was formed by the order the stickers were placed. Remarkably, Leo remembered what sticker was needed the following day. Considering Leo was unable to read during his lifetime, it amazed me when he would initiate certain details like it being Columbus Day after I told him the month and date. I am not sure how he even knew such a holiday; it wasn't one that was discussed on a regular basis.

Leo then took his attention from the calendar and fixed his eyes on his pet gecko, T-Rex. "Check his water." With no time wasted in between, he said, "How many crickets are left? Please turn on his heat lamp." These repetitive statements rolled off his lips from the thoughts in his mind hours prior to them happening. Leo had an amazing ability to know how long the lamp should be on and, most days, he told us to turn it off at approximately the same time. His internal clock was very in tune. This also kept me on my toes for all the required medications that were needed throughout the day. He honestly was so in touch with his pain that he knew almost to the minute when the next medication was going to be administered.

Leo was 100% dependent on our care. Throughout the day, he would need to be changed. Leo humbled himself and graciously accepted our assistance. Reclining the hospital bed to a flat position, I began to attend to his needs. Things became even more personal in the final years when bowel movements were a struggle and didn't always happen on their own. A system called digital disimpaction was needed. We assisted him with not only occasional laxatives to help soften his stool, but also inserting our gloved finger into his rectum to assist in extracting the stool.

This procedure took respect for the body to a whole other level as I watched my child not be able to perform this on his own. Due to his lack of movement and core strength, low liquid intake, and the multiple medications he took, Leo's body had so many elements fighting against nature's natural way.

Once fully attended to, I sat him upright on my lap to relieve him from any pressure points. Those moments when the two of us would be eye to eye, Leo embraced in my arms, were the moments I treasured most. He would look at me with such love. Although his verbal communication was limited by the tension his lips held, I felt his appreciation for his care when our eyes locked.

Leo spoke softly, "Hi, Momma."

These precious words were never taken for granted, especially after they were stripped from his abilities for months. I gently fed my hand up under his shirt and fanned it in and out, releasing the heat that was held in from hours on his backside upon a vinyl air mattress where little circulation occurred.

"How does that feel?" I asked attentively.

"Good." His head shifted and gently rested upon my shoulder, releasing a heavy sigh.

"Do you think some ice cream would help you cool down?"

There was only one brand of ice cream that he wanted. There was a particular occurrence when I ran out of his favorite type and tried to pass off another brand to him. I approached his bedside and he peered into the bowl.

"This is different."

"How do you know that? You haven't even tasted it yet." He continued to peer into the bowl. "Let's just try a bite."

Leo opened up his mouth as I took the spoonful and laid it upon his tongue. He begrudgingly swallowed and gurgled.

"This is different." You truly couldn't fool him. He somehow just knew.

For safety purposes, it was best to stick to foods that didn't require a lot of chewing. This once again depended on his strength and the muscles utilized to swallow safely. Surprisingly, Leo was aware of the days things just worked better. On those days, he would capitalize on enjoying some of his favorites like chicken nuggets. Some of my favorite memories are from the days when I could go through the drive-thru, order one happy meal, and Leo would enjoy the nuggets while Oliver indulged on the fries.

Leo's menu consisted mostly of soft foods such as: mashed potatoes, boost pudding, applesauce, and ice cream. Leo was so keen on details.

In addition to juggling ways to feed Leo, creative measures had to be taken to hydrate him in a variety of forms. Even though the feeding tube was removed, Leo still had good and bad days with muscle control. We would watch each attempt at eating and drinking attentively so he wouldn't aspirate. We needed to avoid dehydration, and help keep his digestive system moving properly, considering his limited movement. We administered fluid to him by spoon, straw, syringe, sipping from a cup, and even what I would like to call the pelican method.

I would say, "Open up, Leo!" and gently fill in the floor palate of his mouth. The muscle strength and struggle he was facing in that moment determined the way we needed to make things work. He wasn't always able to suck from a straw, but boy was he proud when he could do things on his own.

Leo wasn't always thrilled about having to drink, and these moments were more frustrating each time we "forced" his mouth open. He would usually rebut this attempt by clenching his jaw or allowing the fluid to fill his mouth, but then release it from his palate onto his shirt. We tried to encourage him.

"Come on, Leo, you need to drink."

This was when his true colors of being both Italian and German would surface with a stubborn response of either the silent treatment and looking away from us, or a strong, "No!"

Bath days were often tied into haircuts and both presented challenges. Sometimes Leo would request a sponge bath, but the reality of it was he was a teenage boy and teenage boys can get stinky. Baths were essential, and they entailed me first going into the bathroom and getting the bath chair all set up and properly placed at the center. All the needed supplies were collected within easy access. In addition to the bath preparations, I made sure the bed was ready with blankets and towels so that when Leo was finished, he could be wrapped quickly and warmed up. Once everything was in place, I would get Leo stripped down.

"Are you ready?"

"Yeah," he released with a whimper.

I gently picked up his naked body and carried him to the bath chair.

"Be careful," he would say. His tailbone was so exposed, protruding from his bottom with little padding, making any sliding motion turn into a painful experience.

Turning on the water, I would begin at his toes which was a good place to ease into the situation. Goosebumps would cover his frame as he expressed it was too cold. Adjusting the temperature, I would begin once more. He loved the water sprinkling over him and getting the soap-suds all lathered up.

"How does that feel?"

Sometimes, it was expressed better through his smile and eyes, but he would almost always reply, "Good."

He knew what was coming next. The part where the water was drained and his body became cold. Even though he was refreshed and renewed, he expressed his frigid concerns.

"Hurry. Cold."

I slid one arm under his knees and the other under his neck. I cradled him close to my body as I carefully transported him back to the bed. There, he was wrapped snugly under the blankets and towels as I attended to his personal grooming needs.

"The lotion," he expressed as if I might forget. Leo loved to be lathered up with lotion. He enjoyed the gentle massaging, while I knew the importance of keeping his skin healthy.

Gently lifting his arm from the elbow, I would lean in and sniff his armpits. "Phew, we missed a spot."

He would giggle as the air from my nose tickled his sensitive skin.

After I swiped the deodorant stick back and forth, Leo would smile, saying, "Better."

"Do you want cologne?"

"Yes, so I can smell like Papa."

This was followed by teeth brushing which had its own set of challenges. While still lying on his back, we would attempt this task. His limitations for opening his mouth wide made it difficult to properly clean in an upright position, but we did risk his gag reflex due to Leo not being able to spit or swallow the foam building up in his mouth. This would cause an excess of saliva, making it extremely important that we found the right balance of the amount of toothpaste used to successfully clean, but not harm him if some was accidently swallowed. His basic hygiene needs took time and dedication and remarkably, during all his years, he escaped with only one cavity which stemmed from a period of time where Leo was physically unable to leave our home.

Dental visits in general were a production. The simple task of getting Leo to the office was exhausting on his body, and if I am completely honest, mine too. Once we arrived and made our way to the dental chair, I would need to lift him from his wheelchair and place him in theirs. Slowly, they would recline him back and proceed with the cleaning. On the one occasion that Leo required a filling, I was amazed, along with the staff, as he laughed during the procedure.

The doctor asked, "Are you ready to begin, Leo?" The drill began humming and Leo giggled. In my mind I thought, *He won't be laughing soon.*

Leo responded, "Yes." He opened his mouth slightly.

"Wider, Leo."

Somehow, he managed to giggle in harmony with the sound of the drill. I have no explanation as to how he could have found that experience funny, other than the fact he was trying to impress the beautiful blonde doctor.

With additional physical challenges, Leo needed multiple medications administered to regulate his pain. It was extremely important to make sure each of us who attended to Leo's needs knew what he had already received. Considering he was utilizing medications such as Lorazepam and Morphine, it was crucial not to duplicate. The chart we implemented also helped us keep track of when he ate, what he ate, and the number of ounces he drank. When you do a task repeatedly from day to day, it isn't uncommon to question if you already did it. The chart eliminated the guessing game.

One of the biggest battles we faced was Leo's ever changing physical structure. From head to toe, Leo's body progressively changed with contortions consuming his spine, limbs, joints, internal organs ... everything. Leo's body was compressed, pulled, turned, and twisted. He couldn't escape the changes that the disease dragged his fragile structure through. From a dull ache to severe nerve-ending pain, the limbs of his frame never found relief.

The change that broke my heart the most to watch was ultimately tied to all the other areas failing; the curvature of his spine. Leo's spine was out of position for most of his life, but there was a moment that really stuck with me. I remember sitting him upon my knees. My eyes teared up as I traced my fingertips along the spine of his bare back. His spine was so distorted, like an oversized hook. An overwhelming ache consumed me as I retraced my actions once again to signify the truth of the pain his body suffered. His spine was so distorted and off-centered, it kept his head turned to the left. It grazed against his right shoulder blade and continued outward as it edged within inches of his outer body frame, forcing his rib cage out of position before curving inward, and finally winding itself back to the center of Leo's frame at the pelvic region.

The pain Leo felt from his skeleton being so distorted was evident in a pleading conversation that he had with Jesus when he was fourteen. "Jesus, is it my time to go to heaven?" Over and over, he repeated this statement. "I have a lot of aching pain everywhere."

"I am so sorry Leo." I held him close as tears streamed down my face.

"Please Jesus, is it my time? I have had enough." My emotions consumed me. I could not hide my sorrow. One of the hardest things to do in life as a mother is tell your child, "I love you so much. If Jesus is ready for you and the pain is too much, it is okay to go to Him."

Over the years, we attempted a variety of orthopedic options to help not only stretch, but straighten and strengthen his core, limbs, and spine. Trying to maintain some form of flexibility so that Leo could still participate in childhood activities, while also attending school for a period of time, presented their own challenges and often had us thinking outside of the box.

Whether in his wheelchair or in his bed, his body needed to be propped up and supported. Every inch of his body required attention to details. Pillows needed to be positioned precisely to support his needs. Finding the right height for his head rest on both his wheelchair and bed aided the comfort of the rest of his torso. The incline of the back support not only relieved the stress on his neck, but also avoided pressure on his bottom and hip flexors.

We attempted to use a Thoracic lumbar-sacral orthosis (TLSO), a back brace used for scoliosis. This restricted prefabricated mold helps by applying corrective pressure on the outer side of the curve while aiding relief on the inner side of the curve so the spine will gradually migrate in a corrective direction. This apparatus was cumbersome for me to manage alone. Trying to lift Leo's body while simultaneously sliding the device under him and into position put strain on him. In addition, the material retained heat causing Leo to become even more sweaty in his vertical position.

"Leo, time to put on your gladiator vest," I would say to make light of the situation.

This was quickly responded to with a strong, "No."

Remarkably, considering the years Leo spent restricted to his wheelchair and his bed, we managed to only encounter one bed sore on his tailbone which healed with time.

Leo's hands fought stability as one muscle group battled with the other, forcing his wrist to bend downward. This caused tightening in the tendons from which he found some relief while wearing hand splints. But over time, the splints appeared to cause him more pain, and he would express, "Off," wanting them removed. He was no longer able to fully extend at the elbow, making it difficult to get him dressed. We did utilize air splints, a double-walled transparent vinyl plastic pumped with air, which allowed us to stretch his arm and gain range of motion. This appeared to be yet another battle difficult to win. It was better to just accept, instead of trying to change. As Leo's physical condition failed more, we found it was just a better solution to cover him with blankets instead of going through the stress of getting him dressed on the days we remained home.

Surprisingly, with so many obstacles within Leo's body, his legs remained straight. Yet, both of his ankles dropped, leaving his feet to hang forward. This caused a great deal of pain if they were left unsupported. We solved this initially by having Leo wear soft supportive footies, but as time passed, and Leo desired less confinement, we opted to use a rolled-up blanket under the arches of his feet for support. We also attempted a procedure called serial casting. With the use of ankle foot orthosis (AFO), we attempted to stretch and support Leo's feet to an obtainable position. Then casting Leo's feet helped correct the positioning of his ankles. This was done over a period of about four weeks, but the illness conquered, defeating the results.

Leo's hip flexors were extremely tight, leaving him without the ability to straddle anything too wide. Even lifting him, and supporting him upon my hip, became a challenge which also became more difficult as his core strength declined. We were extremely limited in the ways to improve this portion of his condition. Stretching, massages, and sessions with his healer provided the most relief.

We capitalized on the enjoyment that massages brought Leo, and sought the assistance of an in-home massage therapist. The amount of excruciating pain that Leo was enduring daily was painful to watch, and I can only imagine what it felt like to be held within the pain. Tony and I were willing to find and provide ways of relief, even if it was only for precious moments. Leo fully embraced these sessions, and often became irritable with me if I spoke too long to her prior to getting started.

With the use of a portable massage table, we transformed our bedroom into a temporary escape. Soft music played in the background as Leo was all buttered up with lotion, releasing the tension that consumed him. During these one-hour periods, Leo was relaxed. He would often express moans of satisfied pleasure from his body releasing its pain. It was hard to actually disturb him and even more difficult to pick up his limp slippery body to remove him from her table. The long-term results didn't last long, but the hour of relief was definitely worth it.

Even though Leo's body worked uniquely, it didn't relieve him from the hormonal rage of a normal young teenage boy. Innocent at his core, the pleasant things of life still have their allure. I was so happy to see my son become a teenager that I forgot what comes with that package. Even though I had gone through puberty with two sons prior, it had been over a decade since I had to deal with it. Luckily for me, Leo was easier to manage and required less correcting than my two older boys. I still remember the first time Matthew's girlfriend came to his football game in middle school, and all the attention he received from girls in sixth grade. The Italian blood in Matthew had him mature early, with a cast of a mustache sitting upon his lip. Trent was so engrossed in hockey, yet I often overheard the whispers of girls in the stands, unaware of me being his mother, ogling over his handsome presence.

I laughed at the memories as the tires of my vehicle rolled over the pavement in the driveway. We navigated a few turns on the back roads before we entered the on-ramp that stretched out across the hour-long freeway drive from our home to the healer for an appointment. Leo asked me on one occasion to address something after the song ended on the radio.

"I have some questions about sex."

"What do you want to know?" The lack of maturity of his face made it hard to believe that these thoughts crossed his mind.

"I want to ask Ray."

"Don't you think that Mommy can answer?"

"No," he stated, exhibiting zero confidence in my ability.

"Okay then." My pride was damaged a bit, but I knew not to ask anything more.

We pulled up to the office, a beautiful white home, with curbside appeal, nestled on a quiet city block. I parked the car, walked around to the passenger side, and opened the door. It swung open, exposing Leo, smiling from his car seat. Unbuckling him carefully, I cradled him in my arms and carried him down the sidewalk. I then walked up five stairs to the landing. I exhaled as I reached the porch and adjusted him in my arms. I struggled to reach for the door, but eventually found the knob.

Leo yelled out, "Hello, Dr. Ray."

Ray turned and smiled before finishing up with a prior patient. I laid Leo down on the couch. I was shocked at how eagerly Leo greeted him upon arrival.

I whispered, "*Shhh*, Ray is helping someone else."

Patiently, Leo waited. He heard the door open as they exited into the waiting room.

"I want to ask you some questions about sex, Dr Ray." Leo managed to get the whole sentence out, although it took time to exhale all the words.

"Alrighty, Mr. Leo, let's get you transferred and see how I can help."

"Momma, you need to leave the room," Leo stated.

Reluctantly, I left, respecting his wishes. The wall that separated me from the exam room prevented me from listening; I wanted to hear so badly. The time spent away from him felt like time stalled. The mature nature that lived within the frame of Leo's body was years beyond the frame that held him in. As I stood there, waiting for a cue to reenter, I remained confident that Dr Ray answered Leo's questions with respect, honesty, and love. I could tell from his face that Leo seemed satisfied with the session. I guess even when you don't think you have to have the "sex talk", you really still do, and should.

Leo's body wasn't the only one feeling the effects of time. I know for myself, my body wasn't always feeling strong, or willing and wanting to participate. My body endured a lot of challenges during the years of caring for Leo: strain on my back and my neck, compression in my vertebrae, not to mention emotional stress that led to body aches. I tried to remain mindful of the importance of my own self-care. I knew being able to give Leo opportunities stemmed from keeping myself not only physically strong, but mentally and spiritually strong as well. Caring for Leo, when all those items lined up, was difficult enough. Then there was the time when I was healing from a fractured elbow that really enhanced my creativity.

While out rollerblading, a thought entered my mind about how hard it would be to care for Leo if I were to fall and injure myself. I put that negative thought out into the universe and, moments later, I found myself falling. It felt like a slow-motion tumble. Here I was, two miles away from home, alone in the ditch, thinking *How did this even happen?* Then a biker rode by and stopped to see if I was okay.

Embarrassed by being seen, I managed to get myself back up to my feet, "Yes, thanks for asking," I replied. I rolled the remainder of my outing. Once I got home, the swelling continued and the pain enhanced.

This led me to be in a sling for six weeks. Thankfully, no cast was needed. My own daily tasks for self-care were a challenge, but trying to lift and care for Leo was elevated to a whole new level. I became inventive with ways to get things done. Let's just say there were teeth involved in changing Leo and many props were needed to get things accomplished. Somehow, I managed to get through it. Leo was so patient and extremely tolerant of my creative ways.

Every day was a battle of some sort. There was a sense of urgency to live a lifetime in only a moment of time. We tried to remain strong as we marched around and around in circles without any answers, but the ticking of the clock echoed in our ears as moments slipped away. And, as one clock's pendulum appeared to swing quickly, in the distance another clock began to keep time.

Chapter Twenty-Five

BLINDSIDED BY DÉJÀ VU

The years overlapped, and as one son continued his fight for life, we discovered yet another would begin his. Another life-altering moment was brought before my family which could never have been foreseen. At this point, for years, I watched Leo suffer and it weighed heavily on my heart. As I stumbled forward on my journey, I called upon the strength of God and Leo to see me through. If it weren't for what Leo had instilled in my heart, I am certain the weight of my own cross would have crushed me. Had the foundation of Leo's path not been pounded and stepped upon for years, my feet wouldn't have had steady footing to walk the path of my second son's unknown journey.

I found myself in a cold room. The hospital may have been different, but the same sterile uneasiness filled the space. Long corridors stretched thinly along the way like the smiles nurses portrayed with welcome. Lost in the commotion of the ER, I needed to make decisions without a moment to think. I heard phrases and terms that somewhat resembled those I heard before, yet my thoughts were clouded by the realization that my other son might now be stripped away from me too.

My mind had been preparing me for this moment while my heart raced to keep up. At this point in time, after a decade of caring for Leo, I knew the loss of a child was part of God's plan. Even though we filled each day to the fullest, there was still the harsh truth that Leo's light would be diminished at some point on his earthly journey. There was life in his face and in his eyes, but the physical twists and turns of his body still remained. All the while, Trent grew up in the same house, on his own path that became stronger like the forearms he regularly tended to. What I wasn't prepared for, as I was taken away from Leo, was the bend in the road within my sight, but that I was unable to look past.

It was January, the weekend prior to Trent's 26th birthday. He was out of town visiting a friend, when he noticed his equilibrium and depth perception were a bit off. He told me about it, and my first thought was a possible side effect due to his recent Lasik surgery. I told him to monitor his symptoms and keep me informed. The following weekend, I received a call that he had been in a car accident. This caused Trent's life to slow down. He now no longer had a car, but there were still things in life that mattered to him enough to borrow one. He loved going to the gym, and spent hours per day there, while also continuing his job as a referee for ice hockey. Later that month, while refereeing a NCAA game, he stepped onto the ice and fell. After one period, he approached the trainer, seeking out an explanation.

Trent explained his symptoms and a few moments went by as the trainer examined his body. Not having much time to spare between periods of the game, the examination was thorough but quick. After an uneasy moment, Trent was informed that it looked like he had a concussion. He was told that he wouldn't be able to finish the game. Defeated, Trent didn't feel comfortable driving home, so he spent the night at my sister's place, which was close by. I received a call from her the next morning, and she was extremely concerned.

"Trent is walking like he is drunk."

"Oh, that is strange. Do you think he is well enough to drive home?"

Her tone became serious and replied, "I am very worried about him."

"Okay," I instinctively responded. "Can you ask him if he thinks he can make it here, or do I need to come get him?"

Trent managed to drive home, closely followed by one of his colleagues, and I examined his posture carefully when he arrived. He still looked like the son I had known his whole lifetime, but I could see why there was cause for concern. His words were a bit slurred, and he drifted to the left a bit as he walked. I took Trent to his primary doctor to be evaluated.

"It looks like post-concussion syndrome. Most likely from the car accident."

I adjusted myself in my seat as I gathered my thoughts. "What do you suggest we do?"

"I would have him stay with you for the week to keep a close eye on him."

I looked over at Trent to see what he thought of the idea. His eyes widened by the severity of the situation, but he still returned my gaze with a slight smile. Then, he nodded and shrugged his shoulders, "I am up for whatever you think is best, doc."

At that point, I looked back to the doctor, my heart racing. "What should I be watching for?"

"Keep a close watch to see if any of his symptoms change, and if they don't get better, come back."

We returned home and things became concerning quickly. Trent was so off-balance that he drifted more to the left as he walked, and his vision and head pain increased. On February 17, 2017, I took Trent to the ER, but this time for a CT scan. Upon arrival, we were greeted by a rude nurse.

"I called ahead for my son to have a CT scan. His name is Trent Nienas."

"What seems to be the problem, sir?" Her voice was stern and without emotion. Trent looked at me with such confusion. He was unable to answer.

"He is having balance issues, along with head pain."

She looked at me and interjected, "I was talking to him, ma'am."

I felt my body becoming tense. "I understand that, but as you can see, he is not able to advocate for himself."

Reluctantly, she listened to me, and we completed the check-in process. I waited in the waiting room while they took Trent back to the exam room. I watched as he struggled to walk down the hall. He held the wall as he passed through the doorway and out of sight. When the nurse returned, her whole demeanor had changed. My gut instinct knew this was more than a concussion.

The diagnosis was serious. Not fully explained initially, but there was a mass on his brain, and hearing that Trent needed to get transferred to another hospital because the current one wasn't equipped to handle his condition, quickly made the situation real. He was loaded into the ambulance as I followed behind with my sister who came to meet me. The drive felt like hours when, in reality, it was only thirty minutes.

Meanwhile, as all this information unfolded before us, Matthew was still living out of state and Tony remained home with both Leo and Oliver. In their time together, Leo began to prophesy to Tony. From their perspective, all they knew at this point was that Trent had a possible concussion. Tony put Oliver to bed, and then carried Leo from the family room into our bedroom. He carefully adjusted the pillows, and turned on the star gazer machine that cast images of different color moons and stars across the ceiling.

Leo gazed up at the lights as Tony crawled into bed next to him. He rested his hand upon Leo's thigh, providing comfort that he was not alone. In the silence of the room, Leo asked, "How many days?"

Uncertain as to where this conversation was going, Tony replied, "How many days for what?"

Exhaling slowly, "The red truck?"

Tony had just purchased a new Dodge truck and it was getting prepared for delivery. "It will be ready in two days."

"Hmmmm." Leo said softly. "Trent should have the first ride."

"Why?"

"Hmmmm."

"I can put you in the front seat and Trent in the back."

Leo smiled and remained quiet for a moment. "Trent is having surgery for the tumor. The whole tumor."

"What tumor?"

"He is going to have multiple surgeries. Jesus is starting to get ready for Trent."

Tony held Leo's leg a bit tighter and just looked into his eyes unable to say anything, as the light show reflected off of them in the darkness.

"I'm sorry, Papa. Trent is going to Heaven." Leo slowly turned his head to the right, which is difficult for him to do, and looked directly at Tony's face.

"I have never seen this look on Leo's face before." Tony expressed to me later.

"Are you sad?" He stared at Tony, and waited for a reaction.

"Yes, that would make me sad, but if Jesus takes care of Trent, then that would make me happy."

Leo turned his head back to the center, and as the star gazer turned off, he said, "Jesus told me, I told you, now you have to tell Mommy."

"Okay,"

"Trent will have to leave his body in the hospital bed. It's his…" He tried to express another statement, but his tongue kept getting stuck. Then as the room was filled with darkness, it dawned on Tony what he was trying to say, and he listened one more time. "It's his spirit going to Heaven." This whole conversation stretched out in a span of an hour as Tony's thoughts raced in an endless loop.

Meanwhile, as I arrived at the hospital, the hustle of the doctors elevated the seriousness involved in Trent's case. One of the doctors approached me to explain what they knew so far. "Your son has a mass on the thalamus. This is located just above the brainstem."

I tried to remain steady on my feet. "What does this mean for him?"

"This is the part of the brain that is the gateway between the brain and the body. It controls sensation, strength, emotions, cognition, memory, and alertness."

My heart was racing, and my body felt numb. "What needs to be done?"

Referring to his notes in the file, he continued to be informative without a great deal of emotion. "Unfortunately, he also has a tumor blocking the flow of fluid in his brain. This is causing pressure to build, which is why he is having side effects. We need to place an external ventricular drain and a temporary shunt to alleviate the pressure from the spinal fluid that is pushing on the brain."

"Thank you for explaining," I took Trent's hand in mine. "Please help my son."

As I called Tony the following morning to share what I knew so far, Tony replied, "I already know. Leo told me." Then he informed me of their conversation and what he witnessed in Leo's expressions.

The procedure was successful, allowing a moment to exhale. As Trent was stabilized, his file was reviewed by a team of doctors to assess the best plan of action. Trent was admitted to the Neuro ICU unit at the hospital. My heart ached, as my thoughts tried to catch up. Once again, I found myself in a familiar place. Just as I presumed Leo had a sprained ankle and my eyes were opened to the reality of Leukodystrophy, I now stood beside Trent with the initial thought of a concussion, being told he most likely had Glioblastoma multiforme (GBM), brain cancer.

The shunt provided relief, and the combination of that along with steroids to reduce the swelling eliminated the headaches while we waited to hear what the next step would be. After three days of waiting, a plan was in place. A functional MRI was requested to map Trent's brain activity. It checked for the critical areas of the brain that are responsible for thinking, speaking, and movement so the doctors would know which areas to avoid during brain surgery.

Trent was then scheduled for an *awake craniotomy*, a surgery to obtain a biopsy of the mass. They made an incision across the top of his forehead from one side of his head to the other. It was successful, and the doctors were able to obtain the biopsy needed to test and confirm that Trent, in fact, had a GBM. This was a rare and extremely aggressive and terminal form of brain cancer, and Trent's status was already at stage three-four.

Shortly after this procedure was performed, Trent underwent another brain surgery. The doctors removed the temporary shunt, and it was replaced with a VPS (Ventriculoperitoneal Shunt), which was a permanent method to drain the extra fluid on his brain. This was an internal tube that stemmed from the ventricle part of the brain and ran under the skin at the hairline, traveling behind his ear and over his collarbone and draining into the belly.

Since the location of the tumor was in such a high-risk area of the brain, debulking or removal were not an option. There was no ability to attempt this without removing the essence of who Trent was, for the tumor lay in the hub of the brain that controlled everything. The only option Trent had at this point was to place a port, an Ommaya Reservoir. This would give direct access to the tumor from the quarter-sized plastic device placed under the scalp and connected to a small tube into the brain. This incision left a horseshoe shaped scar on the back of Trent's head.

Trent spent weeks in the ICU while he recovered. The process was physically exhausting for him, and emotionally draining on all of us. As a mother, my heart was once again pulled in different directions, trying to be present with him, and still meet the needs of the rest of my family. I was fortunate to have a sister who faithfully remained to cover moments I was unable to stay.

I was in complete awe of Trent's acceptance and strength during this transitional event in his life. He showed such appreciation and tenderness to those who cared for him, and looked out for their well-being. Despite the daunting news of his prognosis, he was eager to get home for recovery. It was laid out before us that this type of GBM brain tumor, and its location in Trent's brain, would limit his life.

We moved Trent from his apartment back home with us. When we initially left the hospital, things appeared to be shaky. It seemed unlikely he would be okay to care for himself. After a few weeks home, life moved in a different direction and Trent continued to make positive strides in improving. Day after day, normalcy came back to life.

With Trent spending more time in the house, and Leo's bed at the center of the living room, I witnessed a reconnection of brotherly love. It had been years since the two of them lived under the same roof. It was as if Leo took Trent under his wing to guide him through his own journey with God. Their bond grew while Trent recovered and spent time sitting by Leo's bedside, as they watched TV shows and movies together.

In his quiet moments, I could tell endless thoughts stirred in Trent's mind. He looked at me, and under the glaze of confusion he asked, "How do I fully believe in God?" He was processing so many details that were downloaded to him in a short period of time.

I turned to Leo and repeated the question, "How do you believe in Jesus?"

He turned his focus to Trent, "I am a disciple of Jesus, I have a special soul in my body. That is how I can talk to Jesus."

"Can you help me brother?"

"I will help you find your way."

I was in awe of Leo's words, astonished by his faith and his true connection with God. This response appeared to provide comfort for Trent and strengthened his own relationship with God.

When Trent returned home from college, after majoring in Biology, I saw my son who had attended catholic high school drift away from his relationship with God. It seemed he was acting out to some degree, and got caught up in several bad decisions. This behavior was difficult to watch and accept because we knew Trent's potential. His gifted mind, his athletic abilities, and his big tender heart were all being overshadowed by an unwillingness to move forward in life. As a mother, I obviously don't know all the ins and outs of the things he took part in while in college, but something drew him away from his belief in God.

What I then bore witness to was Trent rediscovering his love for God through the visions he saw Leo experience. This ultimately prepared him for his own journey of life and how he approached his battle with cancer. He, too, seemed to surrender himself to God's plan. I believe some of that was influenced by the love of his brother, who had nothing but the love for Jesus in his heart, mind, and soul. Over the next few weeks, their connection and conversations grew stronger, and Trent witnessed on multiple occasions Leo's transcending appearance while in training with Jesus.

Trent shared with me one night, while we sat beside Leo's bed, "Leo saved me."

I hugged him and asked, "How?"

"He restored my belief in God. After hearing and seeing what I witnessed next to Leo, I am confident in God's love."

"Leo saved me too. After what I have seen, I would be a fool not to believe."

Leo didn't add any further words in that moment, but his smile made it clear this was another mission achieved.

It had been only a few weeks since his discharge. As his incisions healed, the panel of doctors on his case presented their plan to Trent. Removing the stitches, they concluded it was healed properly and Trent could begin his radiation plan: six weeks of daily treatments totaling thirty sessions. Trent and I sat and listened to the side effects; it was a lot to take in for him, knowing there was no cure, just hope of prolonging his life.

The doctor spoke softly, "If you chose to not proceed with treatment, you most likely have about six to nine months. Even with treatment of radiation and chemotherapy, we anticipate you have less than two years of life remaining." This news was delivered to him one month after turning 26 years old.

His eyes swelled up with tears, and he turned his attention to me, "So, no matter what, this is going to kill me?"

My own eyes pooled with tears, "I am so sorry honey, I know this is a lot to absorb."

"Is this worth putting my body through?"

Trent was balancing so many thoughts as they raced endlessly in his mind. I asked for a moment alone with Trent and held him in my arms. "We are in a moment of trust, Trent. Do you want to trust the process?"

"I don't feel like I have another choice." The room began to feel heated as the warmth of our embrace escaped from us.

"I will support you no matter what you decide."

"What do I have to lose … well besides my hair and possible memory damage?"

Trent proceeded to move forward, and without any time to take in the severity of that decision, he also had another hurdle of trust to conquer, chemotherapy. This consisted of multiple treatments, both oral and infusion, multiple times monthly. I clearly remember the first time he held a bottle of oral chemo in his hand. The prescription arrived by mail in a bag with a skull and crossbones on it. He looked at the bag, held it in his hand for an extended period of time, and numbly stated, "I can't grasp the thought of polluting my body with this."

"I can only imagine how hard it must be," I replied with empathy.

"I can't fathom ingesting a product into my system that has been clean for so many years."

"We don't have a lot of options. I know it is tough to accept, but this is how the doctors suggest you move forward. Please remember though, I support you if you decide this route isn't for you." I reached out and ran my hand along his arms before bringing him in for a hug.

"I understand," he said tenderly.

"This is the plan of action your doctor put in place. We could look into a more holistic approach instead."

"It is definitely something to consider. For now, I guess I will follow the plan."

Trent was determined not to allow cancer to define who he was. He wanted to fight for his life, and no opponent, not even cancer, was going to weigh him down. Instead, he lifted the weight of his circumstances off his shoulders, literally. He found himself back in the training environment he loved. He even managed to go straight from radiation treatment to the gym. Although he had weight restrictions put on him, he looked at the doctor and said, "Are you serious? I was lifting hundreds of pounds prior to this."

"It is protocol, Trent."

"Maybe for some people."

They came to an understanding, yet Trent did push the limits. He was a warrior of strength, and it was incredible to see him succeed. As he reunited with his second family of iron men lifters, he inspired and motivated them to push their own limits. It was only a matter of time before he met his previous achievements of deadlifting close to 600 pounds and bench pressing 440 pounds. Life seemed to be normal.

He also returned to ice skating, which the doctors proclaimed he would never do again. As he gained strength and confidence, he slowly made his way back to the level of refereeing hockey games prior to his diagnosis and was welcomed by his colleagues. He began to feel normal within his abnormality. Then, about three weeks into his radiation treatment, he felt nauseated and became sick. When he got back into bed, he noticed hair on his pillowcase. As he rubbed the back of his head more began to let loose. He was shattered on the inside and didn't want to go anywhere.

"Mom, I am only 26. Why is this happening?" The physical reality settled on him. He was already coping with visible scars and now his flowing hair was letting go. "I know there is more to life than appearance, but this hurts."

"I am sorry, Trent."

"How am I ever going to find a partner in life? No one will ever love me." I was completely crushed. My heart ached at this comment. He just wanted to be loved.

Just like Leo, we hoped Trent could live his life being happy and put a smile on his face each day. Boy, did he ever have a smile. Between his piercing blue eyes and love that showcased across his face when his brilliant white teeth were exposed, he too had a way to draw people in like Leo.

With a positive mindset, and a health regimen any average person would benefit from, Trent appeared to be conquering the battle. After completing his radiation plan, his next MRI revealed that his mass had shrunk 30—50%. Things seemed to be positive, but later that month, he ended up back in the ICU with an infection in his Ommaya reservoir port in the back of his head. He had surgery to remove the port and had a PICC line placed to help him receive antibiotics to treat the infection.

With the success the doctors were seeing from the combination of chemotherapy and radiation, they also wanted to introduce cyber knife treatment. So, in November, 2017, Trent underwent this high dose radiation treatment. This procedure used a robot to deliver a concentrated dose of radiation to penetrate the mass more directly while keeping the surrounding tissue safe.

It was through his illness that Trent found himself and, with that, came the realization that his life was not his own. He discovered he too was a vessel being used for God, and a bigger plan that He had in mind—letting others discover God's love as they watched how he accepted his path.

When Trent was diagnosed, he didn't skip a beat. He had just a moment of tears, and then years of only looking forward. In his heart, I believe Trent believed he was the case of discovery. Between his determination and the brilliant mind of his oncologist, the two of them felt a breakthrough, and possible cure, could occur during his specialized treatment. With laser focus, Trent looked forward and moved one day at a time, hopeful to defy the odds stacked before him.

Trent was faithful to his plan, kept his tumor stable, and remained steady with his nutrition and daily activities, which helped keep his mind in a positive state. His story inspired others and caught the attention of the local news station. He was showcased on a local segment called "Monday Motivation". Trent strongly believed that mindset, along with good nutrition and exercise, was the key component to extending his success.

As the weight of the illness sat upon his shoulders, Trent power-pushed his way through. With every rep on the bar, he cleared his mind. Seven days a week, two hours a day, he let his mind rest in the clarity provided by the iron stacked on him, denying cancer room to take up space in his thoughts.

Chapter Twenty-Six

THE YEAR WAS 2018

The prominent mountain rose above its surroundings. The steep flowing slopes were disrupted by sharp and rounded ridges. The climb was rigorous, but the fight was for one's life. Stabilizing his footing on the ledge, allowing a moment of exhale, a moment to recall all the events that had occurred within the previous year. Trent was in the moment of the climb, Leo in the moment of exhale, and together they tried to stabilize each other's journey.

The year was 2018, and it was time to capitalize on life's adventures. A month after the cyber knife was performed, Matthew and Trent flew to Miami (a Christmas gift), to watch the Wisconsin Badgers play in the Orange Bowl. Trent was not only able to reconnect with his brother from years spent in different states, but he was also able to enjoy time with a friend from college and his family. The days overlapped, and while Matthew and Trent were away on their adventure, preparations for a celebration at home began.

New Year's Day. Leo woke with a sparkle in his eye. He knew the day ahead was special, and that he would be surrounded by love. The excitement expressed was visible in his facial expressions and squirmy jitters.

"Good morning, Leo!"

"Hi." His body trembled sending a vibration across the mattress.

"Is there anything special about today?"

Cuddled in my arms he expressed, "It's my birthday."

I wanted to remain within the warmth of the sheets, but asked, "Should we get up and get things ready?"

"Yes." Leo's leg twitched with excitement.

Once the morning routine was all behind us, I asked, "Should we start to make the cake?"

His eyes grew brighter and said, "Can I help?"

"Yes."

I gathered all the ingredients and stood before the kitchen table, hunched over the large mixing bowl. Swirls of brown mixed with the spoon to form a rich cream. The spatula dripped from layers of creamy chocolate as I walked over to Leo's bedside, and then they trickled off the edge onto his tongue. The reaction jolted his senses.

"Is it ready to pour into the pan, Leo?"

"It needs more stirring."

"Do you want to help?" Hand over hand, I guided Leo as he helped me. Then I dabbed a little more onto his tongue.

"Ummm, it is ready." I poured the contents into the pan and gently placed it into the oven.

I continued with my party decorations when a voice from the other room shouted out, "The timer!"

"I hear it, Leo. Thank you." The aroma of chocolate filled the house.

"Is it time to decorate the cake?"

"Not just yet, Leo. It needs to cool off."

Slowly the house began to fill with loved ones. As they paraded through the front door, their attention went directly to the birthday boy. The house was full of energy and commotion and Leo took it all in as he was the center fixture of the gathering. He was the chandelier from which all lights flow through, draped from the high ceiling of the heavens. Little visits kept a positive commotion moving through the house.

Before Leo became fatigued, it was announced that it was time for cake. The cake was topped with layers of frosting, and coated with a variety of chocolate candies, leaving little room to place 16 candles. With everyone gathered around Leo as he sat proudly in my arms, we began a family tradition. Since Leo's third birthday, we discovered his love for the birthday song. The reaction this simple tune brought to Leo's demeanor is one that is almost hard to capture without physically witnessing it. Trust me, if you were one of the lucky ones to gather around Leo in this special moment, you would completely understand why it was needed a second time.

Leo's position changed over the years, sometimes on a chair, others on my lap, and a few strapped in his stander, but the reaction always remained the same. Complete and utter happiness. The purest form of joy overcame his whole body and he lost control over what little he actually had control of. In my lap, he would thicken with excitement as he threw his head back and erected his body straight out, almost slipping from my hands with laughter. In his stander, his joy would once again have him thrust his head back and since he was already stretched out straight, his strength would take hold of the stretcher and rock it to the point where we thought it would tip. Celebrating Leo's birthday was one of the greatest gifts in life. It was a moment when we saw the truest form of happiness through the eyes of a child. Whether he was two, or 16, the result was the same.

Just 10 days later, the celebrations continued. Trent and I celebrated his 27th birthday in Cancun, Mexico, along with my sister and niece. We wanted to capitalize on every possible opportunity while he felt strong and healthy. We went on a few adventures while we were there, but mostly it was a time of relaxation and recharge. In the sun we found peace, and on long walks in the sand we found serenity.

This season of stability allowed me to feel comfortable with a few additional outings. Not wanting Oliver to get lost in all of the commotion that he was living within, Tony and I decided to each partake in a special trip with him. I ended up taking him to the Bahamas over spring break with one of my sisters and my niece. This trip was more about adventure and less about relaxation. We engaged in so many outings, including swimming with the pigs, snorkeling with sea turtles, and swimming with sharks. This trip allowed me the time to reconnect with Oliver when so much of our life was being disconnected. Oliver's fun continued a few months later when Tony and he enjoyed a Raging Russian Boar hunt in the Upper Peninsula of Michigan.

Even though Leo didn't get a chance to partake in these adventures, he enjoyed the stories shared and experiences of his own. He attended the nationwide Tim Tebow, Night to Shine, prom event, an experience he was unable to participate in within his own high school. This was an annual event made possible by donations and volunteers for those with special needs. Everything was free and unlimited services were provided by those who gave freely of their talents and time. Each participant was given the opportunity to have a date (chaperone) provided, their hair and makeup done, choose from dresses that were donated, flowers, pictures, and a limo ride around the parking lot in addition to the incredible music and red-carpet welcome.

The anticipation of what lay ahead overtook Leo's body as he became rigid in his frame. One piece of clothing at a time, I began to dress his body for the occasion. He was so handsome in his suit, topped off with his red bowtie. As we entered the facility to celebrate accompanied by several family members, he was greeted by a lady who extended his corsage. His smile grew wider. Prior to entering the decorated gym of the local YMCA®, Leo was cheered on by the paparazzi as we strolled down the red carpet together.

"This is awesome!" Leo shouted as reflections from the flash lit his eyes with a sparkle.

"It is pretty awesome, Leo." I walked proudly with him as his date.

We enjoyed the photo booth and dancing for a period of time until it became too much stimulation. Then we waited for our turn to take a ride in the limo, followed by Leo's favorite part of the night. Leo just dazzled inside the ride with laughter and good spirits. That ride in the limo made his night, and it also made ours. He lasted only a few hours there, but the memory of the event lingered in his mind and continues to bring a smile to my face as I reflect on it.

Our whole family had an incredible reason to celebrate in June. Matthew married his bride, Valerie! This event allowed my four sons to stand together and celebrate love. With Trent as the best man, Oliver as a groomsman, along with several of Matthew's friends, and Leo stealing the show briefly as the ring bearer.

The heat of the afternoon settled upon us as we prepared for an outdoor ceremony. The location was a beautifully restored barn sitting on gorgeous grounds. Nestled in the woods, Matthew made his way down the wood chipped aisle arm in arm between Tony and me. Then, each of the couples made their way through the path. Trent glistened as beads of sweat poured down from his head in the extreme heat, and stood next to his brother after making his way to the front. A moment of peace filled my heart. Matthew found his true love, and Trent and Leo were alive to see it.

I saw Leo fight through a great deal of pain in our time together, but what I witnessed during Matthew's wedding was strength from a higher source to help him persevere through the day. Leo got dressed up and took his role as ring bearer very seriously. The crowd warmly smiled as Oliver lovingly escorted his brother to the front. Leo's face was radiant, like the sun on the leaves of a shimmering maple. He beamed with pride as shadows of light filtered through the trees, glistening rays of love off both his smile, and the rings that lay tied to the pillow sitting on his lap. Then a powerful moment hit me. There stretched out across the green grass, under a canopy of branches, stood my four boys united.

Valerie made her stunning entrance. Her pure, porcelain skin glowed in the radiance of the sunlight, only to be outshined by the crisp white gown that hugged her body. She was a thing of beauty, and she was the one who captured my son's heart. Leo giggled and cheered on the happy couple as they exchanged their wedding vows, shouting out a "Hurray!" once it was official. He maintained his composure through the pain and released it with a cry once he knew it was safe to do so. He smiled through pictures as his body fatigued, battling to keep himself calm during his inner storm and the scorching heat. Finally, he was free from the chair and stretched out in the dining room in the comfort of a lawn chair allowing his body to fully extend, relieving it from the pain that settled on his spine and tailbone.

Attending Matthew's wedding was one of Leo's finest last moments. With Matthew living on the east coast, we were pretty certain Leo would not be able to attend the celebration. The trip there would have stripped him of every ounce of energy. To make the situation a little more concerning, we were also facing the possibility, during the time of planning, that Trent would be questionable in his attendance as well.

This beautiful occasion was made possible for us as a family to all be together thanks to the unconditional love that Valerie's family had for Matthew. Knowing that Leo would be unable to make the trip out east, her family sacrificed the celebration being held in New Jersey and willingly came to us. Because of this beautiful gesture, I now have a final memory of my four boys being together in a sacrament of love.

The year continued to shine down on us, and Trent continued to beat the odds. Two months after the wedding, he competed in the Wisconsin State Fair Bench and Deadlift Competition. With abundant family and friends cheering him on, he managed to take first place in bench and second place in deadlift. It was an incredible achievement to watch, and it meant a lot to Trent to achieve the standings.

Prior to Oliver returning to school, to my surprise, another unplanned opportunity arose when Oliver was selected to play on Team USA for hockey, and I had the honor of accompanying him to Italy. Tony graciously offered to remain behind to care for both Leo and Trent.

As we prepared, I suffered from a series of vertigo episodes that stemmed from a concussion I endured the previous year when I struck my head on the frame of my vehicle. Keep in mind this wasn't just a random act of hitting my head. For some reason, my head seemed to find surfaces to come in contact with often. This occasion, however, occurred due to me hurrying to load pumpkins from the farm. Leo's pain had increased, and his need to be removed from the wheelchair escalated. I hit my head so hard that I managed to dislodge a crystal into the second canal of my ear, which resulted in vertigo.

This incident made it difficult to care for Leo. Simple tasks like bending over to change him, lifting him, and assisting in feeding were a real struggle. Even walking through the hallway became worrisome. There were times I would have to crawl to get around because my balance was so impaired. Through all this, Leo took on my pain and sensed my worry. He was so empathetic, which limited my window of opportunity to release my own heavy burdens.

I was alone with Leo one day when my vertigo was in full swing. I awoke in the morning and made my way to the kitchen to get Leo's medication from the fridge. I walked back to the bedroom, administered the medication to Leo, and then proceeded back to the kitchen to flush out the syringes. On my path back to the kitchen lay a large turkey feather on the floor. The same space, only moments before, where I walked across the floor and had nothing in sight. I picked it up, looked around, realized it was not the same breed as the mount we displayed from one of Tony's hunts, and found the event to be quite curious. I gently laid the feather on my husband's dresser, with the intention of asking him about it when he returned from his business trip.

Tony, being Tony, said to me, "What the hell is this turkey feather doing on my dresser?"

"I was hoping you could help answer that question for me." As I spoke these words to him, I could see, out of the corner of my eye, Leo smiling. I turned to him and asked, "Do you know where this feather came from?"

"Grandpa put it there for you. He wanted you to know he was looking out for you."

"How do you know that?" I drew closer to Leo and crouched down to his eye level.

"Grandpa told me."

My dad had passed away a few years prior to this moment and he was a big turkey hunter. He had several turkey mounts proudly displayed in his home from hunts over the years that brought him joy. Tears immediately trickled down my face as I felt the warmth of my dad beside me. The realization of my dad's presence, along with Leo's ability to communicate with him, was astounding.

Oliver and I successfully made our trip across the ocean in the comfort of first class. The treatment we received was incredible, and while nestled in our cocoon, we arrived refreshed and rested. We spent ten days touring northern Italy and Switzerland. The team competed and won all their games! As we traveled across the countryside, we were fortunate to have a translator with us to expose us to all the highlights of the country. With screensaver images surrounding us in every direction, I captured hundreds of photos trying to take in the beauty in which I was immersed.

Shortly after Oliver and I arrived home, our family came up against another giant. My mom was admitted to the hospital with symptoms of fatigue, weakness, and lack of appetite. After an extensive exam, the labs revealed severe anemia, indicating that she was experiencing internal bleeding. My mother opened up further and shared with the doctors that she was experiencing black stools which led to further investigation with an endoscopy.

After the review of her findings, the doctors discovered a tumor in her stomach along with suspicious nodules. A surgery was performed to remove the tumor which led to a very painful recovery. My mom became weaker, and her appetite continued to decline. My mom then decided, at age 87, to proceed with the recommended chemotherapy treatment plan to fight her diagnosis of lymphoma.

Everyone needs to make their own decisions in life, I personally was surprised that my mom wanted to proceed with treatment, yet we did see her rebound. Underneath all the physical pain she endured lay an emotional pain that outweighed her suffering. She was so lonely in the absence of her husband. Tears flowed from her like endless streams pooling into the reservoir of Jesus' love. Fighting to be amongst her children she loved, and drawn to the fight of surrender to reunite with the man she shared a lifetime with.

By October, Leo struggled with his own pain management. He was unable to make it to the pumpkin farm himself, but he could hardly contain his excitement as he gazed upon the pumpkins we brought home later that day. He knew exactly what he wanted to carve, a gecko, to show his love for his real gecko that sat by his bedside. Leo had such a love for this little creature and even though he couldn't physically care for him by himself, he did a great job reminding me to be attentive to its needs.

Leo worked hard poking the holes with hand over hand assistance as we carved out the lines that formed the shape of the gecko. He tolerated the weight of the pumpkin compressed upon his stomach because he was determined to do his part. In the end, he missed out on some of the traditions he grew to love over the years, but from the smile on his face to accomplishing the jack-o-lantern, you would have never guessed something was missing from his life.

When Thanksgiving arrived, we decided to take up my sister's offer to join her family along with some others. I am not sure what instinct triggered us to attend. Leo was still struggling with his pain, and we found that the less we moved him, the better he would do. An inner strength overcame him, and before we knew it, Leo was loaded up in the big red truck, revving the engine and laughing with his dad on the thirty-minute drive. All these steps took a toll on his body. From moving to the vehicle, transferring into the home, finding the right position on an unfamiliar couch, being stimulated by conversation and commotion, and then to once again traveling back home.

Leo did, however, discover his love for pumpkin pie. It had been offered in previous years, but always declined. At my sister's home, I took a slice of pie to Leo, as he cuddled next to Tony on the couch, and scooped a small spoonful.

I held it before Leo's mouth, asking, "Do you want to give it a try?" Without answering me, he opened his mouth. I placed it on his tongue before he closed his lips and smiled.

"Yum. More."

One bite after another, it disappeared with ease. Seeing how much he loved to indulge in this new pleasure, I took an additional slice home with me. The following day, to my surprise, it was missing. I turned to Trent and asked, "Do you know where the pie is?"

"I ate it. Was it saved for someone?" Leo began to cry uncontrollably. "I am sorry brother, I didn't know it was for you." That only made him cry harder for several hours.

I searched high and low for a new pie, stopping at multiple stores … nothing. I tried to find ingredients to make one … everything was sold out. Finally, a few weeks later, a pie was found, and the joy of the flavor brought happiness back to Leo.

No matter how bad the pain was, there was one tradition Leo never missed. This, of course, was his time with Santa. The local town hall held a very special yearly tradition known as cookies with Santa. Leo loved this event, and as time went on and we got to know Santa, we had special arrangements made where Leo arrived fifteen minutes earlier than the other children and was given alone time with Santa. This not only provided Leo an opportunity to visit without distraction, but more importantly it avoided Leo using energy waiting his turn and allowed him to sit in the sleigh immediately upon arriving.

These intimate encounters were so precious as Leo handed Santa his list and they discussed it together. Leo retained eye contact with him the whole time. He never lost focus, and pain never won over in these moments. Leo completely immersed himself into his time with Santa and joy came out on top. These tender moments also left a lasting imprint on Santa and the town hall. Together they created "Leo's Legacy". Families with special needs reserve a fifteen-minute time slot and get to enjoy time with Santa without the wait and distraction. This beautiful opportunity gave children who normally struggled to see Santa a stress-free environment to enjoy the experience.

Every year, our family tradition was to get a real tree. Our home would be filled with several artificial ones, but the main tree was real. Our home would be completely decorated and then on Christmas Eve, we set up the real tree and decorated it together. Depending on the year, we either went to the farm and purchased a pre-cut tree or cut one down ourselves.

Our final tree with Leo was a symbol of strength and determination. The day was cold but the sun was shining brightly. Leo's body was weak, but his mind was strong. He refused to be left behind and pulled himself together enough to participate in the outing. We drove about 15 minutes to get to the location and Leo bounced around reclining in the truck. Once we arrived, we transferred him into the wheelchair, which had recently been adapted to allow him to lay back more, and it had bigger wheels on it to allow for a smoother ride. There really wasn't anything smooth about being pushed through an open field with divots from tractor wheels, roots, and multiple stumps exposed. Aisle upon aisle, Leo studied the trees as Tony pushed him by. He remained focused to find the perfect one. I could see that he was getting cold; his body tensed up, but he fought through.

After an hour-and-a-half search, which was way beyond the normal timeframe that his body could endure sitting upright, Leo discovered the one that he called ours. He waited patiently as Tony cut it down, and loved being a part of dragging it back to the truck and watching it loaded in. From the comfort of his bed, he took pride in seeing it placed into the tree stand, and his body and mind could finally rest knowing that he accomplished what he set out to do.

The year ended with the same elevation of celebration with which it began. Christmas Day, the day Leo's eyes sparkled and shined with the reflection of lights enhancing his glow. We gathered as a whole family at my sister's home like many years before, but this time on December 23rd. Leo wasn't always strong enough to attend, but this year he made it and he was fully engaged. We placed him on the family room couch and allowed him to stretch out in comfort, surrounded by the social gathering from all sides.

This year was different from previous years. As a family, we were confined to a smaller area in the home which benefited Leo and kept people close by and in his view. He enjoyed multiple conversations with aunts and uncles, his grandma, and cousins as the evening progressed. He enjoyed some snacks, but he became fully invested in the experience when he heard the shaking of jingle bells and the deep, "Ho-Ho-Ho!" as Santa entered the room. Leo literally appeared as if he was going to elevate himself up from the coach. He laughed and giggled in between each "I" that he released and the pure belief of a child's heart beamed from his face as he gazed upon Santa leaning over him. It was so beautiful watching Leo encounter time with Santa.

The love for Christmas continued in our home on Christmas morning as Leo awoke with such excitement, anticipating what was awaiting him in the other room. True to character, Leo was more excited about the gift that he requested for his beloved gecko. I carried him into the other room and we sat on the edge of his hospital bed together with him in my arms. He peered over my shoulder as I explained to him that Santa had brought what he asked for—a bigger tank for his gecko to explore along with a larger resting shelf and bigger rock. He laughed so hard and stiffened his body that I almost lost hold of him. Although he was extremely excited about opening the rest of his gifts with his dad and brothers, nothing gave him the same level of joy that he found from his pet having what he needed.

Laughter turned to silence as Christmas Day progressed. Leo laid contently on his bed and seemed to drift off to another place as we watched a family movie. Leo was peaceful and when the hour came for us to all go to bed, we carried him into the other room. Tony helped tuck him in, said his goodnights, and together they said, "I love you." I climbed into bed beside him, rolled him to his side, cuddled close, and talked about the day. There was nothing more precious in my memories than Leo lovingly raising his eyes to meet mine as his face rested upon my shoulder and chest and gazed into my eyes to say, "I love you."

We spent the year on top of the mountain praising God for all that He made possible. The brilliant blue sky provided a beautiful backdrop to our view. Every direction we looked we saw beyond the other peaks and no obstacles stood in our way. Then, without warning, the ground shook and the mountain crumbled. We fell and lay amongst the rubble.

Chapter Twenty-Seven

LEO'S CROSS TO BEAR

We were now in the valley. The view was obstructed, and the direction was unclear. Uncertainty took hold, and so did the fever. The space that held celebration and laughter was now filled with silence and heat. I had been here many times before. There was a familiarity to the scene, but the outcome would not be the same.

When I placed Leo in bed next to me, the thought never crossed my mind that it would be the last time I held him close, my beautiful child. I didn't realize when he said, "I love you," before he dozed off, that those would be the last words spoken by him, and the last time I saw his brown eyes. A sound broke my slumber, and I awoke at 3:00 am on December 28, 2018. I instinctively checked on Leo's condition as he lay still next to me.

My heart dropped into the pit of my gut as I glowed a dim light onto him and witnessed the disconnect, his eyes slightly rolled back, his mouth ajar unable to swallow with ease as saliva built up, causing foam to collect at the corner of his mouth. The fever continued to build, and heat overtook his body. A state of comatose had crept in during the few hours since his last *I love you* was spoken, and I could see Jesus lay His hands upon Leo. I embraced him in my arms. His body grew limp as the heat took hold of every inch of his frame. I carried him into the family room and held him close, allowing him to hear my heartbeat. I then placed him gently onto the cool sheets of the bed, which had embraced him for so many years, in hopes that the coolness would refresh him.

I ran cold water across several towels and positioned them on his forehead and underarms. I curled up next to him in my chair and carefully slid my arm through the side rail of the hospital bed, like so many times before, but this time, I knew it was different. I placed my hand upon his chest. I sensed his spirit was preparing for the journey ahead. I felt the rhythm of his heart change, slowing down as mine increased. His breath labored, the inhales and exhales held less strength, and the space between them grew longer and longer. Life was escaping his body, little by little I witnessed him slipping away.

I walked to the kitchen to get some water to moisten his lips. I was halted in my tracks. A large turkey feather was laying on the ground in the middle of the kitchen, precisely in my path. The same turkey feather, which I had placed in my bedroom in a drawer, somehow made its way back to the kitchen floor.

I couldn't believe what I saw, yet to confirm what I knew to be true, I went to my bedroom and slowly opened the drawer of my dresser. The feather was missing. I knew then in my heart Leo's final moments were coming. I knew it was my dad's way of saying, "I will be waiting for him." Just like Leo was there for my dad in his transition, my father was now present during Leo's fever, and appeared to be playing a role in Leo's conversion as well. The movement of the feather filled my heart with complete splendor and left me in awe of the power of God's grace and ability to comfort me in such a time of distress.

With the feather held in one hand, I returned to Leo's side. I held Leo's hand, leaned in slowly, and stood over him. His gentle breaths slowly mixed with the air around me.

I whispered, "I love you, and if you are ready to fight, I am ready to fight with you. But if you are ready to go see Jesus, I am ready to let you go." He released a heavy exhale as I paused.

"Thank you, Leo, for everything you taught me and showed me about life. Thank you for opening my eyes to God's love."

I pulled back to look at my beautiful son and began to walk to the other side of the bed as Tony entered the room. Leo released his final breath as Tony reached his bedside. Simultaneously, as no more life filled his lungs, a luminous glow came over his face and all imperfections faded, replaced with purity and a glow of light as if the Holy Spirit made Himself be seen, and in my mind, I could hear Jesus say, "It is finished." In a moment's time, my life forever changed.

I watched the grace of God literally lift the spirit of Leo from the body it called home for almost 17 years. As Leo's soul reunited with God, I was left with a body that no longer held the gift of life. He appeared to be sleeping. He remained motionless, but it simulated a similar appearance I witnessed for so many years. His body was empty; it no longer held Jesus within it, and this emptiness filtered into me. In an instant, my son was gone, removed from the frame that allowed us to hold and love him.

The vibrant smile that captivated endless hearts, and the deep cocoa eyes that carried wisdom beyond his years all vanished. The warmth of his love remained within him as his body retained heat for hours. I held his hand and expressed once again my love and gratitude to him for the life he shared with me. I placed my head upon his chest and the hollow silence caused my eyes to swell up with tears. Then a coolness came over him that confirmed my days of holding him in my arms had come to an end.

I felt empty as I watched family members say their final goodbyes, disbelief as I talked with countless police officers who arrived on the scene, reliving the final moments of Leo's life. Although we had a DNR (do not resuscitate) in place, Leo was not under the care of hospice. Because of this, we had to place a non-emergency call to 911 instead of the funeral home. This added another layer of dynamics to an already heart wrenching moment. Even though the officers were compassionate and respectful, it took away the intimacy of letting a loved one go.

Busyness filled the room as stillness filled the bed Leo lay upon. Life continued on for all of those in our home, as one life ceased to exist any longer. There was a grace in God's love for us that allowed us to move forward past our pain and loss. It doesn't come easily. We had to make a conscious choice to allow Him to fill our hearts with His love to replace the void of emptiness that remained as Leo was called home. I felt like the darkness could consume me and bitterness could control my mind, but because God was a part of my life, He was able to reveal the beauty of the loss I was suffering. "We have come to know and have believed the love which God has for us. God is love, and the one who abides in love abides in God, and God abides in him." (1John 4:16)

Leo was a submissive servant of God while he bore his cross in life, and I was reverent of the moments of intimate conversation I witnessed. From this, I found peace, knowing that at his death, he no longer endured pain.

Almost from the beginning, Leo walked through the journey of his life with the knowledge he was going to die; his body in continuous battles of twisting and pulling, tightening and pain. He felt the weight of the world in his failing body, heavy and unable to free himself. He couldn't escape the suffering he endured on his journey, while well aware that it only led in one direction. There are few toddlers and young boys in the world, I imagine, that cope with thinking about their lives ending. Most run carefree in life, exploring the world before them.

"My time is getting closer." Leo expressed these words months prior to his death. For some reason, I sensed that Leo's visions would be changing roles. Leo would be at Jesus' side, and I would be the one he was coming to visit.

"I love you, Leo."

"I love you too, Momma." I absorbed these precious words into my soul as if they were nourishment to aid my ability to continue in life.

The painful experiences in life don't occur to bring us down and destroy us. Rather, they are tools to build the foundation of trust and belief in God to make us stronger. The continued chronic pain Leo endured kept his eyes fixed upon God. He talked to Him, and allowed Him to provide security and courage to cover his whole self, making it possible to continue through his days. Over the course of Leo's illness, I was often asked, "How can a god inflict so much suffering on a child and be a loving god?" God is good. God is love. It is the fall of mankind and our sinful nature that brought pain and suffering into the world.

Over time, I learned that although it is never easy to see anyone you love experience pain, pain is not a punishment, it keeps us running back to God and holds us in His protection, showing us it is better to live a life with Him, instead of a life on our own. We release our control into His arms, so He can help maneuver us through our decision processes. Pain is the beginning of healing from which character is built.

I believe the years of Leo's pain grew with purpose, and his journey was the path God designed for him, not as punishment, but rather for others to bear witness to the power of God's love. "So that the works of God might be displayed in him." (John 9:3) Leo was the light that glowed on all of us who surrounded him, which helped show the love of Jesus to those who had lost their way, me included. Is it possible God provided this beautiful gift of a son to me to help guide me while I was lost?

When this thought crosses my mind, I see it as both amazing and sad. It's so profoundly beautiful that God connected to me on such a personal level, to provide a son I loved so deeply. His presence changed the trajectory of my life. At the same time, it's all so heart-wrenching; my life was so off track that my son had to endure years of pain to open my eyes wide enough to allow my heart to feel the pain of God's love—and see it as a gift.

What a gift to know that in this life we will have trial and pain and from that, be led to a life of no tears and no pain in Heaven. Pain exists now because we need gentle reminders that God is close, and He wants to be in our lives. It is God's way of pruning us to be more like Jesus. When we eventually reach our final destination, we won't need pain anymore. We will physically see God before us and faith will cease to exist. We will no longer need to believe in what we can't see, because we will be seeing!

After years of watching the stations of Leo's journey, I realized everyone carries a cross. We all have suffering, rejection, failures, pain, and death. Leo's body was tested, beaten down and rose again. Time after time, I saw him fight to recover and then obediently relinquish and let go. I watched him regain what little strength he had to carry on, not wanting to let us down or see sadness in our eyes. I saw the illness try to make life unbearable. I was his constant companion and nothing in life weighed more heavily on my shoulders than the weight of his pain. I tried to hide the anguish in my eyes as his fever built and would not break, but he always saw through me, past the surface and into my soul. He provided the courage I needed early on and showed me his life had a plan and a purpose.

By no means am I implying I don't ache inside to the depths of my core. After all, I not only lost my son, I lost a piece of me. Our souls intertwined, making it hard to know where he began and I ended. We became one while I was his mother, his caretaker, his friend, his companion, for his full but very short life.

Loneliness consumed me in the days that followed. Everything about my life transformed in the absence of Leo. Prior, nothing separated us other than two different bodies. Our souls were so united; we felt each other's joy and pain, and our lives enveloped into one journey as time went on. Now I couldn't breathe. Our unity was so tightly fitted, our breaths had become one, and with one of us no longer filled with life, it felt as if I couldn't get enough air to fill my lungs. A compression rested on my chest that was so heavy, panic set in as if I forgot how to breathe naturally. It became a conscious decision to remind myself to inhale and exhale, training my body to work alone. Then God somehow reminded me, *You're not alone.* He remained with me, and because of His love, I found ways to keep Leo close to me, to carry him with me. Leo became a spiritual child I held in my heart instead of a physical child I held in my arms, and he now holds me.

I believe at the core of my heart, my children are only mine to borrow, and when the time comes, they are God's children to call home; allowing the process of loss to go on with acceptance and without anger. With this acceptance came the peacefulness of letting go of a loved one who never was really mine. He was only mine for a while to teach, learn from, and experience love with.

Leo was love, and after his passing, he continues to be love. He has come to me in the form of spiritual signs such as feathers and in strangers who have now become friends. With the grace of God's love, Leo continues to be a part of my life. This occurred because God helped to keep my eyes open and my heart soft, allowing pathways for Him to still enable me to experience Leo's presence in my life, even though he is now present with God.

We all have the capacity to love. It is a choice and at the same time, the most important commandment from God: to love Him above all else and to love our neighbors as we love ourselves. It all goes hand in hand, and if you stem every aspect of your life from the core concept of love it will bring you so much joy and happiness. It is a conscious decision, one I choose so many times throughout the day. Leo made it look easy—he appeared to love without thinking. It came so naturally to him because Jesus was his center of life. All of Leo's being stemmed from Jesus. Jesus was Leo's rock that he built the foundation of his life upon.

It didn't take long for Leo to make his presence known after his passing. His physical body was no longer visible, but spiritual Leo was everywhere. So many emotions washed over me daily. Every day felt like a wave; some mild, hitting the sand with ease, and others crashing ashore leaving me crushed and unable to breathe. Yet, Leo began to leave me little signs; encouragement, love, and strength for me to continue on.

There were days when tears poured out without warning as I slowly lost control of how I felt, and could no longer contain what bubbled up inside. A complete void of his absence and longing to hold him once again consumed my thoughts. I crawled into bed and I expressed how much I missed him out loud. How I missed his laugh and questioned if I handled my time with him appropriately, or had I missed out on an opportunity to gain insight on what he knew and saw. My face was wet with tears as they flowed off my face onto the pillowcase. I begged him, *Come to me, let me feel you close.*

I extended my arm out and placed it in the position that it instantly went to, the exact extension where my palm would place itself upon his thigh as we slept every night for years on end. Within moments I felt movement, I felt a force from under my palm pushing upward against me, causing my palm to arch as if there was a physical object beneath it. The force turned into a pulsing sensation similar to a massage chair stimulating a particular part of your body. I felt a wave of energy transfer from my palm towards my abdomen and this rush of flutter came across me. I have never experienced anything like this before. I thanked God for sending Leo to me and I pleaded with Leo to not leave my side. I told him how much I loved him and missed him and how grateful I was that he came to me.

I fought the urge to fall asleep, knowing he was close to me and I didn't want him to go away. The pulse stopped, a sharp pain centered in my palm, and leg cramps settled in my left leg and remained for some time. I lay there grateful for what I had just experienced, but at the same time sad I now remained alone. I began to wonder, what was the meaning behind everything I had just experienced? The pulsing under my hand made sense. My hand felt the pulse of Leo's life since I had slept in this position with my hand upon his thigh for years. This position reassured Leo in the dark that I remained by him; he would wake up at the slightest movement in our sleep over the years to see if I remained next to him. The sharp pain in my palm connected me to Jesus, imagining the suffering He felt as a nail was pounded into his flesh and the cramping in my leg reminded me of the pain Leo felt on a daily basis in his body. This moment of comfort, tied with pain, left me with a profound connection with Leo and Jesus showing me that even through our suffering, Jesus finds a way to bring us hope and joy.

My heart finds peace when I envision Leo beside his Master. Leo described the beauty of Heaven, and at every mention of Jesus, his eyes glistened and his face glowed with love. How could I be sad knowing he is in a place that held such wonder in his heart? He was my son, he was a piece of me, but ultimately he was reunited with his true Father. Leo bore a heavy cross during his time on earth and I am grateful he is free of his pain. His transition into God's loving arms was peaceful. I pictured him running free, spreading his beautiful red angel wings he earned in his training, soaring over all of us and continuing to shine his brilliant love upon us. I feel the presence of his love in the warmth of the sun and the kiss of his spirit in the blowing of the gentle breeze.

Leo left an imprint etched deep into my heart that will allow his legacy of life and the lessons he taught to continue to transform me. Just as Jesus left and gathered his 11 remaining disciples to the mountain in Galilee and spoke to them about The Great Commission, "All authority has been given to Me in heaven and on earth. Go therefore and make disciples of all the nations, baptizing them in the name of the Father and the Son and the Holy Spirit, teaching them to observe all that I commanded you; and behold, I am with you always, even to the end of the age." (Matthew 28:18-20) I feel like Leo, too, left me and many others to make the mission ours to continue the work Jesus did through Leo. The years of pain and suffering cannot stop with Leo's death. His story needs to spread the good news of God's love that even in hardship you can find glory.

Leo had nothing but belief in his heart and his actions made others believe. The strength Leo possessed within him was beyond the years of his age. This was not a physical ability, but rather a spiritual one. He trusted in God's plan, and as a result, beautiful things were revealed before our eyes. If we would have only focused on the physical limitations within Leo, we would have believed most things in life for him would be impossible. But his spiritual being rose above, shielded our eyes from what he couldn't do, and opened them to all he *could* do through God.

My life sometimes felt like a massive bonfire. As the logs ignited, the pile of ashes grew bigger, but I stood on top of it all and my flame burned brighter. From the ashes we rose unwilling to let the enemy steal our joy. "To bestow on them a crown of beauty instead of ashes, the oil of joy instead of mourning, and a garment of praise instead of spirit of despair." (Isaiah 61:3) Leo spent too many years training us to now wallow in pity. So, I said *yes* to moving forward. I said *yes* to opportunities that came my way, even on the days when I preferred to stay home. It wasn't always easy to be by people who felt joyful when I wanted to cry. But I believe for my own story, the year of saying *yes* following Leo's death, was pivotal for me avoiding depression, and kept me moving in the direction of God.

Chapter Twenty-Eight

NO TIME TO GRIEVE

I took a deep breath. The red light glimmered through the stained-glass window and was lifted by Leo's red wings. Held by both God and Leo, I gazed out upon the crowd and saw love looking back at me. How long had I been standing here? Then a moment of being in the present struck me conscious, and the realization of the journey I looped through my mind was my reality once more.

Pews were full of loved ones who adored my son and cared deeply about my family. I began to speak, strength in my voice, unwavering, honoring the hope that Leo's life displayed. I delivered a fifteen-minute recap of an almost seventeen-year lifetime, trying to pay respect and re-capture the essence of a young man who lived out a lifetime of love and adventure in a short time frame. There were moments of laughter, and moments of tears, as together we became one with the boy we all knew as Leo.

After speaking my tribute to the crowd, I managed to walk from the altar back to the front pew and join my family. Tony and I sat on one side of the aisle and my remaining sons on the other, with Leo centered between us. I embraced Tony and sat myself beside him. A beautiful ray of sunshine illuminated only our row, and the intensity of the light grew brighter as the service went on. As the sun penetrated through the variety of beautiful colors forming the images of the stained-glass windows, ironically, only a red spot of light hit perfectly upon the white cloth covering Leo's coffin, displaying the color of his angel wings. He was present with us.

The service continued, and the readings were so beautifully spoken. They delivered a message about how Leo lived his life, while the homily captured Leo's being to the depths of his core. As the priest blessed the coffin walking around it with the incense, a supernatural moment took place. The smoke hovered over Leo's body. It formed what looked like tiny white wings all coming together, and instead of dissipating, it continued to flutter over him. It was such a beautiful moment bringing to life that particular portion of the mass (where the angels come down to lift the spirit), and we actually witnessed it! This display of love captivated me. My eyes remained upon Leo as the light from outdoors continued to intensely shine upon him, making it possible for all of us to see the incense transforming in such a miraculous way.

This beautiful image that brought so much peace to my heart that day played out again two years later in Leo's playful manner. I was on a beautiful snowshoe hike with a close friend, one Leo had stolen the heart of. As we made our way through the woods, a calmness enveloped us. The sky was gray in complete contrast to the sunny day that lit the sky with Leo's light on January 4, 2019. This day, January 4, 2021, was slightly foggy as the air struck the coolness of the pure white snow. It formed a haze, as if God was wrapping us in a blanket of love, not allowing us to see too far off into the distance, causing our space to appear more confined.

There was stillness, no one else in sight, just the two of us alone with nature; or so we thought. The branches on the trees were coated with a stunning layer of crystals from the hoarfrost that had taken hold overnight. In addition to the blades of prairie grass managing to escape the weight of the snow, the scenery looked as if it were pulled from a Christmas card. God's masterpiece of glory surrounded us.

I stopped to take a photo of us in the midst of all this beauty. What was captured in the background took my mind back to two years prior, when I couldn't take my eyes off the swirling effects of the incense. Above us in the photo, a similar swirl of snow floated above us, forming a halo above our heads. We weren't alone in the stillness, and as we proceeded with our walk, a large clump of snow fell from the sky directly into the hood of my jacket and down my back. Leo made it known to us with his playful nature that he was there, walking by our sides.

As the funeral mass came to an end, I watched Leo's pallbearers gather at his side. Matthew and Trent took the lead with Oliver right behind them. Three brothers united with the help of several uncles; each held tightly as they let go of a piece of their hearts. As they took hold of him and escorted him out of the church, the reality struck me hard. My boys, who each took their turns holding their brother in their arms, now held a box with only the remains of what was life as they knew it, no longer alive. I looked upon my son's physical body for the last time. Never again would I hold him in my arms. Never again would I hear the laughter coming from his physical being. I felt my emotions bubble to the surface.

Tony and I walked behind our son's coffin as tears formed in my eyes and unbearable anguish took hold of me. As we passed through the doors of the lobby leading us to the outdoors, my eyes once again caught sight of the hearse. The back door swung open and the coffin slid in with ease, for it held such a young body. I couldn't bear the idea of the door then closing, as it symbolized this chapter of my own life also closing. I looked away for a moment only to hear it shut, and my heart was pierced once more.

I leaned into Tony for support, then looked up and saw my son's special needs school bus with his driver inside, lined up behind the Cadillac hearse. Out in the parking lot, I then noticed the Station One Fire Truck. Leo held endless love for buses and fire trucks. I was so moved by this display of honor for my son that my sister had orchestrated. I saw the lights go on and the siren filled the air with sound showing respect for Leo as the fire truck led the procession, centered by Leo in the hearse, and end-capped by the bus. The visual of this image leaving the church parking lot left me weak in my knees; I clung tighter to my husband for support. I couldn't bear the idea of leaving until the three vehicles were completely out of my view. Somewhere and somehow, I needed to gather myself as we reentered the church to comfort those who remained for the meal.

It was healing to listen to stories and feel the support and love from those who wanted to express more intimately how Leo had impacted their lives. What I wasn't prepared for was the emptiness I felt the following morning when I woke up and couldn't get out of bed. For as strong as I had felt in the days prior, I felt equally broken in that moment. For the first time in years, I didn't have a reason to get out of bed. I was lost and didn't have a purpose anymore. For years I had always attended to the needs of Leo, and in the week after he passed, I attended to all the preparation needed to plan a funeral. But in that one moment of opening my eyes, I felt as if I had nothing, and my heart was still heavy knowing things with Leo were not complete.

The crowds were gone, loneliness settled in, and my heart ached as the final step approached … Leo's cremation on January 8, 2019. As a family, we gathered in the family room, and sat in the space next to where he lay for so many years. I utilized my cell phone to search for urn options, and Leo made his opinion known. As I scrolled, I paused often and lifted my phone from my leg to reveal a possible choice to the family. Finally, I came upon a red one with silver wings and, as I lifted my phone from my lap, a small white feather appeared from beneath my phone. My clothing didn't have any feathers included in their designs. I had not stood up or moved since our decision-making process began. This feather appeared at that moment for a reason. Our choice was made.

Just days after Leo's cremation, my mother's health took a significant decline. She was battling her fight, yet her weakened state indicated her time, too, was coming to an end. Things moved swiftly, and only three months after my precious Leo left his body and left me in grief, it fell upon me again to have to say goodbye to a loved one.

This was the woman who raised me, nurtured me, held me during my times of a broken heart. She was my model who demonstrated strength and taught me how to persevere through extremely painful times. I wasn't done needing her, my grief was still so raw. Yet, I now needed to be there for her and demonstrate my strength in a moment of weakness, while grief consumed most of me.

With so many siblings, my mother was continuously surrounded with love. As we each tried to do our part to comfort and support her with everyone's schedules being different, my mom felt secure in her care and knew she was loved by us all. Then, the physical change in her became more obvious. My mother was a beautiful woman. A stunning head turner in her prime years. Baby after baby, she managed to return to her model figure all the way up to baby number 13, 14, and 15. Her body had been through so many transitional moments, pounds on and pounds off. In her final months, it was heart wrenching to watch her then voluptuous frame wither down to flesh covering a skeleton.

Her fragile structure hit me hard one day when Trent and I spent an afternoon playing card games with her. Trent embraced his grandma in his arms, and in his muscular structure, my mother seemed to evaporate in his grasp. The two of them had deep admiration for each other, a love that grew from the guidance of a grandmother passing on her wisdom to her grandson.

The night prior to my mom's passing, I asked Leo for a sign. I couldn't believe that I needed to go through this loss without him. Then, in the quiet moment when I silenced the world and spoke to him, I realized Leo was still with me.

"Grandma's time is drawing near, which I am sure you already know. Please send me a feather in a beautiful way to let me know that you all found one another in Heaven."

I put all my faith into the way I looked above as I spoke these words. I believed in Leo's connection to Jesus, and the angels, and the power of God. I closed my eyes and knew he was watching over me in my tender moment with his grandma. My body was flooded with warmth as a flutter of love stimulated my heart. I sensed that Leo always watched over me and protected my family, which brought me comfort.

While seated beside my mother and she drew her last breaths—this woman who Leo had adored in his lifetime tenfold—I felt like a sign of his presence just might be strong enough to make it all hurt a little less. Just like the turkey feather appeared for my dad, another sign would shine even more light in life, and all that it brought with each new challenge.

My mom passed peacefully, and once again Matthew would receive the call that it was time to fly home. So many flights, so much loss, endless heartache. Once again, we were in the midst of one loved one's battle, Trent, while another loved one's came to an end. As the funeral home removed my mother from the home where she had spent a lifetime, I closed my eyes to imagine her new home. At this intensely emotional moment, three white feathers appeared in my mom's family room as I sat beside one of my sisters on the coach. One rested on the floor by my foot, one lay on the couch next to me, and the third I discovered underneath me on the cushion after I rose up to say goodbye. Leo. My father. My mother. Leo sent me a feather for each, to let me know they had found one another.

Later, I gathered with my sisters and brothers to discuss the arrangements that needed to be finalized for my mother's service. My siblings turned to me, "We need you to write and verbally express the eulogy at Mom's funeral."

"Are you all sure?"

"Yes."

"I need to think about this." I had the honor of doing the eulogy, not only for Leo, but for my father as well. Uncertain if I had the strength in me, I went for a walk to clear my mind and to hear God's voice. Then, when I got into a rhythm, I found my voice and began to talk out loud to Leo.

"I need your help. Am I strong enough to do this for Grandma? Do you think I can do this?"

A cardinal began to sing. Ignoring my own advice about there being no coincidences, I thought for a moment that maybe that really was just a coincidence. A few steps further into my walk, a feather floated before me appearing from the sky. The way it drifted freely in the breeze reminded me of the whimsical way Leo looked at life. Sure, it may never know which direction it was going, just like Leo's health over the years, but it continued on the journey nevertheless. Stripped of the weight that once kept the feather in captivity, it now flew lightly, ignoring the ways that the world felt so heavy. I imagined the freedom of the feather as it allowed the wind to take it to places it had never been, in just the same way Leo's mind allowed him to escape the weight of his body that held him in place. This beautiful white feather floated past me at eye level, then up a neighbor's driveway out of sight. I thought, okay, that was pretty clear. Then, I spoke out loud again.

"Leo, I need your help to write this."

Then, an energy flowed over me as stillness grasped the air. Within moments of asking for help, the words just poured out of me! The clarity of the message and the flow of descriptive words were sprinkled with the love of an angel. I quickly pulled out my cell phone and began to dictate the message sent from above.

A week later, I found myself retracing my steps. The church was different, but the scenario was the same. Only by the grace of God could I stand before another crowd and deliver another eulogy for another loved one, especially when the wounds from my loss of Leo still oozed with pain. God held me on that platform and showed me His never-ending grace, which provided me with the necessary armor to honor my mother.

There were several more times when Leo appeared as feathers in the days leading to my mom's funeral. Each time filled me with comfort and love. The beauty of feathers continued to rain love down on me. My box holds precious memories, each one a moment I cherish and don't want to forget. Considering Leo is never far from my mind, it is no surprise that they reveal themselves while I am either mentioning his name or asking him for help. In times of feeling lost and looking for my purpose, a white feather floats downward from the ceiling, showing me he is close.

I discovered feathers on walks, driving in my car, walking into stores, sitting by the pond, in the airport, in the dryer, sticking out of clothes, at the gym, stuck in the Christmas tree we selected, floating down stream while kayaking, on the bike trail, on my chair, in my shoe, resting upon my laptop, inside a hockey rink—wherever I spoke of Leo or looked to him for guidance, a feather came to me. In happy moments and moments of sadness. Times of need and times of needing answers. Feathers drifted and appeared before me in places they had no reason to be. My thoughts were heard and my questions were answered by God in a message of love from Leo.

Sometimes feathers soared as a flock of birds in order for God to convey His message. I witnessed a magical occurrence in the sky on my way to church one day in March. The unique formation of this flock of cranes making their migration had me mesmerized. It caused me to pull over and take it all in. The whimsical freedom they demonstrated, as they danced in the air with one another, swirling from side to side, exchanging positions from follower to leader, was limitless.

This moment brought me my biggest blessing of feathers in one location. It heightened my senses to the point where I had a glimpse into the spiritual force that enveloped Leo in his lifetime. I continued to open my heart and mind to the possibility that our loved ones remain close by. I felt Leo lay his hand upon me as if extending his mission to me by seeing life the way he viewed it through his eyes.

My time in nature is about observation and being still. I am grateful for the time with God, and for the beauty He surrounds me with. We often must move quickly throughout our day to complete tasks. Time with God should give us a moment to pause and be intentional about the quality of time we spend with Him. So many signs go unnoticed when we fail to be static. Leo taught me this beautiful gift, and I am able to unwrap the beauty of it daily.

The life I watched, and the signs I continue to receive from Leo led me to act on the nudges I received from God. An inner voice kept expressing that I share further the ways Leo served God. Sometimes in life we may find ourselves loosely expressing that someone in our life is a saint. If we look at the definition of a saint, we will find a person acknowledged as holy or virtuous and typically regarded as being in heaven after death.

As I cared for Leo during his life here on earth, I couldn't help but see he demonstrated godly service, and over the course of his life, I noticed actions from him that appeared to set him apart. The qualifications for becoming a saint in the eyes of the Catholic Church do not come easily. In fact, they come at the cost of your own life, as death is the first requirement.

Not wanting to ignore the action I was intending to take, I set up an appointment with my parish priest to have a conversation explaining the life of Leo. As I left my driveway, a male cardinal sang his song and, on my way to the church, a cardinal flew over the hood of my vehicle. This beautiful occurrence happened so many times since Leo passed, but never once while he was alive. As I parked my car in the lot at church, another cardinal sang in the tree. Three cardinal encounters in a fifteen-minute period confirmed to me that this was what I was supposed to do.

After I met with the priest, we prayed, put up an intercession to God, and left it in His hands. I couldn't help but wonder, "Where does that leave me? What is my role in this now?" To be a true disciple of God, you're supposed to spread the good word, the Gospel, the love of Jesus. Knowing all this, I decided to trust in God to show me the way.

The next day, I experienced a beautiful encounter while out snow-shoeing. As I approached a wooded area going over a bridge, a large number of robins came into view. They were scurrying around, flying from tree to tree. In the chaotic commotion, there was peace. This was the end of January, in Wisconsin. Why were there so many robins? As I paused to watch the beauty fluttering around me, a warm sensation came upon me from my head to my toes, and with it, I was weakened. I looked around to realize I was at the farthest portion of my hike and uncertain if I was going to make it back. Tears began to stream down my cheeks and I could no longer control my emotions.

A spiritual force came over me. At that moment, I was no longer alone. God managed to find a way during this emotionally spiritual moment to send me hundreds of feathers in motion at once. I tried to proceed, but all strength had left me. I fell to my knees and sobbed. Eventually, I managed to get back to my feet. One step at a time, I made my way back to my car. It took longer than I imagined, but as I began to regain my strength, I found myself at the peak after being in the valley.

While this experience happened to me, the priest with whom I spoke had his own signs that God was at work. He mentioned to me that Leo's story is incredible; that the love of God has been woven into my family in the most painful, yet beautiful way. While he was at his office, one of the retired priests who had worked closely with Leo arrived. He asked him about Leo. At the mention of Leo's name, his face lit right up and he shared kind things about Leo and our family. Another priest then entered and said he met Leo during an anointing and knew he was in the presence of something special.

I now envision Leo soaring above me, free from his limitations, and find pleasure in his enlightenment. Prior to his own death, Leo shared details about his wing color. His love for the color red that stayed true to him in his lifetime carried over into the afterlife.

"My wings will be red in Heaven."

"That doesn't surprise me, Leo."

"They are big. Strong and powerful."

"I can't imagine them any other way. After seeing the work you have done here on earth, I know that God has big plans for you in Heaven."

"He does."

"Because of that, it makes sense that they need to be powerful."

Red represents vitality, the life force, passion, physical energy and strength. It also means courage and good fortune in life. I can't think of another individual who has demonstrated courage in life better than Leo. His name alone means courage, like the lion. Just as a butterfly struggles to free itself from the chrysalis, Leo struggled his entire life to earn his wings. He has been my good fortune in life.

Chapter Twenty-Nine

REFLECTION ON LEO'S LOVE

The reflection of time looked back at me as I gazed in the mirror. I saw the wrinkles had become more clearly distributed upon my face, where youth once lay. My eyes were clear and bright, and held a shimmer of hope despite the years of tears they had shed. I was able to see past the scared little girl that looked back at me for many years, and I now saw wisdom from the love learned from my light source, my Leo of hope.

We have all most likely loved someone or something. An emotional pull that drew us to desire. But love is more than an emotion, it is an action we are called to do. It is not always easy to love on this level. People often give us multiple reasons to challenge our ability to love them. Leo, however, showed me how to love beyond the emotions, he showed me how to love like Jesus, by letting me see how Jesus loved him.

When God created Leo, He created a source of hope. He planted a seed that developed roots that grew deep, spread outward, and impacted the lives of more people than I am probably aware of. I saw with my own eyes faith blossoming in not only myself, but also in so many others based on the work God did through Leo. I saw my husband, a borderline believer, transformed into a true believer. I witnessed friends who were not believers at all come to follow Christ. I may not have been around in the beginning, when God created Heaven, Earth, and man, but I saw the beauty of the creation of Leo, and I can say, as God himself said, "It was good."

In Leo's particular case, I believe his lack of mobility may have been a positive thing. Leo was immersed in his interactions; he couldn't escape them and react in a way that some of us may. Leo steadily remained in eye contact with me and engaged his remaining senses. His ears would hear, his eyes would see, my touch was felt when I laid my hand upon him. He couldn't walk away when a situation arose, he didn't slam a door upon its frame because of a conversation that angered him. Instead, Leo absorbed all that was expressed to him and received it with love. Other than a few occasions, like telling Tony to *Go to work*! he would give love in return no matter the circumstance.

Leo's presence was love. Being next to him, I felt the space around him exuding love. There was no room within him to hold judgment or resentment. His heart was filled and overflowed with the type of love many of us pray for. When I was in his presence, I knew I was everything that mattered to him. Even when he was engaged in a TV show he enjoyed, his focus drifted to me if I called upon him. Yes, this called for me to pause the TV, but the point is he would pause to transfer his attention to me; after all, that is what most of us long for, to be heard, to feel and to know we have value.

Love doesn't stop there, it isn't just about focus and attention, it ventures further into an act of giving. Giving of our time is the most valuable commodity, for we can give it but can't get it back. Once you release minutes onto someone, you can no longer retrieve them (except for memories replayed in your mind). For many years, time played against itself to me. I was always uncertain of how much time I had with Leo, while at the same time watching moments of my life go by.

In those years when life was more confined, I was unsure if people knew what was going on in my life, and sad about what I thought I was missing out on. Within those same moments, I realized that what I was doing with my time was what Jesus asked me to do: take care of the needy, the lonely, and those who are unable to do for themselves. My time, or so I thought, was drifting by unnoticed, but actually ended up being the time I needed to find myself and fully understand the purpose I was called to do in this world. I watched, I listened, and I learned how to love. I witnessed the most precious testimony of faith and love as I cared for Leo and saw he only held love for Jesus in his heart, no matter what he endured or how he suffered.

With Leo's limited ability to speak, it became clear that love wasn't just words. I treasured the breaths it took to express those three simple words, *I love you*, as they were released from Leo's lips, but Leo's eyes spoke more than his mouth. He held a glistening glow that reflected love back to me as I looked at him. I saw and heard his thoughts transcend through his gaze. He showed love through his actions, not the typical running into your arms that a child may express, but rather undenied attention with locked eye contact made me feel like nothing else in the world surrounded me.

The Bible says in 1 John 4:19, "We love because He first loved us." God sent His son to die for us, to take away our wrong doings, our sin. An innocent, sin-free man gave His life for our benefit. That type of love resonates with me. It is the type of love that made me want to be a better person. Leo came to me, an innocent child, a gift from God. I watched the love of Jesus shine through his eyes. Leo loved. Leo struggled. Leo gave all he had of himself until he couldn't give anymore, then he was gone. But Jesus never left and He still shines.

As I continued my walk along Leo's side in his painful yet beautiful journey on earth, I began to see myself transform. With every challenge he endured we found a solution, with every struggle he faced, we found a way, and with every breaking moment that could have brought us to our knees, we found God faithfully by Leo's side giving him the peace of His love in the midst of his storm.

It was in these repetitive events that my transformation became my conversion, the moment I decided to give myself to Christ. Circumstances that may lead individuals to turn away from God, blame Him, and become angry with Him, were the same circumstances during which I received Jesus into my heart and my brokenness began to heal. I witnessed things that were bigger than this world; they allowed me to peacefully accept our struggles, stop being concerned with what the world said was relevant, and start living the way of Jesus.

Initially, I remember being uncomfortable with sharing Leo's visions and his messages. I minimized them, not wanting to draw attention to his gift, afraid of coming across as boastful. I never wanted to give the impression my child was more special than any other of God's children. Then one day, God spoke to me and I realized I was actually doing a disservice to God by not allowing Leo's gifts to be known. After all, Leo had paid an ultimate price for the gift God bestowed upon him. One could say he sacrificed his childhood and life for the matter, to be a prophet of God's word.

Just as other parents share information about their children's accomplishments and successes, whether academically or athletically, I too began to see this was Leo's gift, his purpose, and his way of making the world brighter and better. Once I realized this, I felt the sensation of God's love come over me, giving me the ability to articulate the words and humbly deliver the message in a manner that was relatable. It was amazing to me, to feel and see God working through me, often giving me just the right words. Whether it was to send out updates over the years of Leo's life, or to now recapture a lifetime of moments into simple messages of love and hope, He inspired me to convey that we can all see how close God is to us.

Leo's work continues. I honestly feel him in all my steps throughout the day. I am still walking by his side and now he can walk with me. After Leo died, I experienced beautiful moments, moments I knew God orchestrated and Leo played out. These moments of Leo's presence have gone beyond just me. Leo seems to be present in the lives of ones I love, friends who have been by my side throughout my life, and new acquaintances who have now become intimate friends because of Leo. So many of them, who never saw or noticed feathers, now find them perfectly placed before their feet as they step along their paths in life, often appearing while contemplating a decision or looking for guidance.

A childhood friend of mine (who deeply shares my faith and has also endured many family hardships) had a beautiful experience occur while on a short family getaway. She took her two girls to Kohler-Andrae State Park in late August to soak up the sun before school resumed. Kohler-Andrae is a unique, beautiful place located on the shores of Lake Michigan. The natural landscape of giant sand dunes, miles of beaches, and clear blue water makes you feel far away from Wisconsin while you're there.

They had a picnic lunch, played in the waves, and collected many smooth rocks and stones from the shoreline. After some time, my friend decided to just lie in silence and soak up the sun. As she lay there, her mind went to Trent, and his latest news that the brain tumor he had been keeping at bay had new growth. Her heart began to race, and tears sprang to her eyes, as she found herself reaching out to Leo, telling him she knew he was near, watching over Trent and my family, and about this new unexpected path. As her thoughts continued to focus on Trent and Leo, she felt a calmness fall over her, knowing Leo was without a doubt hearing her.

When the time came to go, she walked over to the shoreline with her daughter to call out to her other daughter and her friend that it was time to pack up to leave. As they were motioning for them to come in, they both looked down and saw one large white feather with a few much smaller ones. These were feathers they did not see the whole time they were collecting and marveling at the beautiful smooth stones and rocks. Feathers. Leo's undeniable message that he was right there, by their side. Feathers, goosebumps, followed by happy tears. Leo was there.

As they collected their belongings and started their walk back to the car, my friend had an instant feeling of peace. She experienced this intense feeling that Leo, from the other side, was actually right beside her. This feeling stayed with her for the rest of the day. You know that feeling that something wonderful has happened. As mortals here on Earth, we have times of feeling such pain. But Leo reminds us there is something much bigger to help us through those challenging times.

Another friend of mine experienced a sudden onset around the same time. A stroke had snuck in without warning and, thankfully, her background in nursing gave her the insight to act on it quickly. During her hospital visit, anxious thoughts crept in, and an unsettling feeling consumed her mind. She knew she needed to refocus and regain a positive attitude. She had started to dwell on what she couldn't do, and not on how fortunate she was, considering she suffered only a small stroke and she received treatment quickly. So, she turned to Leo, remembering all the pain he endured, recalling the peacefulness that he maintained, and reached out to him to provide her comfort. Instantly, a calmness set over her and her mind found peace. Once again, Leo utilized his calling from God and a friend's prayer was heard.

One of the things these women have in common is their faith and belief in God. Each embodied an open mind, willing to seek and receive signs showing the Lord is present in our days, and He wants to bring joy and happiness to all of us. We all have the ability to step into the pages of the Bible, to find ourselves in the stories, to live out our lives and be the people God intended us to be. He wants us to be our own unique selves, to follow our own journeys, not trying to duplicate someone else's pages, but to create the pages God has in store for us.

My life seems dimmer now. Leo's light was so bright, it cast a glow on those who were near him. His light still illuminates objects that are associated with him. Even on overcast days, his urn has a reflected glow as it sits upon our mantel in the center of the family room. I have had moments when I feel an inner glow, a sense of him shining through me, guiding me. These moments come when I talk about him, sharing his love and journey with others. His love pours out of me, along with God's grace, giving me the words to show how through his struggle, Jesus was by his side, never once leaving him alone.

Leo had a gateway to heaven and I believe he lived in both realms simultaneously, at times connecting with both the human form of his job to fulfill here on earth, along with his heavenly call to train with other angels. His vocabulary was so limited, and his sentences were far and few in between, but the words he spoke were precise and purposeful. He was not acting on his own will, he was being guided by Jesus, for a greater calling.

Chapter Thirty

SOARING TO NEW HEIGHTS

Trent put on his singlet and fastened his weightlifting belt around his waist. He waited offstage, to the left, for his name to be called. His heart fluttered with anticipation. His name sounded off over the speaker and he began his approach, taking note of the weights stacked on the bar while feeling the weight of his illness in himself. He lay down on his back on the bench, his eyes first looking to God, then guiding his hands to the bar. He inhaled as his grip took hold and he briefly felt invincible, then reality opened the door and walked back into his life.

The world was in a state of stillness, things were shutting down when all Trent wanted to do was move forward. It had been three years since his diagnosis, and the days were ticking by. Weeks turned into months, and Trent felt the urgency to live life, all the while life was slipping away from him. We all have the same reality—death—but for Trent, this was put on a known timeline.

In July of 2020, Trent went in for a routine MRI and it was discovered that a new tumor had grown, about the size of a peanut M&M, right next to the existing one. The doctors wanted to be aggressive with his health plan, so they concluded a second round of cyber knife was necessary. With this news coming to the surface, a sense of importance settled in. Life had already been on hold for the past several months due to the pandemic, and we knew this was the time to not waste time. We began to look at Trent's bucket list to see what had already been accomplished, and what items we could try to make happen.

So, once we got the all-clear from the cyber knife that was performed in August, we began to plan our adventures. October began the whirlwind of events. One of Trent's friends organized a hot air balloon ride. The two of them floated across the skyline and embraced the peaceful flight as they were one of ten balloons taking part in the, "Lifting Spirits Around the World" celebration. They had a birds-eye view of the area in which Trent grew up, as if preparing him for how he would eventually see the world, looking down over us.

This adventure prepared him for what was to follow. My family was blessed with a beautiful gift that allowed us to escape to Colorado. I briefly mentioned on a Facebook post that Trent wanted to see the Rockies as part of his bucket list. I was contacted by a woman whom I had only briefly known. We became quick friends while taking a boxing class at a local health club about a year after Leo passed. I had only known her for a couple months when she extended an offer to use her timeshare so we could fulfill part of Trent's wishes. She saw how Trent's new developments shattered his spirit after he had maintained stability for such a long time, and truly believed he was going to be "the miracle" to beat this horrible cancerous tumor on his brain.

My friend's generosity ignited my flame. I began to research and pull together a trip of a lifetime packed with adventure that pushed me so far out of my comfort zone. But in the end, I never felt closer to God. We filled our four days with paragliding, white water rafting, hiking, horseback riding, and ziplining. Prior to the trip, I prayed to God asking that this experience generate positive and loving memories. God did not fail me; our trip from start to finish flowed perfectly in every way, and Leo surfaced on so many occasions.

As we prepared for our flight, I prayed to Jesus, *Please show signs that Leo is with us.* Again, the Lord did not fail me. Leo was present from the beginning to the end. Before we left, I walked in the backyard talking to Leo, and as I proceeded to place my foot down onto the patio, a feather laid tucked perfectly between the grass and concrete, perched between two leaves that had lost their hold of the tree branch and now were beginning to dry out and crumble. I looked to the sky and said, "So it begins, let's go have some fun, Leo."

Trent and I woke early, gathered our things, and started our drive to the airport. The traffic was light and the sky was still dark, but prior to arriving, the sky began to allow the sunlight through. Simultaneously, a fire truck drove by and both of us looked at one another and said the same thing, "Good morning, Leo." As we checked in and made our way to security, a lone feather sat in the middle of the hallway just prior to entering the security line. No coincidences here, Leo was ready to fly. I picked up the feather and placed it safely within the zipper pocket of my jacket.

Our flight was so smooth and we arrived early. Things continued to flow with ease. Matthew, and his wife, Valerie, met us at the Denver airport and our adventure began! We literally were just minutes away from the airport when we heard sirens and saw lights. We all looked at one another and thought, *No way is that for us*, and as we made our way to the shoulder of the road, the motorcycle cop stopped behind us. Welcome to Colorado, as he claimed to clock Matthew at 87 MPH in a 65 MPH zone. He was, as Leo would state, a jackass; no eye contact, and not even willing to hear us. There was no way we could have been going that fast, but we instantly shook it off and declared there is no way he is stealing our joy.

Our next morning began with paragliding in Glenwood Springs and as we stepped out of our vehicle at the meeting site, a feather rested on the ground next to our car. A serene sensation overcame me and I knew we were about to soar with Leo. Leo remained with us all day. A feather waited for us in the parking structure when I swung the car door open for our meeting spot for our white-water rafting trip. Then, a delicate pure white feather floated in the water alongside the raft down the river beside us.

That evening, it almost became humorous for the number of signs indicating that Leo was right there with us. We were walking down the streets of downtown Glenwood where we came upon a tattoo shop. We all stopped and I began to tell the kids how I was considering a tattoo in honor of Leo when a feather appeared. We continued walking and one after another, feathers floated by. Almost in unison, Matthew and Trent both said, "Leo really wants you to get a tattoo." To seal the deal, a fire truck drove by, and then the sound of the train whistle pierced the air as the train cruised through town. This was one of those moments when I felt like I was being smacked on the head and being told, "Can I be any clearer with you, Mom?" This all circled back to a walk I had by myself a month prior when I first contemplated the idea of getting a tattoo of the words Jesus and Leo intersecting with the "e" forming a cross on my left wrist that laid upon Leo's body as I sat bedside with him for years.

Feathers continued to reveal themselves as the days went on. You would think this was normal considering we were outside with nature. But the thing about all of it was the timing and the placement of the feathers, not to mention feathers are usually not just lying around, even in nature. Leo sealed the deal with his feathers when we arrived at the ranch for horseback riding (one of Leo's greatest joys). There amongst the gravel in the parking lot with not a single other feather to be seen, lay a beautiful feather by the front tire of our car as we pulled into the pretty open lot. It just happened to be where we parked.

Each of us had a horse with very different personalities, much like the ones Leo cherished over the years. Mine was extremely naughty, didn't want to stay on the path, and decided it would be fun to change his position in line along the way as we hit a 9000-foot elevation. Then, as we proceeded our way down, he passed the horses in front of him on a path that was only one-horse width wide, and when that wasn't an option, he would just venture straight down off the path.

One of the signs that hit my heart the most was a young man in a wheelchair who was trying to get on a city bus outside of our hotel. He struggled to line up his wheels properly with the ramp and proceeded to ask us for help. The first thing I noticed was the speed on his motorized chair was set at three which is high for this situation. So I lowered it to one, and with the help of Matthew, we lined him up and safely got him on the ramp. He laughed, giggled, threw his head back, and stiffened his body in a manner I had witnessed on so many occasions. The young man then said to the bus driver, "That pretty lady helped me."

Instantly, tears ran down my cheek. Everything about that moment, from the way he looked, to the way he spoke and reacted, brought Leo back to life before my eyes. My heart filled with joy. My years of caregiving allowed me to know exactly how to assist this young man's needs. Then it dawned on me; he was alone, functional but alone, and for a moment we filled his heart with joy. As we continued with our walk, we reached the lake and made one last final loop around. The night sky continued to grow more red and Leo's presence was felt by all of us.

After our trip concluded, I met with my friend who had given us her timeshare, and we spent hours talking about our trip, faith, life, and Leo. I filled her in on details of some of the miracles that had occurred over Leo's lifetime, and how he continued to work in my life and those of many others. I gave her a prayer card from Leo's funeral, and told her to talk to Leo to see what he could do for her. To my surprise, I received a message from her the next day. Shivers and goosebumps covered my whole body as she explained how Leo worked at her request.

She mentioned she ran some errands after we met and was thinking about, and missing, her mom. After reflecting on Leo, she asked him to please say hello to her for her. When she came home, she found a letter in her mailbox from a childhood friend she hadn't seen for ten or so years. Inside the envelope was a note from her friend that said while she was cleaning out her recipe box, she came across two recipes, in her mom's handwriting! She wanted to make sure she received them. My friend was so grateful for this tiny blessing and stated, "Leo is my new friend."

The precision of this moment is so beautifully orchestrated, a genuine example of the time continuum showing exactly how perfect God's timing is. He had to perfectly place the thought in my friend's mind, send the envelope to be received after I met with her to share Leo's stories, give her his prayer card, and encourage her to talk to Leo. God is beautiful!

The adventures continued and I embraced an item that was on both my and Trent's bucket list. I found myself jumping out of an airplane! I, the same woman who endured years of vertigo, claustrophobia, issues with heights, and flying in general, saw past all of those roadblocks. For the love of my child and with my trust in God, I geared up and went skydiving.

I had never experienced such freedom, complete exhilaration from the free fall. It's a feeling that simply cannot be put into words because it serves a different meaning for each individual. I didn't want it to end, but I was obviously grateful that the chute deployed, shifting the experience from floating to gliding, giving me more time in the sky to soar with Leo and to be still with God. My mind completely transcended to another place. My thoughts ceased from racing and I was 100% in the moment. This was not just an adventure or experience. It was a life-changing moment. It was a gift that put my life into perspective when I realized, *I am not just living, but I am alive to live.*

The following month, after we experienced so many exhilarating events, Trent had a setback. Our pattern of uncertainty continued as we chartered the waters of Trent's health. Like many people around the world, he too contracted the Covid virus that led to pneumonia. With his underlying condition, this was a major concern, and when he endured an extreme fever consuming his body, I once again found myself holding in my arms another child who appeared to be slipping from my life. Trent's fever remained between 101 and 103.5 degrees for about five days and things looked extremely grim. He was initially administered Tessalon Pearls for his cough, and both a steroid and inhaler to help with his lungs. The isolation in his room, and the inability to breathe, played games with his mind.

He called out to me one day while the heat took hold. I entered his room, and instantly saw the fear in his eyes. I stripped myself of all protection and crawled into his bed and held him. At that moment, I was more afraid of his fear than I was of contracting the illness. Together, we put it in God's hands and surrendered to His will.

"Mom, I don't believe I will survive the night."

"God, please rest Your hands upon Trent. Relieve him of his fear and let him feel Your armor of protection."

"It feels like the virus has control of my mind. I have an overwhelming sense of impending doom."

"Remember in your isolation, you are not alone. Jesus is with you. Call upon the Holy Spirit, let Him control your thoughts."

"Can you hold me and pray further for me?"

"Lord, I pray that Trent feels your presence. Father, please go before him, beside him, all around him and within him. In Jesus' name I command the enemy to leave his thoughts and renew his mind with Your love and promise."

Finally, the fever broke, and somehow Trent rebounded from fourteen days of suffering, displaying no lingering side effects. This way of life that so many experienced during this time of the Covid-19 pandemic, was the way of life that my family experienced for almost two decades. Uncertainty can lead you to a dark place, but trust and knowing God can lead you to peace, comfort, calmness, and a certainty He is in control. He wants us to come to Him in times of darkness and bring you to the light.

Through all these obstacles, we still managed to find joy. We cultivated our trust in God. We took a time when it seemed impossible to be happy, with external circumstances that tried to weigh us down, and turned it into our garden of hope. God planted peace in the garden of my heart, where He lives. Weeds grew there too, but the loyal Gardener worked to get rid of them. When I sat quietly with Him, He shined the light of His presence directly into my troubled heart. In this heavenly light, peace abundantly grew and my weeds shriveled up. As trials entered my life, I trusted Him in the midst of my troubles. My peace flourished, and my weeds died away. I was then able to thank God for my troublesome situations; I saw my life flourish more, and the peace that settled upon me outweighed the trials I endured.

Life is full of opportunities, but fear can hold you back from accomplishing them. As a family, we weren't going to let fear consume us. We weren't going to be frozen within ourselves and let joy pass us by. Instead, we put our trust in God and decided for ourselves; a life worth living is a life actually lived. Fear didn't consume us through all the years of uncertainty with Leo, and it definitely wasn't going to control us now.

As I climbed into bed on the night of December 27th, two years since Leo's passing, I replayed in my mind the events that had occurred since his death. The weekend had been a long emotional struggle, processing the absence of Leo from the holidays and everything that was transpiring with Trent. I extended my hand out and laid it upon the mattress in the exact place his thigh once was, and tears flowed from my eyes, for his body was no longer there.

I prayed to God, *Please let Leo come to me, send him to me in my dreams so I can gaze upon his beautiful face. Let me take in every curve of his smile, the glimmering of his eyes, let me feel his presence.* I awoke and realized that possibly my prayer was not heard. Leo never came. I grabbed my phone and took a deep breath to begin my devotional time.

Like so many mornings before, this time with God allowed my mind to be set in His presence.

I noticed a name pop up on my text messages. It was a friend I recently had the pleasure of meeting, one who knew of Leo's stories, but never had the opportunity to meet him. Although I considered her a friend, at that point, she was one I only knew on a surface level. We hadn't had time to develop a deep connection, yet somehow, we were connected. Her message struck me and brought me to remember God doesn't always bring things to you directly. Sometimes He uses other people to deliver the messages you seek.

She stated, "I just wanted to tell you that you popped into my mind this morning when I was praying. I had this image of you with incredible strength, like a fierce, roaring lion." She went further to say, "I don't know what that is about, but you probably do. Sending love and prayers for whatever you are facing today."

With our friendship still being new, this woman had no idea what December 28th meant to me, yet she trusted her faith and her love for God and followed her instinct to share that beautiful image and message with me. When I replied to her that my heart was aching, and that very day represented two years since Leo passed (and his name meant brave as a lion), I told her Leo provided me with incredible strength. He was the one who guided my footsteps to Jesus. I continued on by letting her know I had prayed to God the night before to bring Leo to me, and he had—through her. She said she couldn't believe how clearly and abruptly the image came to her. So, the moment I was awake and saddened to realize Leo hadn't come to me in my dreams is the same moment this image abruptly entered her mind.

She trusted God, she didn't waiver or hesitate to follow her instinct to share. She didn't second guess and, in addition to providing me comfort, she too was gifted with joy. God used her. He relied on her with such a precious message and she delivered. If we take notice of the events that surround us, be present and willing to be used by Him, the end result will fill us with joy. After all, it is within each of us that God lives. By being there for one another, sharing a connection between living beings, we piece together the parts of God and together remain whole. A void felt within could be filled by others if open to the vulnerability of the encounter.

I found myself, a few years later, having my own powerful dream. The clouds were shifting. As some dissipated, others began to take form. What began as a mass of cotton-like material was pulled and stretched into a lamb that emerged. As the image drew closer to me, I saw it changing. It morphed into the head of a powerful lion with its mane somehow managing to flow in the wind. Immediately, the image of the Virgin Mary appeared to the right and simultaneously, Joseph stood strong to the left. When it was all fully in focus, I awoke.

As the night came to an end on December 28, 2020, I once again found myself talking to God, expressing my gratitude for the love He bestowed upon me that day. I showed appreciation for the gift He gave me and prayed wisdom and words would continue to be gifted to me. I began to weep at this moment as I felt the weight of the call: a vision for myself, wanting to be used in a manner to spread His message, sharing the story of my sweet Leo and the way God used him to help so many find their way to Him.

I once again extended my left hand and placed it gently upon the mattress. Ironically the quilted form of the mattress humps in a way that slightly resembles the form of Leo's thigh. I tried to breathe through the tears, longing to hold my son in my arms. I felt heat under my palm, the warmth turned into a pulse. My inner self calmed and a feeling overcame me. I knew without hesitation Leo was beside me. He was still guiding me through this journey with Trent. The veil between us and the life beyond is sheer, it is so close you only need to believe. God wants to shower us with His love. Even in our darkest moments, He never leaves your side.

Although no side effects remained evident from Trent's close encounter with Covid, slight changes in his health transformed into a noticeable decline. Little changes in his grip and a slight catch of the toe during his stride on the left side of his body were the first to be seen. We were concerned that healthy cells were impacted while penetrating the cancerous cells in the brain with the cyberknife procedure. Things escalated rather quickly, which made the follow-up MRI in March of 2021 very confusing.

By the time the scan was completed, Trent had experienced significantly noticeable gait changes similar to drop foot, as his toe grazed the surface before being placed into position. There was weakening in his left hip and knee, which made his stride flow in an irregular motion. These changes were life-altering for him. He demonstrated heightened tone on his left side which caused his arm to hold in close toward his body, not swinging naturally as he took steps. These changes had me revisiting Leo's deterioration and what I had already bore witness to in another son. Simple tasks, the ones we often take for granted and do without much thought, required intense concentration from Trent. He struggled to grasp things like his toothbrush, or even shuffle a deck of cards. He was defeated by the reality of his life changes.

"Who would have thought, at age 30, I would struggle to put on my own socks and pants?"

I sat at his feet and looked up at him. "I can't begin to imagine how you feel, Trent."

He hung his head as he sat before me, holding his socks. "Well, what can you do?"

"I guess all we can do is trust in God's plan."

The scan revealed a decrease in enhancement, size, and thickness of the tumor. The extended growth from the previous scan in the fall of 2020 was almost fully diminished. What appeared in black and white was not aligning with what we saw in the three-dimensional world. His doctor was thrilled with the results.

"Why aren't you both more excited for this news?"

I leaned forward adjusting myself in the chair, "It just doesn't make sense with what we're seeing,"

"Well, that may be, but in my experience, the scan doesn't lie."

Trent replied with quick wit, "Well, my body is telling a different truth."

As we left the hospital, neither one of us could engage in the enthusiasm of the doctor's excitement. We both had the intuition that something was more wrong than right. We began to discuss what we noticed within the past few months, and the unsettling feeling in our stomachs weighed heavily on us both. Trent had experienced so many changes, subtly but quickly. I made an appointment in Madison with the healer our family had relied on for years. Both Trent and I struggled with what we were told versus what was happening.

During the visit, Dr. Ray laid his hands upon Trent's head and expressed, "I feel a darkness within you."

I asked, "What do you mean?"

Before he could answer, he left the room because the experience was more than he could withstand. He exited the room briefly to gather himself. After returning, he laid his hands upon Trent's head again.

"Okay, let's try this again."

"Let's do it," Trent replied.

His hands nestled Trent's head and he expressed, "A light has now filled the space that was once dark." He continued the motion, establishing a further connection.

After some time passed, Trent looked at me and stated, "While I was being treated, I was talking to Leo and Jesus."

"I'm so proud of you for trusting your faith! What were you talking about?"

"I asked Him for strength. I asked Leo to comfort me and bring peace."

Chills covered my body as I knew I had witnessed a beautiful moment. My takeaway from this precious encounter was that in that very moment, when darkness became light, the Holy Spirit came fully into Trent, lighting his way.

This pivotal point was when Trent found complete peace. All the uncertainty and questions ceased, and only acceptance filled his mind. The Spirit was always with Trent, but it now appeared that Trent had surrendered completely. I believe this was Trent's surrender moment when he opened every window and every door and let God fully in to take control. The session with Dr. Ray spread the depths within another son's mind and took him places traditional medicine could not achieve. His energy transformed, and where there once were twists and turns within his beliefs, intentional relaxation and purpose remained. His aura resembled that of my dad's after he saw Leo in the lights of his window. A natural ability to draw others in, like a moth to the light fixture outside the front door, opened, allowing others to share in the glow.

Just a few weeks passed, and Easter was upon us. Trent's safety became a real concern at this point since he slipped and fell down the stairs a few times. Trent's left arm and hand became weak, and at this point, he lost range of motion and he began to hold his arm closer to his side. As this significant decline took place, I was amazed by Trent's gratitude that his right arm was still functional. He kept his mind on God and was so grateful that his functional arm was his dominant hand. He struggled with the simplest tasks, and at this moment his independence left him, and being dependent came into play.

I remember vividly sitting on the floor at the base of this massive structure, so strong, so determined, and seeing my life come full circle. My role as mother once again moved into caretaker. Tears began to form behind my eyes as I pulled up on the tongue of the shoe and slid his foot into position. The right foot slid in with ease, but the left one offered no assistance, and the struggle was evident. I took the laces over and under and bowed them together, trying my best to keep the tears at bay. Trent rose to his feet, determined to not let cancer steal his love of the gym, faithful to his call of fitness, my warrior of strength.

The decline continued to escalate quickly, so we requested a follow-up MRI on April 19, 2021. The beginning of the end. The MRI revealed a single cell layer had formed. The tumor no longer needed blood supply, and it fully intended on using its "host" as its source of survival. Like an egg being cracked into a pan, the cancer traveled both left and right. The doctors prepared us for further weakening, which would most likely be followed by cognitive decline and affect his alertness, ultimately ending with what remained as permanent sleep.

I witnessed amazing grace and acceptance in Trent. As the news was delivered to him, I noticed his unwavering faith grow to a whole new level. He believed within the duration of his illness that there was a greater purpose for his suffering.

Without hesitation, he requested, "I would like to donate my brain to science."

The doctor replied, "There are additional steps and possible costs that would need to take place."

"If my diagnosis, my case, my loss of life, can help find a cure, then I want to proceed."

"Then, upon your death, your body would need to come to the hospital in lieu of going to the funeral home to have your brain removed."

Trent didn't flinch. "I would like to see this through."

"I will look into the protocol and follow up with you."

During the final weeks of Trent's life, I was strengthened by God's love as He bubble-wrapped me in His protection. Trent was radiant, and others saw his glow. I know with certainty that my son, a child of God, led others to Him. My eyes laid upon my beautiful son as his body, that once held so much strength, became weak, yet simultaneously his heart grew stronger in his love for the Lord.

The parallel events that took place transported me back to the struggles Leo's body endured. I couldn't help but feel at moments that I was reliving my loss of one son through the loss of another. Trent's body and mannerisms began to mimic those of Leo. The weakening in his left side left him with a crooked smile which led to his speech softening, becoming difficult to detect. The way he held his left arm close to his body as he lost control of movement reminded me of the limitations Leo also suffered. His gait transported me back to the days Leo would stomp around with the use of his walker, dragging his toes as they dropped, if not supported with an AFO.

What I saw day after day was Leo living within Trent; two of my sons, becoming one, physically and spiritually united. Trent allowed Leo to show him the way to transition into the love and comfort of Jesus' arms. With each passing day, tiny declines removed Trent's abilities until the tiny issues became massively noticeable.

I once again felt alone in these moments. Matthew was out east, desperately trying to get home, Oliver was preparing for finals at school, and Tony continued to help while he could and managed his job at the same time. Friends checked in and wanted to help, yet this was something no one was capable of seeing me through, except Jesus. The uncertainty of each day made it difficult to foresee with what, and when I would need help, often resulting in no one being around when Trent fell and needed assistance back to his feet. Or urgency arising, and not quite making it to the restroom, and then the need to steam clean and sanitize the space and redress Trent, which became more difficult each day while his ability to assist also declined.

Exhaustion crept in as the needs of the day increased. Our door felt like a revolving entrance of visitors, making our home a space of final goodbyes, not wanting to deny anyone their opportunity to say goodbye to Trent, and at the same time surrounding him with love and distraction from his own inner thoughts. Then, there came a point when visits were just too much for Trent, which resulted in a new plan: immediate family only. The energy continued to seep from me as I walked through the preparations of end-of-life events. We discussed funeral plans in detail.

"Mother, can you help me pick out a reading for my service?"

"Yes, sweetheart. Are you sure you are up for that?"

"I would really like to be part of it."

"You are so brave. I am sure there are verses that mean a lot to you."

Together we searched for keywords, like strength, comfort, and shield, until we discovered the ones that resonated most with him. We then repeated the process to find the Psalm and songs that touched his heart most. The following day he asked me for help once again.

"Mother, can you help me assemble my suit for the casket?"

I leaned forward to embrace him as I held back my tears. "Of course, I can."

"Which one of these green ties do you love best?"

As he held them up, I envisioned the events in which I saw him wearing them. "I like that one, honey," as I pointed to the one on the right.

"Me too. It has the most green color in it."

"Is this the suit and shirt you want?"

"Yes. Do I need underwear and shoes?"

Together we laughed, "That is a great question. Since the coffin is closed on the bottom half, I don't believe so, but underwear is probably a good idea."

"Yeah, probably not the time to go commando."

Trent willingly wanted to take part in the particulars of the planning, which demonstrated his strength and his belief. My heart ached inside as I gazed into his brilliant blue eyes that looked at me with such love, knowing they would soon become ashes contained in an urn sitting on my mantel.

This is life. This is death. This is everything about the dash between those two dates. So many people fear death. Death is the easy part. What we should fear is the part in the middle and whether or not we made it count. Did you live a life worthy of God's love? There is only one way to move on after the death of a loved one, and that is moving forward to Him. With every step I took in healing my heart, I was one step closer to a life of eternity with my Maker.

As a parent, I failed. I made mistakes and with that, I often had regrets; which is why it was such a relief to know that my kids have a Father who loves them. There is no amount of disappointment felt by Him, for God's love is unconditional and comes without limits. "Whoever confesses that Jesus is the Son of God, God remains in him, and he in God. We have come to know and have believed the love which God has for us. God is love, and the one who remains in love remains in God, and God remains in him." (1John 4:15-16)

Chapter Thirty-One

MAN IN THE ROOM

The weight of the illness became more than even a trained powerlifter could withstand. Trent's mind powered through when his body failed him. His creative nature of inventing ways to ensure his love of the gym did not escape him took him within weeks of his last day. A routine so embedded in his thoughts that he imagined he could achieve gold, when in reality, streets of paved gold were going to be his reward.

Although Trent's health declined, he maintained a level of fitness for as long as he could manage. And, he waited patiently for Matthew to make it back home. The embrace of my two sons as Matthew walked through the front door and came to Trent's side is etched in my memory. No initial words exchanged, just love expressed through a hug. Matthew seemed to want to embrace him forever.

As he pulled away from him, he looked into Trent's eyes, "Hello, brother."

"It's Matthew!" Trent expressed in his normal playful manner.

"I missed you so much." The tears that pooled in Matthew's eyes were of both joy and sorrow.

"I have been waiting for you."

Matthew shared his final walk with Trent. I drove them to the spot where they used to go off trail and do jumps on their bikes. They looked down the path and held each other. Not to exhaust Trent too much, we loaded him back in the car, made our way to the lake, and stood by the water, listening to the soothing sounds of the waves.

One of Matthew's most tender moments from the visit was on May 11, 2021. He accompanied Trent to the gym. Trent's body was weak, but his mind was determined. He adapted a new system of lifting to prevent him from falling and continued his regimen with what became his last visit to the gym. As if handing over the ropes to Matthew, he walked him through his own personalized workout plan, and the two of them shared an experience that was close to Trent's heart. These "workouts" at the end of his life were more about being with his second family than his normal fitness routine. They highlighted the warrior inside of him and inspired his fellow athletes to push through any barrier that was before them. Matthew later told me about the conversation they had in the sauna that day, where Trent reflected, somehow knowing this was his last time there.

"I can see people and feel like I'm in two places at once," Trent said as the room filled with steam. "I feel like someone else."

"Wow, that sounds amazing," Matthew replied. "It must be a connection you're having with other lives."

"It's like I can feel energy."

"I think that people are connected by energy we can't see. What do you see when you're someone else?"

"Sometimes it's like I'm split between time. I can see a man."

"That is very interesting, Trent. I wonder what that all means."

At that point, Trent stared straight ahead as they remained seated in steam. A few moments in silence went by before he broke it.

"Live each day to the fullest." Trent's words echoed as the timer counted down his final moments at the gym before his last departure.

At this point, previous four-mile hikes with Trent converted into ten-minute strolls, but the beauty of those few precious steps was so worth it. The sun on his face, and the true presence of him appreciating the beauty of God that surrounded him, taking notice of every detail as if he was trying to store it in his memory bank was refreshing. There was a very special moment just weeks prior to his passing when he paused mid-step on our walk. He shifted his eyes to the sky and began singing.

"Sunshine on my shoulders makes me happy. Love you, Grandpa."

"That is so tender sweetheart." His words were like a whisper of love.

Leo was present on many of our walks. Feathers were found in our path, and one was even present as we drove home from the bike trail. The windows were down, as we were moving on the road and a feather flew into the car with us! It sailed through the car, in front of Trent, and out the driver-side window after passing me. Matthew sat in the center backseat, and I saw his jaw drop as the feather drifted by. "Did that seriously just happen?"

"Leo, you are never far away from us." This feather appeared at a moment when we connected over our love for nature and provided us with comfort as we realized Leo would be with us every step of the way.

In the midst of these beautiful moments, things continued to decline. As movement became more of a struggle, we made the decision to place a catheter to avoid further falls due to the urgency to get to the restroom. This pattern stemmed from extensive doses of chemo, resulting in Trent's bladder having spasms which then caused the catheter to leak through the top of his penis. Although it kept us from avoiding falls and rushing to the bathroom, it caused him to have accidents through his clothing and on his bed sheets. With the decline of his memory, he was often confused and forgot the catheter was in place. Trent's mind still believed he was capable of getting up from bed to get to the bathroom, which led to two separate occasions when his safety was in danger.

Although I cherished the moments spent alone with Trent and felt a tremendous amount of strength from God, neither one of these precious gifts was going to be able to help me lift Trent from the floor. He was confused, trying to get out of bed to use the bathroom. In the midst of all of it, he pulled the catheter tube out and tumbled to the ground. It was 4:30 in the morning, and as I opened my eyes to peer at the baby monitor, I noticed Trent was missing from his bed.

I rushed down the hall to find the bedroom door closed. I clearly recall that it was left open before I went to sleep. I was unable to open it at first, as he had somehow managed to scooch himself to the doorway. He lay there on the ground, covered in his own waste. Dazed and confused as to what happened but unharmed. I began to gently wipe him clean, managing to turn him enough side-to-side to remove not only the urine that he was soaked in, but also his bowel movement which was most likely the trigger point for desperately trying to get himself to the bathroom.

The strength behind the man who could once lift unthinkable amounts could not aid in helping me lift him from the floor. I felt helpless, weak, and sad. I couldn't catch him before he fell. Even with the use of a baby monitor, I was unable to foresee an incident before it occurred, and in his weakened condition, he was unable to yell to me for assistance or even have the intuition to remember to do that.

My heart was broken. I told him I would keep him safe. I failed him briefly. Since Trent and I were alone in the house, I placed a call to the non-urgent phone number for the local fire department expressing that I was in need of an assisted lift. I was specific about Trent's weight and size and had to laugh when I peered out the window to see two female paramedics coming down the front sidewalk, both slender and petite in stature. Without trying to diminish their strength, I thought to myself, *Did they hear me when I described Trent's structure to them?* I knew in the back of my mind that they knew what they were doing, and moments later two men also made their approach around the bend of the front walkway. I thought, *Yep, they heard me.*

The paramedics came and beautifully and gracefully got him safely back to his bed. Trent became my 220-pound toddler. I couldn't turn my back away from him for a single moment. He was once again safe and unharmed, but my heart was wounded seeing his abilities stripped away from him.

Just two days later, I was awoken at 3:30 am by a noise that had me running down the hall once again when Trent was not visible on the baby monitor screen. I found my precious pumpkin dazed and confused, sitting on the floor next to his bed. He was staring off into the distance, gazing intently at something or someone, so I asked him about it.

"What are you trying to do?"

He paused briefly and turned his attention to me and responded, "Getting ready to go to the gym." His routine was so ingrained into his mind that he was unable to recognize his body could no longer do what his mind obviously dreamt of.

Thankfully, Tony was home this time and between the two of us, we were able to get him safely back to bed without the assistance of the fire department. Unfortunately though, we did notice the catheter was not just disconnected at the outer tube, Trent somehow managed to completely pull it out of his penis with the internal balloon still filled. He had to have experienced excruciating pain. Astonishingly, Trent had no recollection of the event.

One time could be considered an accident. Two times, it had now become a pattern. For me to get rest at night and know he was safe, we attached full-length bed rails (instead of half rails which were initially installed) to keep Trent from further harm. Trent's mind slipped and he was drifting between two realms. One he was not quite ready to leave, and the other was calling him home.

During these weeks of transitioning, Trent was tender and loving and so appreciative of the care he received. He greeted me regularly with compassion.

"Hello, young, beautiful mother, I love you, and thank you for everything that you continue to do for me." One day, he said to me, "You are way underpaid for the work you do."

Little did he know that I was being overpaid with his love, and the life lessons God was teaching me. But there were moments when his confusion took me aback. He became increasingly affectionate and loved getting and giving kisses. He asked for Chapstick to be applied and insisted that the kisses were on the lips (even from Tony). One of the times I leaned in for a kiss, he grabbed my breast. I pulled back quickly, startled by his action.

He said, "Is that okay?"

"Probably not." I tried to keep myself from laughing due to his seriousness.

"Why?"

I held his hand in mine, "Because I am your momma."

"Why does that matter?"

This conversation showed me how impacted his cognitive understanding had become. Although the incident made me laugh, it also made me so sad.

There was also a funny incident that occurred while I gave Trent a shower. His stability had become unsteady, and it required both Tony and me to transfer him as we began using a shower chair. Once we had Trent in position,

Tony asked, "Are you all good?"

"Yes. I will call for you once we are finished." Tony stepped away and, at that point, I realized I had the wrong catheter in place and didn't want that one to get wet. I looked Trent directly in his eyes and said, "Don't move, I need to go grab something."

"Okay."

When I returned, I found him standing with water spraying everywhere. He had pulled himself up to a standing position utilizing the cord of the shower head. He broke it, of course, because it wasn't designed to assist a 220-pound man to his feet. I turned off the water, sat him back on the chair, and asked him what had happened.

He quickly replied, "I didn't do it." His facial expression was so serious, truly believing the words he spoke.

"Well, who did then?"

He pointed, and with conviction, said, "She did."

I looked in the direction he was pointing and asked, "Who?"

"The woman in the corner."

His illness required a great deal of love and patience from all parties involved. I imagine it may be similar to caring for an individual with dementia or Alzheimer's, involving a lot of questioning, confusion, and a great deal of repetition and continuous reassurance.

Mixed within the confusing moments, Trent shared tender stories about the time he was spending with loved ones who had already passed. He was experiencing, more regularly, intercession, similar to what Leo had exhibited as well. These moments were so comforting as I realized he was growing closer to God and reuniting with loved ones we lost.

Trent spoke of my mom and dad and my brother, Glenn.

"I need a shirt and tie for a special event that takes place on Monday or Tuesday."

"You do?"

"Yes."

Could this be for the banquet in heaven? Ironically, he passed on a Monday, but the death certificate stated Tuesday, due to the time of his passing and when the hospice nurse actually arrived. What was even more interesting about this statement was that Trent would need a shirt and a tie for a Monday, the day of his funeral, (the combination he had picked out with me previously).

Leo also came up in conversation often. There was a beautiful transition that occurred when referencing Leo. Initially, Trent sobbed when he heard his brother's name. Slowly, as the weeks went on, Leo's name provided peace. I am not certain as to why this occurred, but Trent feared the thought of having to die alone. It seemed as if Leo helped in changing this fear of the unknown to the peace of being known by Jesus.

The day prior to Trent's passing, I was standing bedside at his right side. He looked at me and with full confirmation said, "I see a light."

My heart sank, familiar with what that meant. "Where is it?"

"Over your left shoulder."

Wanting to know more, I asked, "Is it only light?"

"Leo is in the light." I began to cry. Trent said, "You are stronger than that. You will be okay."

"I know, sweetheart." A warm sensation came over my body, almost sensing Leo was so close to me. Trent remained focused on the light.

"I see Jesus." These three words had been spoken many times before in our home. I knew the meaning and the reason behind why Jesus was in view. Jesus was standing there, with Leo by His side, showing Himself to Trent. Jesus made it known that He prepared a place for him as if saying to Trent, "In my home, there are many rooms, and one is waiting for you."

This image was the most beautiful vision. My precious Leo standing;

standing beside the One he loved ever so dearly, coming to show Trent the way alongside Jesus, fulfilling what he told Trent he would do. My heart was so full, unable in that moment to feel sadness for the loss that I knew was drawing closer, because all I could see was the beauty of Leo's face in the moments when he talked about Jesus, and now Trent saw it too.

For the previous two weeks, there had been a man in the room; a man Trent was unable to identify. He was not able to tell us if he was good or bad. This man was loyal and appeared daily. This man made his presence known, yet was not ready to be identified. This man watched over Trent, appearing in the same location of the room, sometimes standing and other times sitting. This man didn't reveal himself until it was time for Him to be revealed. It was Jesus.

Sometimes even those with the strongest faith still fear the unknown and battle with being okay to let go. Trent had an incredible faith. His love for Jesus was firm. He knew the truth. Even with this unwavering love, he feared the unknown. Realizing his life was coming to an end, he expressed being afraid of having to die alone. Thoughts of uncertainty raced through his mind as he wondered, *Will those who have died before me recognize me and be waiting?* He struggled with leaving behind the loved ones in his life, concerned if they would be okay.

I saw this battle play out to the end, yet it transformed as the days went by. I had a strong sense there was a battle for his soul to the very end. Not because he didn't believe, but because the devil fights to take you just like Jesus fights to save you. I saw the strength in Trent's belief bring added benefit to his battle. As he wore the armor of God, he was able to fight off the demons of his life.

In the weeks that led to Trent's death, I paid close attention to the details. I watched the signs and stayed in tune with his actions and words. There are many things expressed as loved ones transition. They seem to have things they need to do and places they need to go, all without a sense of time. They see people, often those who have preceded them in death, and if you allow their truth to be told without interjecting what you see as the truth, you just may go on a beautiful journey of discovery with them.

Like the morning Trent awoke, extending his hand out to hold mine, "I was in Africa."

"That sounds amazing." I pulled up a chair next to his bed and drew myself closer to him to hear every detail.

"I was playing with the animals." A peaceful expression covered his face as if he was there once again.

"That sounds dangerous."

"I was surrounded by butterflies while stroking the mane of a lion."

"Only with God's grace could you be in the lion's den and remain unharmed."

Later that day, after taking a nap he said, "Where is Matthew? I am searching for him."

"Where is he supposed to be?"

"Matthew told me to take this bus to New York. Now you and me are here, but where is he?"

"Should we try to call him?"

"Yes."

I dialed the number hoping that Matthew would remember to play along. "Hi, Matthew."

"What's up, Mother?"

"Well, Trent and I took the bus to New York to find you like you told him, and now he is confused as to where you are."

"Oh, brother, I live in New Jersey! You almost made it here!"

"I need my energy back," Trent interrupted.

"Okay, should I meet you somewhere?"

"I need my power pack. It straps on. I am waiting for the phenomenon to occur right before me that will give me the results from my test to see if I become a bumblebee."

"That sounds amazing." The beautiful thing about this simple statement was that after Trent's death, I had bumble bees appear and fly by me while talking about Trent, and multiple bees landed on me and refused to leave my side.

"Well, I will be sure to get it back to you." And just like that, in only a moment of passing, in his mind, Trent and I were back home.

Trent was so present in these conversations releasing the words with such authority. He was caught between two realms, and his reality was such a beautiful place to be. Time didn't control him. He believed he could be in one spot and instantly be in another that was hundreds of miles away.

He expressed on multiple occasions, "We are not safe. They are coming for us."

"Who is coming for us?"

"The bad guys."

"Honey, we are safe."

"How do you know?"

"Remember, you wear the armor of God."

"We need to head north. It is important that you join the 'skinny's'"

"Who are the skinny's?"

"Don't worry, you are pretty enough, they will take you." The whole conversation was so fascinating. Could the north Trent spoke of possibly be Heaven? On multiple occasions, he pulled me close to him, as if protecting me from the danger surrounding me. Trent continued the conversation and mentioned, "I have a GPS."

"You do?" Interestingly, Leo also told me years ago that angels have a GPS and that is how they track and find one another.

With each passing day, I witnessed Jesus come alive in Trent. In conversations, but more strikingly, within the transition of his eyes. Trent's already captivating blue eyes became piercing, as they crystallized into a clear blue that appeared like a prism with light projecting from the inside outward. When he looked at me, I felt like he was looking through me, reading my soul. Many times, it didn't feel as if Trent was alone in these gazes. It took my breath away as if Jesus Himself was looking at me. These moments were calming and intense at the same time like I was basking in the love light of the presence of God. The intensity of Trent's stare transported me to another place, and I felt like he was carrying me along on his journey.

These moments sometimes made me have peace, and other times made me do a quick internal evaluation of my own soul. I questioned if I was a true servant of God, and acting and reacting in ways Jesus would. It was amazing how quickly I adjusted my mindset, at the fleeting moment where I felt like I was transported in front of my Master. I am so human. My flesh led so many of my decisions, yet I felt transformed by the trials of my life, that my level of love for God elevated as He purified me and my faith to a place where I didn't want to disappoint Him.

In Trent's weakness, I found strength. My big strong man, my son, once capable of so much, now relied heavily on me. The embrace of his hug that had once made me feel secure, now securely held on tightly to me to remain steady. When the final weeks of his life were upon him, when he was unable to walk any longer, he looked long into my eyes searching for comfort and answers as confusion consumed his thoughts. His big beautiful blue eyes pierced my soul and melted my heart as I gazed back at him to see Trent was there, but not really *there*. The sound of his voice expressing his appreciation with a gentle "Thank you" and "I love you" fueled my ability to push through the exhaustion.

He looked long into my eyes, just days before his final breath, and said to me, "I am trying to see what your next prophecy will be. Seeing your face brings my heart to fullness."

"That is such a beautiful thing to say."

"God has big plans for you, Mom. I love you."

"I love you too. Tell God I am ready."

My gentle giant. My son slipped from my grasp, but I was comforted by knowing, as he slipped from my life, that he was falling into the loving embrace of Jesus. My son, who was once so capable, was now incapable of leaving his bed. His food intake went down to just a spoonful a day and fluid intake from what was absorbed by sucking on a sponge swab. My son, who was once able to lift unthinkable amounts of weight, now weighed down by his failing body. My son, who was once filled with life, now drained of the life he once knew.

It was difficult to witness the slow decline of the physical form. To watch it play out again required every ounce of strength gathered from the resources within me. I put my trust in God's plan. Yet, there was something very tender and beautiful that occurred, and something so powerful about being present in the company of a loved one who was leaving this life for a fully new and restored eternal one. So much revealed because I was willing and able to be still and listen.

The morning of May 31, 2021, the sun pried its way through the shutters. The room in which Trent spent his final months faced east, and two of the four walls were mostly windows. With a few of them ajar, the room was soothed by the sound of flowing water coming from the waterfall and stream outside. Christian music played softly in the background as it had continuously done for the past few months. The day was bright, but soon, darkness crept in. I brought a lounge chair from the patio and placed it next to Trent's bed, sensing that I was not to leave his side.

I leaned over and whispered, "Good morning, sunshine."

"Hello, Mother."

"I love you."

"I love you too."

I stroked his head and admired the beauty of his face. I etched every detail into my mind. The fullness of his checks, the scars from the battles he endured, the smile that once blazed charisma, now fallen crooked from the effects of the illness, and those beautiful blue eyes grew dim as life was leaving his body.

Just hours into the day, his demeanor changed. His breathing became labored, layered with grunting. He appeared to desperately express something to me, but words escaped him. He stared at me with such intensity, often gasping for air each time he tried to swallow. I couldn't do anything to save him. I knew it was time to provide him with oxygen and a cocktail of medication to provide comfort.

I reached out to the hospice nurse, "I need you to come."

"What changes are you seeing?"

I sighed heavily as my request needed an explanation instead of just a response. "Trent is really laboring and struggling to breathe. I think it is time for medication and oxygen."

"Someone will be there within the hour."

Once again, I sighed. "Okay," as I watched the struggle continue.

My heart broke. Torn between holding on and letting go, as did Trent. I knew it was time for him to go home. Trent fought the good fight. Trent finished the course. Trent kept his faith. By the time the hospice nurse arrived, Trent had slipped into more of a comatose state. He stared out into the distance, not really connecting with anything. The oxygen machine was attached and after about an hour it appeared to provide a bit of relief. Medication was slowly introduced, yet it didn't provide complete comfort until the nurse was administering it hourly.

The nurse stated, "We could be in this stage for days."

"What do I need to do?"

"He will need medication administered every hour. Do you have someone who can help take shifts with you?"

In the back of my mind I thought, *Isn't that your job*? but replied, "Yes. We will be okay."

As darkness filled the room with the subtle glow of moonlight, I told Tony to go get some sleep in case I needed him to take over. My sister sat with me and took the first-hour shift so I could attempt to close my eyes. She held his hand and rubbed his head knowing her precious godchild was closer to meeting God Himself. She gave Trent his medication at 11:00 pm, kissed him, and said, "I love you, Trent."

"Thank you for your help," I said as she kissed me good-bye.

"I love you."

"Love you too. I will call you if anything changes."

I closed my eyes. My hand extended through the hospital bed railing, resting upon Trent. I lay there, listening to his breaths. The span of time between exhales grew longer. I knew this pattern. I knew the outcome. I opened my eyes briefly to watch his chest move up and down. I stared at my son not wanting to miss a moment of his life. My eyes grew heavy. I closed them, and as Trent let out a breath, another one didn't return. Startled by the silence, I spoke his name, "Trent!" My actions called him back to me for a moment; it wasn't my intention to disrupt his transition. Then, a final breath, and it was finished. He left me at the tender age of 30, at 11:15 pm. I was prepared for days of care, but they would no longer be needed. I left his side momentarily to inform Tony of the news.

"Honey, wake up."

Startled, he sat upright in bed. "What's happening?"

"Trent died."

"What?" He followed me down the stairs. I hesitated as I walked past Oliver's room.

"Should we wake him?"

"No. He will need all the strength he has to endure the days ahead."

I called my sister. She had only left our home 20 minutes prior. "I need you to come back."

"What is going on?"

"Trent died."

"Are you serious?" The soft sound of tears filled my ears through the phone.

I placed the call to the hospice nurse, letting her know that Trent had passed. She arrived at our home about an hour later. She then placed a call to the funeral home. It was such a different experience. No police officers, no strangers filling our home. No loved ones coming to say their final goodbyes. The night grew darker, and in the hush of the shadows of night, Trent's body was removed from our home.

I held Tony in my arms as we watched another son leave our home in a body bag. The emptiness consumed me. Together, we sat in the family room with my sister and shared stories about a warrior named Trent. He was courageous and he wore the armor of God's love until his last breath. His last day was a battle. It was a representation of the fight he had fought. Although his body tried to let go, his heart did not understand because it was so strong and so well conditioned. It did not know how to pump its last beat.

Consumed by grief, lost in survival mode, it dawned on me in the stillness that after Trent was removed from our home, the doctor failed to follow through. My precious son, just 30 years old, willing to give a piece of himself for the better good of the next one, fighting to help find a cure, and no action was taken. An opportunity was lost at the cost of possibly more lives. The moment we left his office after the final diagnosis, we were no longer a concern. The years spent being a patient seemed to be deleted from the doctor's memory, and what should have been a gift for a future life, ended with the life of my son.

The realization of my broken routine surfaced as I searched for something to fill the void of my days. My body ached as the toxins held within it finally released, causing me to feel weak after a stretch of feeling so strong. Every inch of my frame felt the pain of another lost son and my heart hurt as the beat of its rhythm searched for what used to make it whole. My breathing became labored while I replayed the struggle Trent fought to keep his breath from failing, as his incredibly strong heart pumped, almost refusing to release its final beat. My brokenness consumed me as I sat alone, and then the crowds that surrounded me for days diminished. I pushed through, searching for what lay ahead, and the plan and direction God wanted me to follow.

During our trials in life, you can choose whether you want to be held captive in anger or captive in hope. As soon as I began to alter my perspective years ago, I realized what a blessing all my struggles were. God saw something in me, and the more pain I endured, the stronger I became. I was worth investing in. God knew He could use me based on what I had learned through my sons. He saw in me more than I could ever see in myself.

For life is led by where your focus lies. Our family chose to focus on God, and because of that, we found joy in our deepest sorrow. God is why I had the strength to endure the death of a second son. God is why I had the strength to stand and deliver, yet another eulogy, for the life of a child. God is why I could smile and comfort those in need of support and love, recognizing that our loss was also the loss of others. God is why I could transition emotions from celebrating one son getting his wings and entering eternal life, to another son spreading his wings and getting ready to expand on his life. Within only four days, we went from a funeral to a high school graduation for another son.

Chapter Thirty-Two

WHISTLE BLOWN

I awoke. Exhausted, my limp body stretched across the silk sheets, weighed down by long days without sleep. Heavy eyelids struggled to open, crusted together and strained by the months that led me to this moment. The tears from the evening before remained. I rubbed gently to release the particles that felt like dried glue as if prolonging what the day would bring. My eyes slowly came into focus with the realization of another son lost from my grasp. It was time, all too soon, to rise and prepare for Trent's funeral.

The sky was overcast and reflected the dimness I felt inside. Only two years separated the death of my two sons, and the events blurred together from the similarity of their suffering and my heartache. Like a dragonfly hovering over the rippled water, distorting its ability to reconnect with its loved ones, anxious thoughts became distorted in my mind. My boys were their own individuals and I wanted them to be represented without comparison.

I remained still in my bed, searching for strength. The sun blocked by the clouds reminded me of the way my heart was blocked from feeling joy. The darkness in the room settled in and I couldn't find the light. I managed to roll my lifeless body over and rested my feet upon the floor. I made my way to the bathroom and hoped that the east window would shine warmth upon me, yet darkness prevailed. I shifted my eyes from the window to the mirror and heard Leo's voice once again, *You got this, Mom*, as he reflected light into my darkness.

Peace began to fill me. I imagined both of my boys for the first time running free together, pausing to look back at me. One shining light, and one providing strength. Slowly, things became brighter within me as the darkness outside remained. There was no need to rush. Stillness consumed our home. No one needed my help. I didn't have to watch a monitor or listen for a noise, rushing down the hall to see what it was. My role as caregiver had come to an end after almost twenty years. My mind felt empty, unable to grasp my purpose in life and where it was leading me.

The dense clouds remained prominent like a shield, representing power and strength, as the day continued. I stepped into the shower, once again hoping to cleanse the sorrow, washing the tears away as the water fell upon me. As I dried myself off, I paused to look in the mirror. This time, I heard Trent, *You are stronger than that, Mom.* Hope and strength echoed within the walls of the room as I heard the love of my boys speaking to me.

I stepped into my dress, green this time, honoring Trent and the color he loved. I combed through my long hair as I prayed for strength and blew it dry, hoping to blow away the pain. I applied my mascara, trying to brighten my withdrawn eyes, lost in the tears of sorrow. As I curled my hair, I could hear Trent's voice echo from the mirror, *You look beautiful, Mother.*

I gathered my things and began my drive to the church. Once again, I left prior to the rest of my family with Trent's personal items at my side. I noticed pockets of light where the sun shone through as if the sky portrayed my life. Slowly, the sky opened and light prevailed. I walked to the church doors, halted as the view of the hearse came into sight, and my heart skipped a beat. The back door swung open as I watched two men gently, yet with some struggle, remove the coffin that held my son. From a distance, I stood, exhaled, and gathered what strength I could find to step forward.

As loved ones helped display Trent's life upon the tables in the lobby, I walked arm in arm with Tony and our two remaining sons to the front of the church to say our private goodbyes. Trent's massive frame filled the structure of the coffin. My son's earthly vessel lay before me, but the spark of his eyes and his brilliant smile were gone, confirming he was no longer with us. As his hands crossed upon his stomach, I gently guided his official refereeing whistle over his knuckle and into position, displaying the dream he once had.

We stood as a united family alongside Trent as a trickle of those paying their final respects turned into a steady flow of endless love. Acquaintances from years ago along with endless friends, family, and co-workers made their way to Trent's side. Most in disbelief of the reality lying before them. God remained with me, providing me strength, as we consoled and comforted all those who came to say their final goodbyes, even as my own heart was breaking. The flow increased, causing our family to separate to help with disbursement. I looked up occasionally and was so proud of the way my two sons handled themselves. Oliver maintained a mature composure. His structure stood tall, and he kept eye contact and carried conversations with people, many he didn't even know. Matthew too, stood before others with his wife at his side, in his own grief, and provided comfort to others.

Loved ones settled in and found a seat. I sat in the front row with Tony beside me, along with Oliver, Matthew, and Valerie. The realization of my family slipping away from me came into focus as I noticed we all fit in one small pew. I held Tony's hand firmly as if channeling strength from him, preparing myself for what I knew was only moments away. I kissed him and paused a moment by Trent's side, gently kissed the coffin, and retraced my steps up to the altar.

I looked out into the crowd. In disbelief, I said to myself, *I am here once again.* I delivered the eulogy for yet another son. God held me up. I felt Him beside me along with Trent's presence. As I read the words out loud, I saw Trent's face in my mind. The image of his facial expressions resurfaced from the day I had the privilege of reading to him the words that would be spoken at his funeral. I saw the moments that made him smile, the ones that made him laugh, and the words that made him cry. What a gift to be able to share that tender time with him, letting him hear the words that would honor his life.

There was a booming sense of approval. As I flowed through my delivery, the sky grew darker, yet the weather remained calm. A gentle rumble began to form in the background, subtle, but there. Then there came a point in the eulogy where I expressed how Trent was a warrior, not just for his physical stature, but for what God intended him to be, *a spiritual warrior*. As those words rolled off my tongue, the thunder cracked loudly. It shook the walls of the church and penetrated my body with a force of energy that immediately strengthened me. Instinctively, I confidently stated, "That's right," as if receiving God's affirmation that Trent indeed was a spiritual warrior, and then proceeded without missing a beat. God's timing in this was precise and meaningful and left many in the church feeling His presence. This moment represented Trent's strength, his power, and the ability to finally "drop the weights" which were forbidden for him to do in all the years of weight training at certain gyms.

I left the altar after finding my footing, made my way back to the pew and consoled Tony. I saw his pain and witnessed his tears while we were separated from each other. Unable to hold his hand and embrace him in my arms, while tender words were spoken about our child. As mass proceeded, I heard Trent's voice in each of the readings he carefully selected. I recalled holding his hand as he sat across from me and we read the scripture aloud to each other. Each song, hand selected by Trent, made the words pierce my heart. I could hear him sing the verses to me.

I kept my composure for most of the service until it was time for the pallbearers to take their places. Tears flowed steadily while I watched Matthew and Oliver come to Trent's side. Front and center, each grasping a handle on the coffin; the coffin that held their brother. They were joined by my brother-in-law and a parade of thirty-year-old men, friends experiencing the first death within their tribe. Tears welled up in their eyes, emotions of the loss could no longer be held back.

With all of them in place, Casting Crowns, "Only Jesus", sounded over the speakers. I closed my eyes and saw Trent singing and displaying his motions of adoration. We began to follow the procession down the center aisle, when something overtook me and Trent came through me loud and clear. As I walked behind my son, my soul was lost in the music and mimicked Trent's motions, pointing to Jesus, holding my arms up to Him, knowing that life is lived for only Him.

Afterwards, the celebration of Trent's life continued. We exceeded the capacity of the space in the restaurant as countless loved ones gathered, not quite ready to let go of their time with Trent. It was beautiful to witness the love and energy that filled the room. Endless stories were told, reminiscing about the past; some I had never heard, and some that, as his mother, I probably shouldn't have heard. Laughter and tears carried all of us into the night well beyond closing time.

I awoke the next morning exhausted from the weeks that preceded, but with no time to grieve. Our family shifted our mindset quickly. Only four days separated the celebration of life at Trent's funeral from the celebration of Oliver's high school graduation. I was amazed by Oliver's strength, considering the loss of two brothers during his high school years. He maintained focus and graduated in the top five of his class. His incredible dedication provided him with a partial scholarship to UW-Madison. As his world crumbled around him, he built a foundation, stood upon it, and persevered.

Then it was all over. Matthew and Valerie returned to New Jersey while Tony returned to work. Our home was still and quiet. The void grew even deeper when Oliver left for college. Within only a few months, Tony and I went from major parenting and caretaking to true empty nesters. I was indeed empty and searching for my purpose. God was gentle and loving in the care of my tender heart. In my loss, I found significant gain in life, heightening my senses of the spiritual world surrounding me. Signs of Trent's presence became known.

One of the most beautiful conversations I had with Trent, prior to his passing, was also one I will forever cherish. Being able to have meaningful conversations with loved ones is obviously something that is accessible to us every day. But do we take advantage of that, or sometimes regret missing the opportunity to know the thoughts that transpire in their minds before it is too late?

Trent witnessed the significance of the signs that enabled me to feel close to Leo. He knew the meaning behind the feathers that were found and he often heard me say, "Hi, Leo!" as a cardinal flew by. Weeks before he died, he asked me, "Is Leo the only one who can be a cardinal?"

"No. A cardinal is a symbol that a loved one who passed away is close by, looking out for you."

"So, I can be one too?"

"Of course." I could see that he yearned for something more, something personal that would symbolize him for me to know that he was present in my days the way that feathers made me feel with regards to Leo.

We began to talk about different events from his life and, as we discussed his childhood, we focused on his time in youth hockey. We began to formulate something that represented him both in power and in grace. He played for a team called the Warhawks and, ironically, every time we traveled together for a tournament or game, we saw a red tail hawk sitting on a highway sign, in a tree, or on a post close to the road. We began to call it our "good luck hawk" since it often led to Trent having a great game and scoring a goal. Our discussion went further into his college days where he studied for a semester on birds and loved birds of prey, especially the hawk.

As our talk wound down, he looked at me and blurted out, "That's it. I will be a hawk."

Trent didn't waste any time allowing me to confirm that he in fact was going to soar over me, protecting my heart and providing me with strength to see God present in my days. The morning after he passed, Tony and I went for a walk. We got to the top of the hill just out of our subdivision when a strong, massive hawk swooped in front of our pathway and landed on the tree limb overhanging the street. Goosebumps shot down my entire body as I paused to look at Tony.

"Well, it is confirmed. God used a sign of Trent as a hawk to assure us that he is safe."

"That was incredible!" We stood, frozen in the moment, and watched the hawk gaze at us.

"God's timing is perfect."

"Look how it is just sitting there watching us."

We embraced each other as warmth overcame us. "It is amazing."

The symbol of a hawk was so fitting for Trent. It represented his strength and courage, the warrior that he was. Since he left his earthly form, Trent has shown up in so many situations and I honestly saw more hawk sightings in the months that followed his passing than in all my years living in our home. The day of Oliver's graduation, a hawk soared above the football field as his ceremony was performed. On my way to church, a hawk flew above my car and traveled with me for about 30 yards. I have seen endless hawks on my walks. Sometimes, they are waiting on tree limbs until I pass, sometimes they fly right towards me, and other times, they swoop down in front of me as if saying, *Hello.*

One morning, God found a way to bring my two boys together. I was on a walk, thanking God for all that He has done in my life by comforting me with signs from above. As I passed by a neighbor's driveway, a large hawk took flight from the top of a pine tree near the road. I was so close; I felt the power within him. My eyes stayed fixed on him as he flapped his wings, demonstrating both strength and grace. Out of the corner of my eye, I noticed something and as my eyes drifted, I noticed that something caught the attention of the dogs as well. There on the driveway between the noses of my two dogs, lay a beautiful feather that the hawk left behind, allowing God to give a sign from both of my boys simultaneously. My heart was filled with such joy as I bent down to hold the feather, despite not physically being able to hold them.

One evening, Trent came in full force and power as I witnessed over my home a migration of night hawks assembling. What began as ten continued to multiply and every time I looked to the sky there seemed to be more. It came to a point that at any given time, there were between 50-100 soaring above me. I couldn't take my eyes off the sky! It became easier to lay down and look up. It was a vision that had me wondering if Trent was recruiting others for a greater purpose.

All these encounters brought peace to my heart. During that time, my light could grow dim in my darkest hours. Yet, I choose to let it shine brighter than ever to give glory to God, for I will strive to be a beacon for others to see His light and find their way to Him. It is His light that lets me know that my boys are right at my side.

On one particular walk, I noticed a hawk sitting on the telephone pole about 25 yards in front of me. I grabbed my phone and began to record knowing that as I approached it would take flight. It did as I expected and as I looked back at the footage, I was in complete awe. The spiritual world was literally walking right beside me. A bouncing green orb was keeping stride with my pace and as the hawk began to fly, the orb sped up and drifted toward it as if one spiritual force belonged to the other. The green orb followed the hawk into the sky!

A month after Trent died, I sat alone in my family room. The front door was shut, but not latched. A breeze picked up, and as I brought my gaze to the front hallway, I saw an image of someone who looked like Trent walking by the front door as the wind pushed the door open. Fear was not what this moment brought, but rather peace. It reminded me of the beautiful pulsing sensation I felt under the palm of my hand on my bed after Leo died. I have come to recognize my boys are not physically with me, but instead spiritually known. In that reality, I close my eyes and clearly see Trent in his spiritual form, just the way Leo described he would be.

"Trent's wings are beautiful," Leo slowly described to Tony the day he informed us, "Jesus is getting ready for Trent."

"Can you tell me what they look like?" Tony leaned in closer not wanting to miss any details.

"They are green angel wings with blue edges."

"Green is Trent's favorite color."

"They are brilliant, like Trent's eyes. The colors change as the light hits them."

"They sound amazing."

Uncertainty lies ahead of us, a way of life we are more than acquainted with. None of us know where our lives are leading. We can only hope we learn from where we have been. Fear can take hold of us when we forget to keep our eyes on the Lord. Fear can take hold of us when we lose our faith. Without the years of life lessons and visions Leo shared with us it would have been so easy at this moment to fall to my knees in desperation. Yet, what Leo left behind for us to hold onto was belief. Leo gave us the gift of Jesus to hold close to our hearts in these times of uncertainty. Leo showed us the way to trust in God's plan: be still, trust, believe.

Trent's journey followed a similar path to Leo's in the sense that time allowed him to grow, surpassing the initial prognosis of 18 months. This additional time allowed the seed in Trent's heart to grow. What God planted and Leo nurtured became Trent's undeniable faith, love, and trust in God's plan. He took up his own cross and became an inspiration for many. He remained positive as he spoke of God's presence in his life to friends, family, and strangers, and showed others that you can overcome adversity when God is by your side.

Trent had the mindset and spoke, "Cancer will not control my life. God will lead it. Cancer will not keep me from the things I love to do. God will provide me with the strength to persevere."

When doctors told him, "You will never lift weights and skate again," God answered by saying, *Hold My hand, and I will show you the way.* A shadow can only be cast when there is light present. So, in every moment of darkness in our lives, there was also light. We need to choose which way we are going to turn and follow. Trent walked the miles of his discipleship. He stepped into each new day with acceptance, and the love of Jesus was then able to shine through every pore of his sun-kissed skin. Although Jesus wasn't visibly seen, He was known through Trent's actions.

In Trent's darkest days, Leo smiled at him and showed him the light of God. Trent took that light and turned it into his very own flame to ignite the torch that enabled him to fight his fight and with God by his side, he found his way home.

Chapter Thirty-Three

CHOSEN THROUGH BROKENNESS

Like the seasons change in Wisconsin, from life sprouting in spring, to unpredictable harsh winters, my life's journey also weathered the storm. My metamorphic stage of being trapped in a cocoon without a voice couldn't be held forever. I pushed through hardships, gathering strength with every inch I obtained, and broke free. I remained still as my wings dried, waiting for God to guide me in my times of sorrow. He patiently blew life into me with the breath of His wind, giving me hope with every swoosh of movement. As I came into my own, free from the brokenness that held me captive, my whole self was restored from the foundation of Jesus' love and Leo's guidance.

This process of growth allowed me to see that all my failures and all the hard times made me who I am. My pain didn't destroy me, but rather, it drew me closer to God thanks to Leo's acceptance of suffering and patient guidance showing me the way. Leo allowed me to see life through his eyes. The reflection of light that flowed from his presence lit my way and kept me on a path that strengthened my heart through my weaknesses. The more I observed, the more I wanted that same level of life. As I began to follow, surrender, and believe, I, too, found peace.

Like a bolt of lightning striking an unsuspected tree in the forest, I was blindsided multiple times and shaken by the words, "I am sorry, there is nothing more we can do." In a moment's time, the faith I was then rooted in left my limbs and heartbroken. To hear those words expressed once shattered my world. Being told them twice for two separate children was more than the heart of a mother should ever have to bear. Yet, Leo rooted me in a stronger belief. With three words, "I see Jesus," my life was changed forever. A new sprout formed and blossomed into a life meant to live for God.

Leo blocked out the distractions of the world partly because of his physical limitations. What he lacked in motion, he gained in spirit. His calling, his gift, came with a price—mobility, and eventually his life. Jesus carried him through his ordeal when he was no longer able to walk it himself. His physical changes made me look at so many things in life in a different light, a light of a loving God using an earthly vessel emphasizing what matters most—love. With love in your life, all things are possible because you will not allow emotions to alter your way. Emotions get in the way of love because they are feelings, altering the concrete concept of love. Love is a way of life. When we turn it into a feeling, it becomes something else, something that someone else can steal away or change in us.

Trent also accepted his life-altering circumstances, yet as an adult man, he asked, "Why is this happening to me?" believing he had lived his life in a way pleasing to God. Trent continued to have things stripped away from him, but he adapted and moved forward, letting his steps be guided by God. Both may have accepted it differently, yet each of them trusted God's plan and knew it was wiser than their own. I love how each of my sons looked past their circumstances and saw the evidence of God's goodness surrounding them.

It can be hard to shed our old ways. Things of the past are woven into our being, even as we try to transform and move forward. They tend to resurface, trying to pull us back in. All we can hope for is that by acknowledging them, we learn from the things we did in our years before and try to become better because of them. As I continue to step into each new day, I not only carry the loss of Leo and Trent, but I also feel the weight of their mission upon my shoulders. Leo's purpose here in life was intentional. He was a true warrior of God and I was amazed at how quickly God turned Leo's death into a garden of beauty. Leo barely stepped out of this world, and God's grace was already stepping in renewing and healing me.

If we look at love as a necessity, it can only lead us in the direction of God, for He is love, and if we need love, then we need God. God is already with you. He has taken up residency within you and all you must do is accept Him. Lay down the welcome mat for Him and others, and just like that, you have accomplished the two most important foundations Jesus stated. First and foremost, love God. Secondly, but equally important, love yourself and others. If you do this, there will be no room for hatred. This was Leo's way. He gazed upon everyone with the same deep affection of love, shining light on others, choosing to be chosen.

Leo brought to life, "For to me, to live is Christ and to die is gain." (Philippians 1:21) Just as the scales fell from the eyes of the apostle Paul, Leo, too, had his eyes opened during his transformation from an active toddler to a bedridden follower of Jesus. Once he encountered this life-altering change, Leo's mind centered on God. There was only one narrative playing in his mind on a continuous loop, and no background noise or distraction stole his focus. To live was to live for Christ.

There is so much peace to be found in the simplicity of that one line from the Bible. Nothing in this time on earth is more important than living for Jesus. I learned that by putting Him at the center of my thoughts and actions, I couldn't help but make better decisions. Leo helped me see that. Somehow, during all his pain, discomfort, and uncertainty, he was able to love and enjoy life. He embraced the trials in front of him because he saw the finish line. To die was to gain. He knew his circumstances here were temporary and with purpose, and because of his willingness to be still and listen, he was filled with the gift of the Holy Spirit and allowed God to work through him.

He did not let Satan's lies consume his mind. He fought, not on his own, but with the armor of God's love, to conquer daily battles and not spiral downward into depression or self-pity. Not once in his lifetime did Leo state, "Why me?" He did not question God's path for his journey; he embraced it, took up his cross, and carried it.

Such belief filled the pools of his chocolate brown eyes and somehow managed to reflect the light of God's love in the darkness. Leo showed me that if you want to hear the heart of God, then you need to be silent. Only then when you are still, will you be filled with the spirit of God. Don't hide from God, dwell in His love. Let the wings of His shelter cover you, protect you, and shield you from what may be hurting you.

Leo once told me, "Jesus has the most beautiful wings. They are made up of every color. This is what makes them so brilliant and white." What an image to be wrapped within and sheltered by.

There is a Japanese art form known as Kintsugi, an art of renewal. The philosophy is to embrace the flaws of broken pottery by highlighting the cracks versus hiding them. I was the imperfection etched into Leo's life. He covered me with his beauty and made my scars become something worth admiring. My brokenness needed time to mend. Leo took his "gold lacquer", the gold thread of love that connected him to a higher power and healed me. Leo showed me a way to take all my broken pieces, the events that had shattered me in so many ways and highlight the love of God to help me find myself once again. I was able to erase the shame and display my wounds instead.

Through God's grace, Leo came to me as my own personal savior, helping to cleanse me of my past wrongdoings and giving me the ability to see a new beginning. For when he entered my life, God also entered. My mind shifted, and my thoughts and actions followed. My past life was no more, and my life moving forward was cleansed and restored. God brought Leo to me, and in return, Leo brought me to God, saving me. He was able to bring the Bible alive in my home so that what I didn't know became known. I witnessed my own version of the passion, and my heart was transformed by the agony I viewed and became a part of. I walked alongside my son as he carried his cross, honoring God and faithfully following His ways. Through God, Leo played a part in miracles while here on earth. I can only imagine the ways God will continue to use him while beside Him.

What Leo left behind was a transformational legacy, building a foundation for others to step upon to build their own faith. He demonstrated the building blocks needed: love, compassion, patience, trust, faith, and belief. His cross was weighted with more than his own personal mission. He was presented with the task of bringing others to God. Through his actions, he demonstrated that even through adversity, God will not waver or leave your side, but rather strengthen you and provide you with abilities beyond human possibility. Leo walked with Jesus through the way, the truth, and the light, and he illuminated the way for others. I strongly believe there are souls in Heaven now only because Leo helped others believe, and that more will follow because of his example. Leo has the greatest legacy in heaven; he can look to someone beside him and hear them say, *I am here because you guided me in knowing God.*

Through my brokenness, Leo led me to God and He cultivated my life. God plowed over my past and planted a new seed in my heart. He watered me with the dew of His spirit and, with Leo's light shining ever so presently in my daily life, my faith grew. God took all my failures and hardships, and as I allowed the dew to penetrate deeper, God laid His hands upon me and remolded me into something new. "Create in me a clean heart, God, and renew a steadfast spirit within me." (Psalm 51:10)

God knew me from the beginning, aware of all the mistakes and trials along my path. Knowing this, He saw what I couldn't see, taking me from a broken little girl and rebuilding me. He didn't throw away the essence of who He created me to be. Instead, He held me in His strong yet gentle hands and remolded me into the strong woman I was always meant to be. For His glory and by His design. The pieces of my heart that were pierced and removed with the death of my two sons were replaced with the love of God. As He poured His undeniable love for me into my wounds, he filled the cracks, making my heart whole once again by reinforcing them with His love.

As a believer, I know God is good and only love flows from Him. He allowed affliction and difficult things to occur in my life because we live in a sinful world, not because He wanted to punish me. These experiences helped shape my character for spiritual growth and discipleship. They trained me and prepared me to live with Him forever, much like the way He worked in Leo's life. As a follower of Christ, I believe Jesus stretched out His arms for us and shed His blood to cover us so our sins could be forgiven.

Leo knew and learned his purpose early in life. He willingly accepted it and became a teacher using God's lesson plan to help refine me and many others who were fortunate to be part of his journey. Leo seemed to understand without question; his brokenness was needed as a visual tool to show others that our weaknesses, struggles, and suffering are all necessary to gain the wisdom for our spiritual growth in order to live an eternal life with God. Leo taught me to shift my focus from the ways of this world and to see life through the lens of eternity. To live my life here on Earth with a purpose, answering the call that God has for me. Because of this, I saw life is not about the duration, it is about how you live it and build your character for eternal rewards.

I am in awe of the young man Leo was. He was a student who trained and later became a teacher to many. Only God could have worked such a miracle within such grim circumstances. God did it His way, the perfect way, through the sacrifice of my son who ultimately was His. Only because Leo had a willing heart fully turned to Him, God was able.

When God sent me Leo, his loving ways and tender heart cleared the fog before my eyes, and slowly pulled back the curtain to reveal Jesus to me in a way I had never seen. Leo provided glimpses into the promise God has for us. When you believe in Jesus, you will live with Him forever. Leo's insight made it impossible not to believe. The purity of his heart and unwavering faith even in his darkest moments let the light of Jesus' love shine through him. What Leo experienced, in both his conversations and his visions, was without influence and intimate between him and Jesus. Leo's speech was made possible because God wanted those particular words noted.

Ironically, as Leo revealed more to us, I felt myself loosening my grip on him. My brokenness became a strength, releasing my fear of clinging to Leo like the day of the photoshoot in his youth, and ultimately finding peace in surrendering him to God. I saw in my own visions, Leo free from his cross and capable of doing a more efficient job of showing God's love by being *with* God. This fact allowed his light to shine through me by the peace He bestowed upon me, despite the loss of four children (two lost before taking their first breaths). He took me through a transformation. He broke my shell and built me a new one made up of total reliance on Him.

The 'me' that existed before I knew God was lost, struggling in life. I now have peace. That peace stems from surrender, the point where I let go and released my control and handed it over to God. I no longer recognize the girl who lacked confidence and saw little worth in herself. I now confidently live for God, knowing He is the One and only One that I live for. He established my course. I chose my direction. He met me at every right and wrong turn, willingly taking me in and loving me. That kind of love is a love that only my Maker could give me. Nothing of the flesh can provide that type of security.

God elevated me to a whole new level, a level of trust and love that fills me with calmness inside. Without the purity of Leo's spirit and the enormous sacrifice of losing children, I would have missed the life God was trying to provide for me; a life preparing me to live in His glory and to reunite with all loved ones lost, whole, and well for eternity.

We must be broken. We must accept our brokenness and be open to the way God then wants to use us. Our broken moments are for our benefit, a way to help us grow spiritually, even when we can't see it. We need to be open to the process, willing to let go of the things and ways we cling to while wanting to believe they are what is best for us when in reality, dependence on God is what is best for us.

I would have fought this concept and fought it hard if it weren't for Leo. He surrendered his control to God, and what I saw was beauty through pain. All the odds were stacked against Leo. The doctors didn't provide hope, but Leo pondered the love and trust of Jesus in his heart and allowed Him to work His ways. Just as the doctors discarded Leo as a case that had no cure, Jesus scooped him up in His arms and carried him for the rest of his days. Once Leo completed his mission and his calling in life, Jesus set him down beside Him and allowed him to run free. I see it in my dreams: Leo standing, running, and smiling, released from the shackles of illness and continuing his mission from a bigger platform. His work is not complete. He now works through me and with many others.

One thing is certain in life; you will have pain. Suffering, on the other hand, is optional. Our family endured pain, yet God provided an immeasurable amount of strength to us, not because we are special, but because we are open to His love. I want to glorify God through my pain. I am willing to be an instrument of His love to shine through. In my darkest moments, I want others to see light. That light is God shining from within me.

Pain can destroy you or it can lift you to a higher level. I choose not to suffer. It is a conscious choice I must make each morning. What benefit would it be for my loved ones or myself if I get stuck in suffering? No one benefits from that. The moments you remain still and don't move forward after a loved one dies are the minutes of your own life that can't be regained. By allowing joy to fill my soul instead of sorrow, I give God a perfect vessel from which others can see His beautiful grace and perfect love.

When we hide behind a mask and portray an image of only good things, we take away the reality of ourselves. We become less approachable when we do this because those around us who may be flawed feel they can't measure up to our standards. If we are transparent, we reveal we are flawed too. There are pages in my story that I sometimes wish I could remove, but then I remember that God helped create my story, and I am more than one incident. I am a daughter of God. My strength is God's strength, not my own. For alone, I would crumble and fall to pieces.

As I move forward in life, I look up to God and His light shines down on me. As I absorb His love, I try to allow it to pass through me and then out of me like the cross of Jesus' love, so those around me can feel and see His good works. The cross is more than just a wooden symbol. It is a way to show that when we interact with God, we too can stretch out our arms, extending His love to others.

I want to shine in my darkest moments because I want others to know God and feel His peaceful presence. I want others never to feel alone, even in their own darkest moments. God is the friend you can always count on. God is the One who will never leave your side. God is the One to see you through all your moments in life.

When things begin to fail all around you and you are left standing, then you know that you have succeeded in life. Don't hide your brokenness. Don't dispose of your shattered pieces. Instead, accumulate them and stand proudly upon them as if they were a platform for your voice to be heard. Always keep in mind your mistakes don't own you, rather, own up to your mistakes and move forward. Your mishaps don't just happen, they occur with a purpose God intends to use, and can be used for good if you allow them to be used that way.

Amidst the changing tides of life, when we are often tossed and turned and lose direction, resurface and draw yourself to the light. When we overcome our challenges, we help others navigate by being a beacon of hope, like Leo. There is a little bit of him in all of us. There is strength in the connections between people. So together, if we don't hide behind the clouds of our past, we can burn brighter than only a small flicker, and glow like a wildfire spreading through whatever may be in its path. Dissipate the burdens that hold you captive, and let your light shine bright with the love of God in your heart.

Diane Nienas is a mother, author, speaker, and certified life coach with a degree in life experience. With two decades of caretaking for terminally ill children, Diane has learned how to navigate through many unforeseen circumstances with grace. Diane is a woman of faith, family, and friends. Many would comment that she has been shaped and molded from the events of her life by God's hands.

Diane was raised on a farm in Southeastern Wisconsin as one of fifteen children. The world was changing as she grew, and although farm responsibilities lessened, the weight of worldly events sank in. A survivor of abuse at a young age and wounded by the death of her sister, Diane was forced to mature quickly, and with that came a relationship with her high school sweetheart, Tony. When it came time for her to have her own family, she found stillness in the eyes of her third son, Leo.

While raising her four sons, Diane spent her time in the community as an active parishioner at her local church, a volunteer at school events, a librarian's aide, and advocated for special needs. She has influenced a group of friends around her with grace and has joined a network of women who guide one another through grief and accomplishments.

Author of the number one best seller, *Living Life with Leo*, Diane highlights the activities that children with disabilities can partake in, as well as encourages children to play with all types of friends. Her name stems from the Hebrew name *Dinah*, suggesting she is meant to be a light-bringer and teacher. It appears God knew her mission, as she spends most of her days breathing the breath of light into others' darkness thanks to lessons she's learned from Jesus and Leo, as well as from her own tale.

ACKNOWLEDGMENTS

To my Heavenly Father, my most sincere gratitude for the limitless love and strength You provide me. For bestowing upon me the gift of motherhood, and allowing me to witness firsthand the supernatural miracles of life.

I'd like to extend my deepest thanks to my husband, Tony, for the endless years of love and support, providing me with the ability to be a stay-at-home mother and caretaker. Your tireless pursuit to provide financial stability is beyond appreciated, ensuring that our sons had the best care possible within the safety of our home.

To my extraordinary sons, who embraced our circumstances and became more courageous, more compassionate, and more patient, demonstrating the power of God's love.

To my loving parents, William and Alice Nettesheim. Thank you for raising me in a home full of love and preparing my heart to hold the weight of the world.

To my family, siblings, church, and friends who faithfully supported us over the years and walked the journey alongside us in every "Leo update" received, so grateful for your never-ending love and encouragement.

To my beta readers; Matthew Nienas, Liz Smirl, Jen McGraw, Andrea Leigh, and Teresa Benson, thank you for investing your time and providing critiques and encouragement.

To the publishing team at FEW International Publications; Kimberly Joy Krueger, Trace Chiodo, and Amy Oaks, thank you for lending your heart to God's wisdom for guidance to enrich this book with your expertise.

Finally, thank you to the non-profit organizations that invested their resources, time, love, and energy in making opportunities possible for families with special needs and leaving us with an imprint of Leo's love to cherish.

Twenty years ago, God sent me a gift that I held close to my heart. I placed Leo "under a bushel" to protect him and keep him close. Then, at age two, God had other plans. Leo was meant to shine, and his life transformed in the process. God then placed Leo on a lamp stand, radiated His love from Leo's weakness, and proved that all things are possible when you trust in the Lord's plan.

"You are the light of the world. A city set on a hill cannot be hidden. Nor do people light a lamp and put it under a basket, but on a stand, and it gives light to all in the house. In the same way, let your light shine before others, so that they may see your good works and give glory to your Father who is in heaven." (Matthew 5:14-16)

Like the Virgin Mother Mary, I watched my son trust in the Lord's plan. I witnessed him carry his cross up the steep terrain with his broken body, determined to fulfill his purpose. The crushing impact my heart felt was only made lighter by knowing Leo's discipleship would serve even greater purpose alongside his Heavenly Father.

Leo was only two years old when the weight of his cross was placed upon his tiny frame. He pulled and struggled as others watched him try to find his footing. The burdens came quickly, yet he clung to the cross, keeping his focus on Jesus and the call of home.

Leo's body was beaten down, distorted but never broken. His faith remained strong. He was stripped of all he knew, yet grew to know more than many ever manage to believe.

Leo was nailed to his limitations for all to see, unable to hide being lame. He was drained of life, while filling others with belief upon releasing his final breath. His body transformed and purified as a radiant glow overlaid all his imperfections. But Jesus was there beside him, as was I, and together we saw him through to the very end.

Leo rose, the weight of his burdens lifted. He stood before the Lord and He expressed,

"Well done my faithful and loyal son."

In the moment of pain and sorrow, it can be hard for some to see the beautiful garden being planted. I have been blessed to be a "bee" amongst the "flowers". I chose not to suffer, but rather hold firm in God's promise of eternal life.

FEW INTERNATIONAL PUBLICATIONS
An Extraordinary Publishing Experience

FEW International Publications is a #1 Bestselling Publisher for women authors at all levels who are seeking more from telling their stories than just a printed project. We are privileged to watch FEW Authors connect, learn, grow, and heal through the creation of a written work that impacts others and glorifies God. Find FEW's books at thefewwomen.com and on amazon.com.

Extraordinary Women; Extraordinary Stories

thefewwomen.com

Made in United States
Orlando, FL
07 February 2023

29660362R00192